The PAINTED CEILING

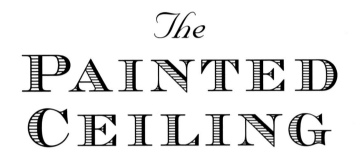

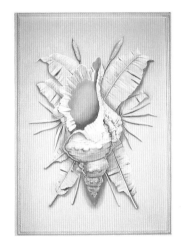

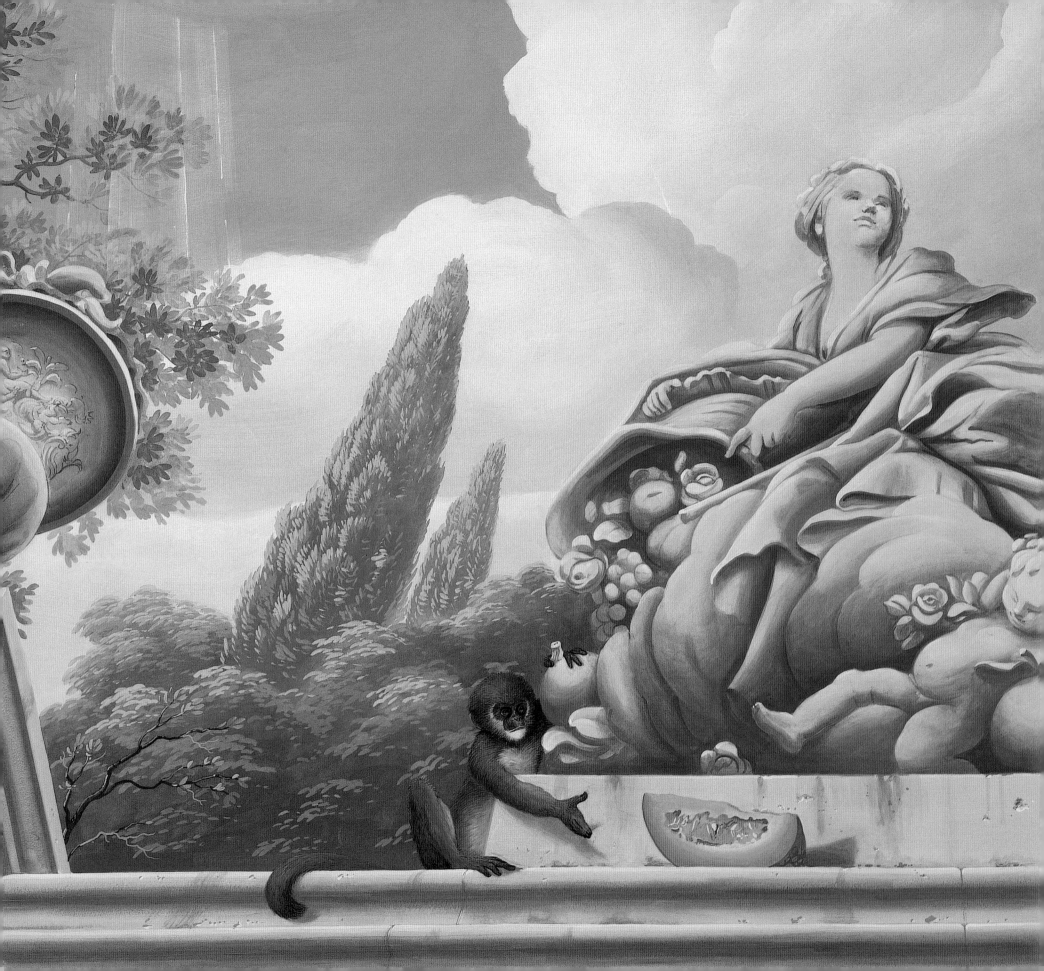

The PAINTED CEILING

OVER 100 ORIGINAL
DESIGNS AND DETAILS

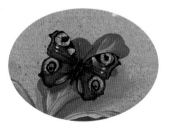

GRAHAM RUST

A BULFINCH PRESS BOOK
LITTLE, BROWN AND COMPANY
BOSTON • NEW YORK • LONDON

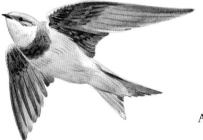

First North American Edition

ISBN 0-8212-2689-4

Library of Congress Control Number 00-111662

Designed and produced by
Breslich & Foss Ltd.
20 Wells Mews
London W1T 3HQ

Bulfinch Press is an imprint and trademark of Little, Brown and Company (Inc.)

Printed in Hong Kong

CONTENTS

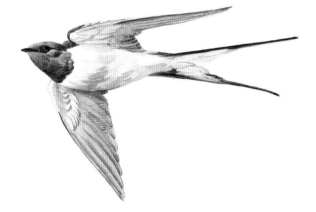

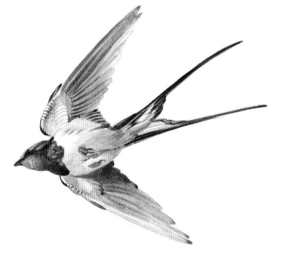

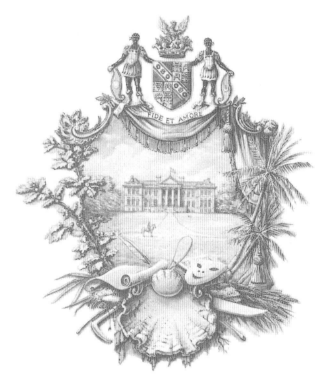

FIDE ET AMORE

In Memory of
Hugh Edward Conway Seymour, 8th Marquess of Hertford
29 March 1930 – 21 December 1997

INTRODUCTION

—

The possibilities for ceiling decoration are endless, from the simplest wash of colour or sky effect, to the most intricate architectural confection or fantasy. A painted ceiling can do much for a room, whether alone or in conjunction with mural decoration. It can in the right circumstances add height, light and of course enhance the decoration of the space, lifting it to another plane.

I am writing this in the Galleria Celeste, one of the many painted room in the Palazzo Durazzo Pallavicini, where I am staying in Genoa. It is the most enormous pleasure to be surrounded by such a magnificent collection of paintings and by so many fine ceiling paintings. I do not have far to go to look for inspiration or for an example to emulate. A visit to Italy is essential for anyone interested in ceiling painting. The colossal output over the centuries and the variety is hard to absorb, but is a constant delight nevertheless. To see the ceiling paintings in reality, rather than in pho-tographs, enables one to comprehend a little of the physical endurance needed to produce them.

I must confess that every time I finish a ceiling painting, I promise myself that it will be the last. Time, however, tends to make one forget how arduous a task painting a ceiling is, so when presented with a blank canvas and an exciting idea my good intentions evaporate.

I have tried on the following pages to provide a few ideas and designs for the decoration of ceilings large and small. I hope that the drawings here will serve as a springboard from which to develop other solutions and variations.

There is much to learn about many different aspects of composition and painting by taking time to look carefully at other people's work, especially that of masters of the past relevant to one's style. I would suggest that anyone who has not worked on a ceiling before should begin with one of the simpler designs before progressing to something a little more demanding. Having taken the mea-surements of the ceiling you intend paint, it is essential to produce a scaled design on paper before tackling the ceiling. Working on paper allows you to experiment with different options and, hope-fully, iron out any problems before you begin to paint. Unless it is a very large or very small ceil-ing a scale of 1 inch to 1 foot (2.5cm to 30cm) is quite workable. Further practical information can be found in Chapter 6 of this book.

It was during my first sojourn in Italy in my early twenties that I visited the Villa Barbaro at Maser near Treviso on my way to Venice. I was bowled over by the frescos of Paolo Veronese that seemed to cover every wall and ceiling of the villa. Fired by this exuberant explosion of virtuosity, I was inspired to paint my first large ceiling paint-ing. This was 'The Temptation' in the south staircase hall, at Ragley in Warwickshire, com-missioned in 1968 by my dear friend the late Hugh Hertford and his wife Louise.

This book is dedicated to his memory.

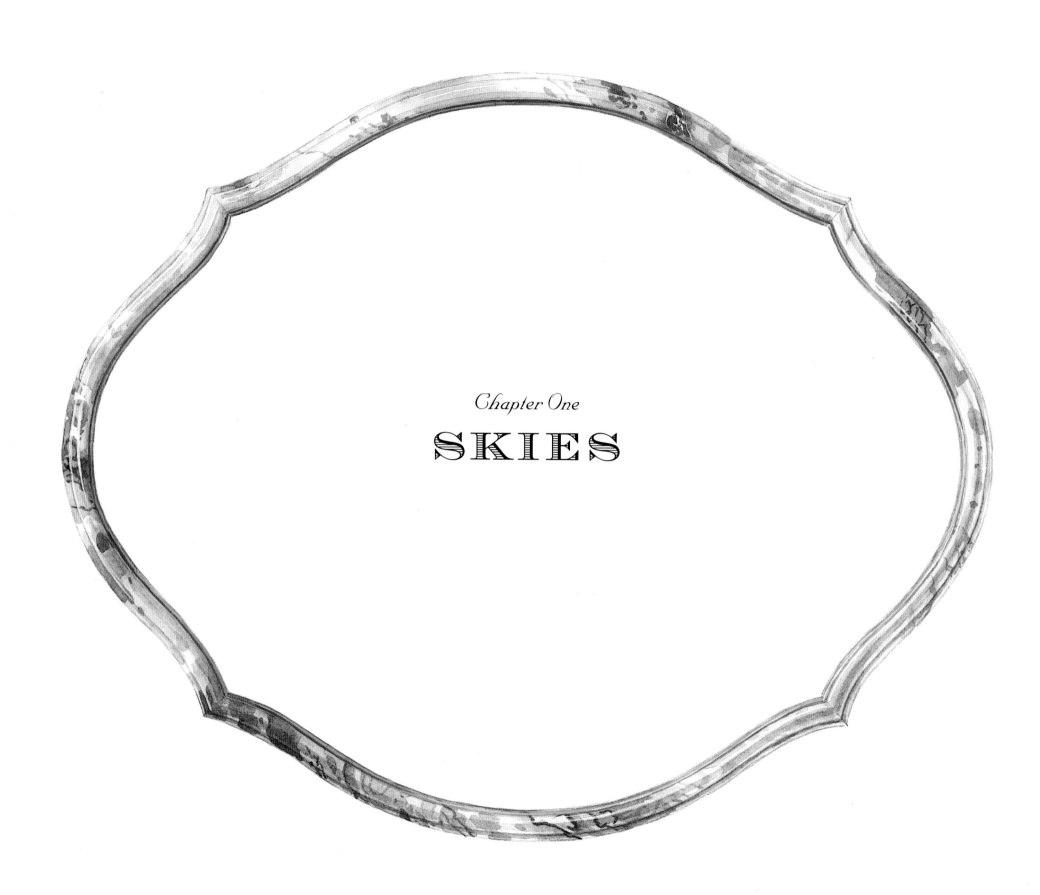

Chapter One

SKIES

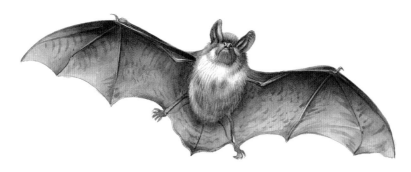

It is known that man has always wanted to 'reach for the sky' and, in the confines of a room, the sequitur is to open the space by simulating a sky on the ceiling. The variety of shapes and colours to be found in a sky is vast, and allows one an enormous range of effects, from clear azure with a few wisps of white cloud, to the thunderous menace of the storm.

It is impossible in this chapter to hope to give more than a suggestion for the different treatments in paint. I live most of the time in East Anglia, a part of England well known for its wide, open skies so beloved by John Constable and other painters. It was indeed another East Anglian painter, the late Edward Seago, who bemoaned the fact that ' no one now seems to have ever heard of a cloud atlas' when we met once in Sardinia. The infinite variety of cloud formations and complex layering are an inspiration to any painter. The opportunity to create a 'mood' in a grand or even a very modest room, whether by painting the entire bed of the ceiling or by opening the ceiling in part, is enticing. A smaller area can be painted within a moulded panel or some *trompe l'oeil* device if a panel does not exist.

It is easy to design a dramatic eruption in the sky for someone else to live with. So often, when it comes down to it, peace and serenity are what is wanted, particularly in a bedroom.

Naturally, the location of the ceiling dictates the nature of the design to a degree, and one of the curses of so many modern houses and apartments is that they have low ceilings, not to mention the ancillary equipment of air-conditioning vents, recessed lights, and so forth.

A high ceiling lends itself much more readily to decoration and, because of its distance from the eye, it is possible to achieve a greater sense of reality, if that is the aim. One has to hope that the client has good eyesight. I was told several years ago, having finished painting a staircase, that 'His Highness wanted to know what the dirty marks were on the ceiling.' They were in fact a flock of birds, but perhaps my client did not have his spectacles on when he looked up!

A few creatures in the sky can help to achieve an even greater sense of space as the eye fixes on the particular bird, bat or insect. Again, if the ceiling is too low, the threat of claws in the hair is not attractive, not to mention an ill-placed bird over a dining table!

I have suggested various shapes for the sky panels, should you wish to limit the amount of sky on the ceiling. One of the most charming small painted skies I have come across is in a closet in the Ca' Rezzonico in Venice (see page 36), a palazzo open to the public as a museum of eighteenth-century decorative arts. As you will see in the sketch, hastily done on site, it is quite simple and depicts a sparrowhawk chasing a flock of sparrows. Something of this size could easily be painted on board or canvas and then fixed to the ceiling.

The night sky is also open to myriad interpretations, whether in a stylistic manner or more natural vision. Perhaps the most simple, but nonetheless effective, design is that of a plain dark blue ground with gold stars superimposed, whether in a regular pattern or reflecting a specific part of the galaxy. On pages 26 and 27 I have shown the placement of stars and planets at the time of the eclipse in August 1999. An added conceit is the *trompe l'oeil* guide to be painted on a nearby wall.

In the oval dining room of a house near Hilversum in the Netherlands – a name on the dial of the wireless I had known and wondered about as a child – I painted another night sky. This time, in the coffered panels, and continued on the frieze below, I added creatures of the night to give interest and amuse those dining by the flickering light of the candles.

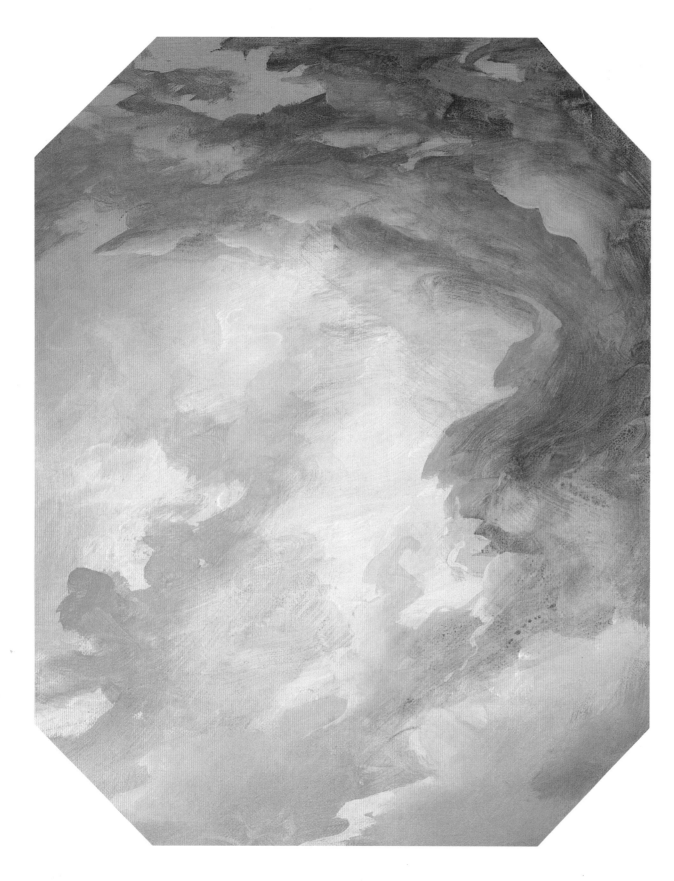

SKY STUDIES

A palette of blues (cobalt, manganese and ultramarine), the earth colours (red and yellow ochre, raw and burnt sienna and raw umber), together with white, is more than adequate to produce this *(left)* and any of the skies illustrated on the following pages. For a touch of warm sunlight, Italian pink or gamboge is a useful addition. For a predominantly yellow sky, Naples yellow too, is invaluable. A limited palette is always preferable to one with too many colours as the various nuances of the selected colours can be explored, making the resulting painting cohesive. For example, the collection of pinks derived from adding white to burnt umber and raw and burnt sienna is quite wonderful.

All the sky studies reproduced here are best viewed by holding the book above one's head, in order to get an impression of what they might look like *in situ*. The shapes of the panel openings are, of course, interchangeable with each other.

RIGHT: This sky has a strong ultramarine cast to it. Lay a sheet of tracing paper over the page if you wish to get an idea for a 'softer' version.

LEFT: The introduction of dark clouds gives a more sombre feel to a room. (Right) The use of pink and yellow suggests how the sky can move away from an overall blue.

LEFT: The clouds in the oval strike a dramatic note. The addition of umber lends a cooler feel. This more tranquil sky (right) is suitable for a bedroom. With all of these studies it is possible to isolate a part of the sky and create a design with a different disposition of cloud mass and colour.

ABOVE: If one talks of 'mood' I think this is a very happy blue, a sky that makes one glad to be alive.

RIGHT: This rough sketch shows a different composition. It draws one up to the very source of light, the sun, with its rays touching the edges of the spiralling clouds.

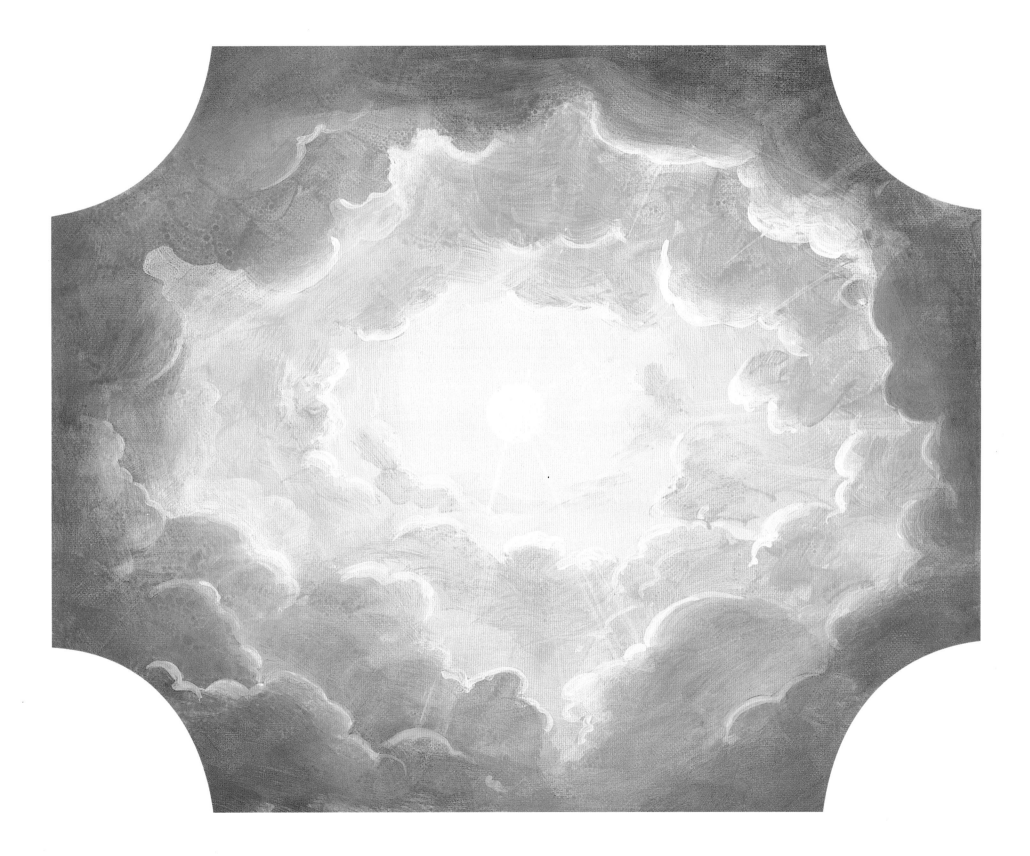

LEFT: *A lyrical sky, the golden clouds bathed in sunlight, this, for me, works alone. There is no need for the addition of man or beast. (Right) Lit by an unseen sun, the darkened clouds suggest a certain drama in the sky. Serendipity can sometimes produce an interesting result when playing with paint, far removed from close meteorological observation but valid, nevertheless.*

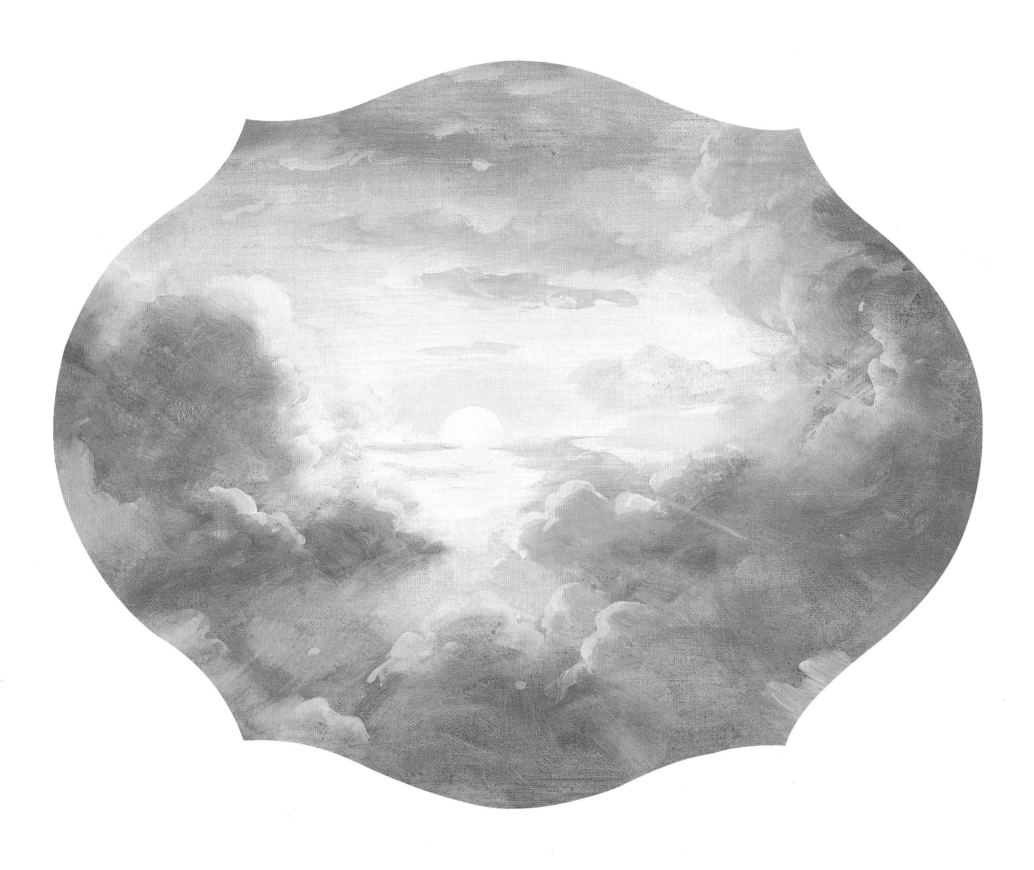

LEFT: *This sky, because of its suggestion of a horizon, would work most successfully from a single viewpoint, such as in the canopy of a bed. (Right) This study was done for a bedroom ceiling. It was to be painted within the existing plaster moulding.*

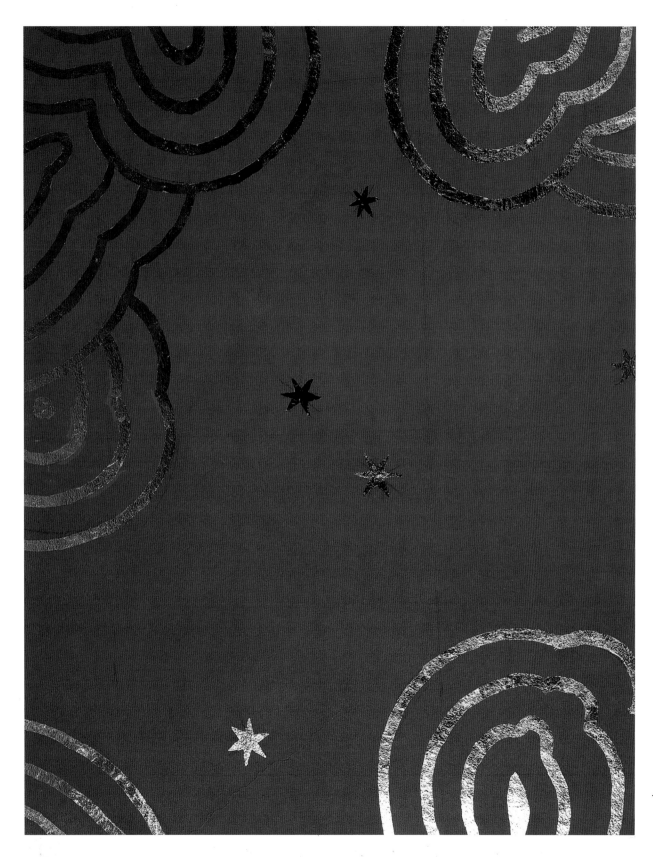

SOMERTON SKY DESIGN

The architecture of my home in Suffolk, the Old Rectory at Somerton, is mainly mid-nineteenth-century gothic. The decoration for this particular passageway was inspired by Horace Walpole's house, Strawberry Hill. It is a rather eclectic mix: the bookcase is formed from confessionals removed earlier last century from a Belgian convent, and the gilded screen at the end of the passageway came from the chapel of a château in southern France. The passageway now houses a collection of plaster casts.

The design of the ceiling is loosely based on the embroidered hem of a sixteenth-century Chinese coat. The stylised gilded clouds create movement in an otherwise rather static space.

LEFT: A detail of the ceiling showing the lines of the cloud formations interspersed with stars gilded by David Cossart. The ground colour, painted by Garth Carter, was achieved by painting a flat blue coat, with three thinner coats of ultramarine and raw umber stippled over it.

RIGHT: To 'hold' the design, two lines of gilding were applied on the cornice.

OVERLEAF: The design, to scale, for the cloud formation and placement of stars. This is a blue ground with line decoration in white gouache washed with yellow ochre.

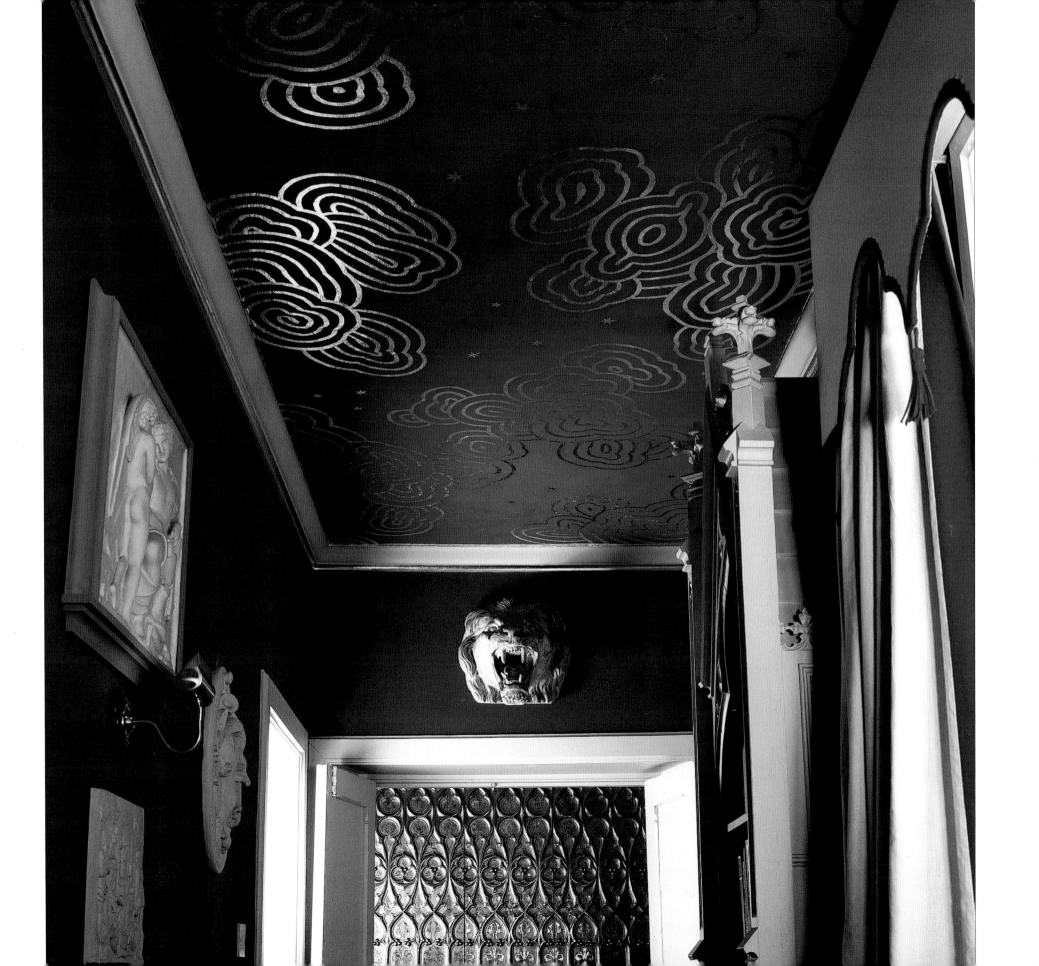

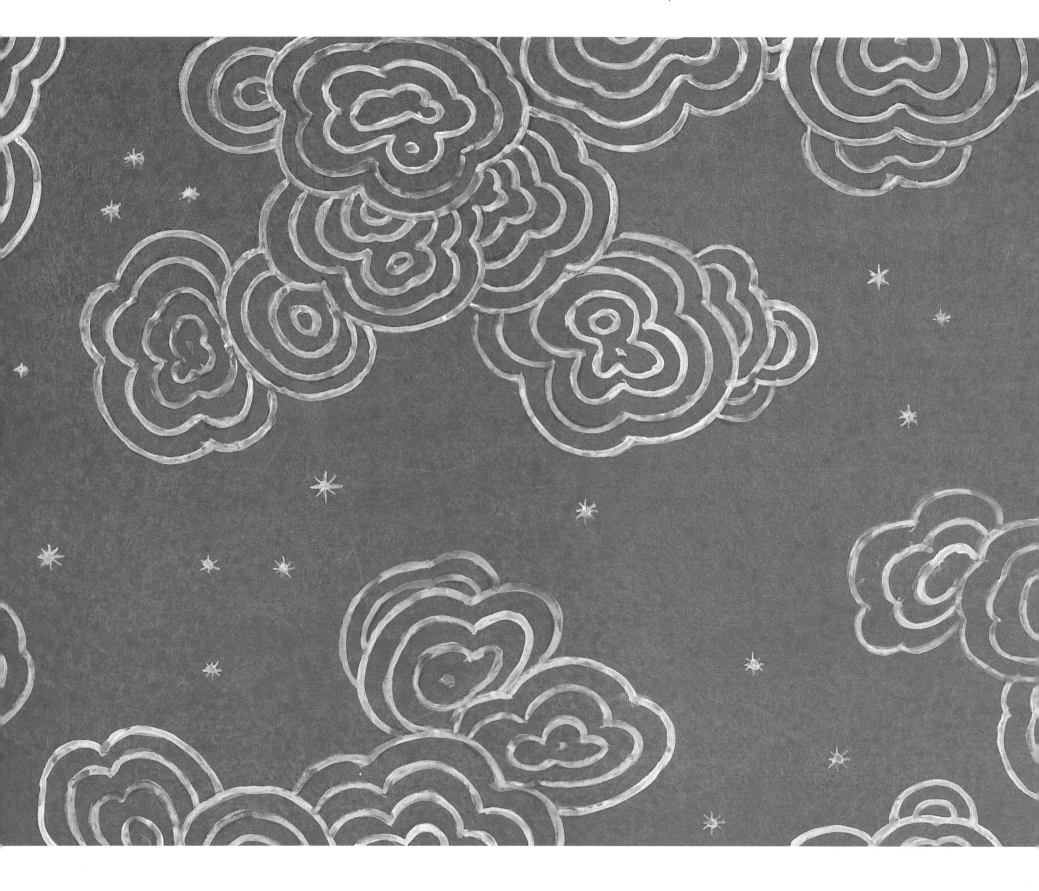

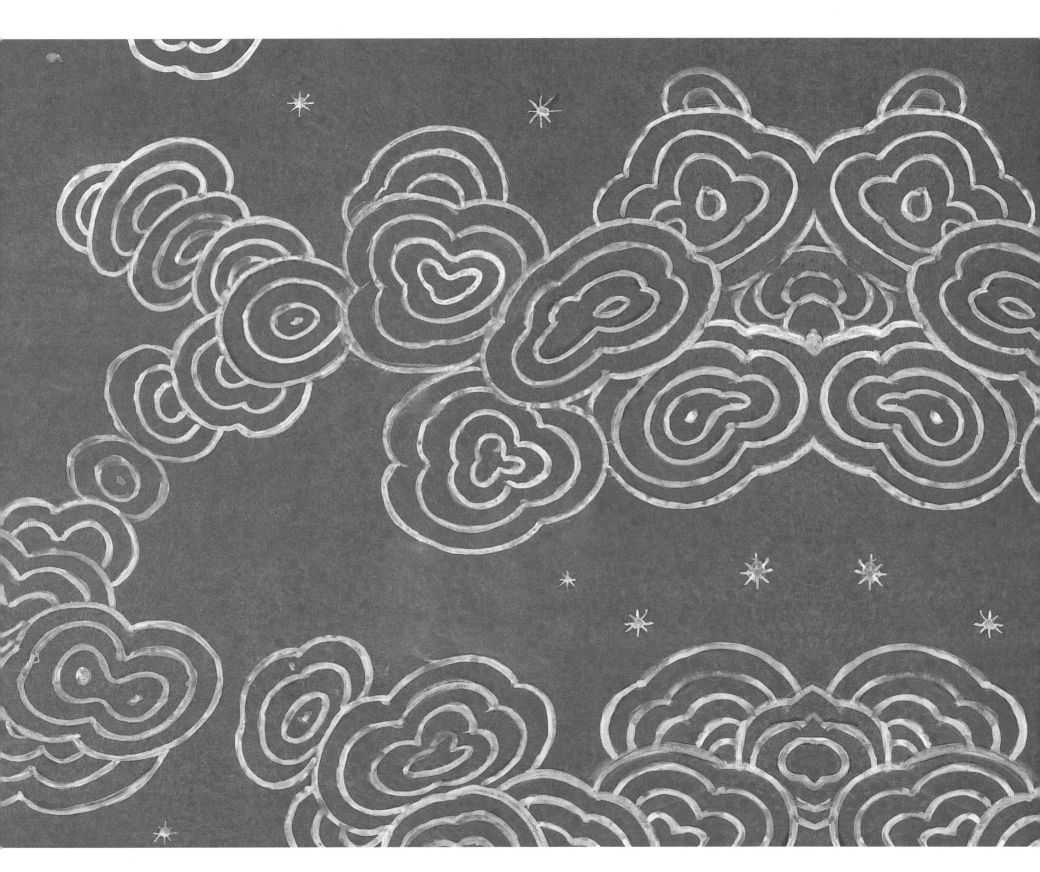

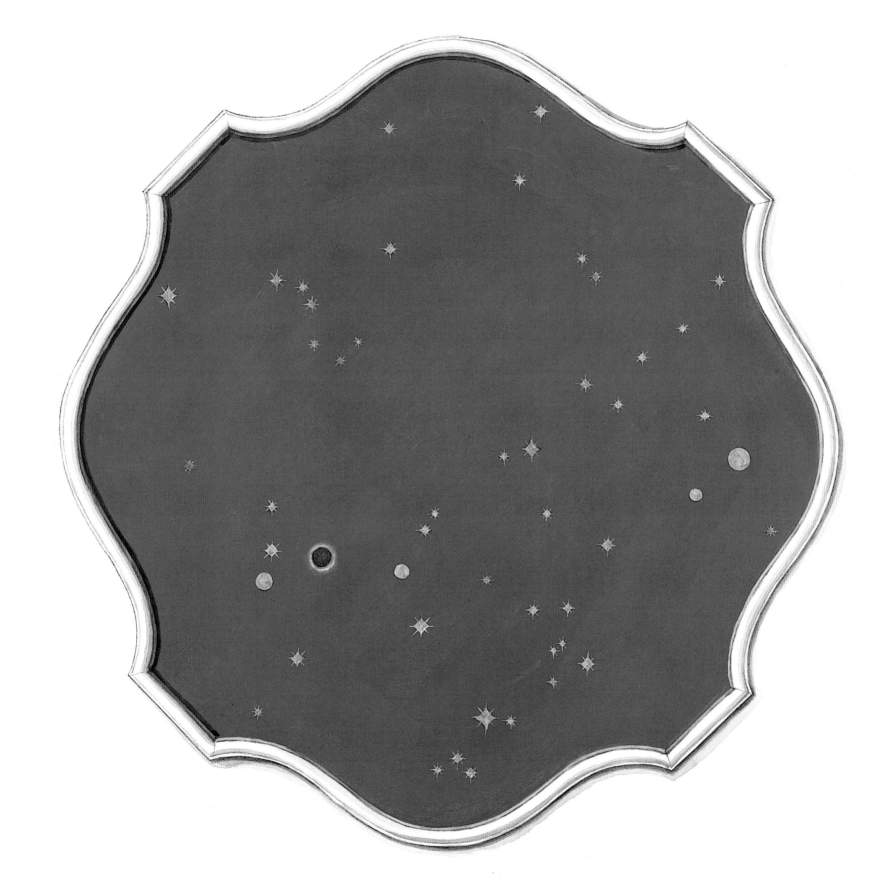

ECLIPSE SKY

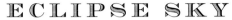

My design for the eclipse sky (*left*) shows the exact position of the stars and planets on 11 August 1999. This painting was intended to be the central panel in an entrance hall with further astrological motifs painted in *grisaille* on the walls. The moulding is painted in *trompe l'oeil* with a gilded filet.

RIGHT: This guide to the constellation in a trompe l'oeil frame is intended to be painted on the wall, as if hanging from a gilt pin, at a height that is easily readable

N

Deneb

AUGUST 1999

Arcturus

Capella

W

E

Jupiter

Castor

Saturn

Sun
Moon

Pollux

Regulus

Aldebaran

Venus

Mercury

Betelgeuse

Procyon

Rigel

Sirius

S

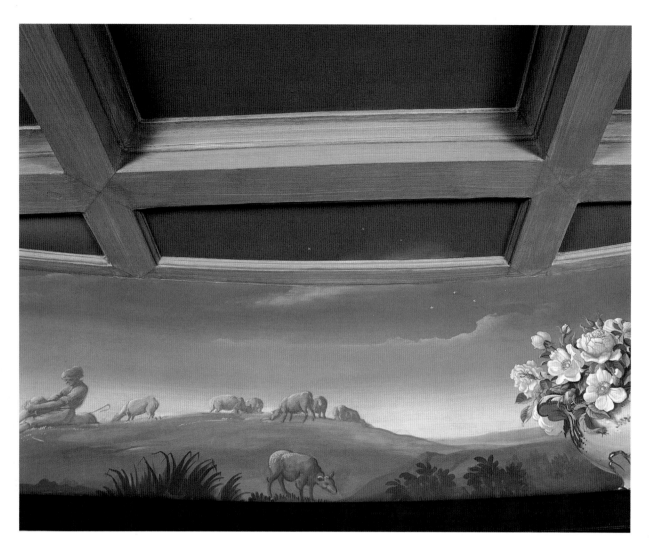

HILVERSUM

Built in the early twentieth century, this thatched Dutch house boasts an oval panelled dining room. The owners decided that the coffered ceiling and the frieze above the mahogany panelling in this room would benefit from being painted.

After discussion we decided on the depiction of a night sky, as though one was looking up through the beams to the heavens above. The sky would then continue on the frieze. In front of this moonlit *paysage*, *trompe l'oeil* bowls and pots sit on the ledge holding flowers.

Opposite: The coffered ceiling showing the night sky with a crescent moon and bats. Supporting pillars were painted so that the beams would not appear to float.

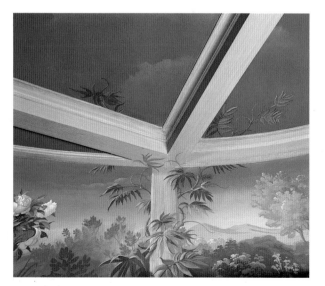

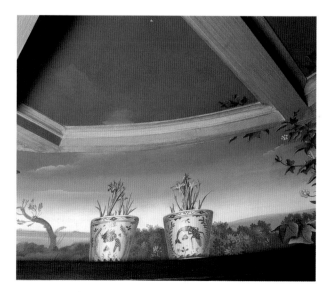

Above: Sheep graze peacefully in the background and a trompe l'oeil *bowl of roses sits in the foreground on the frieze. I was fortunate to have Henry van de Vyver and his colleague Steven Curtis to paint and stipple the beams, which saved me much time in the darkening days before Christmas.*

Left: One of the painted supports entwined by a creeper, this device 'holds' the ceiling.

Right: Dwarf irises sit in blue and white pots on the mahogany ledge.

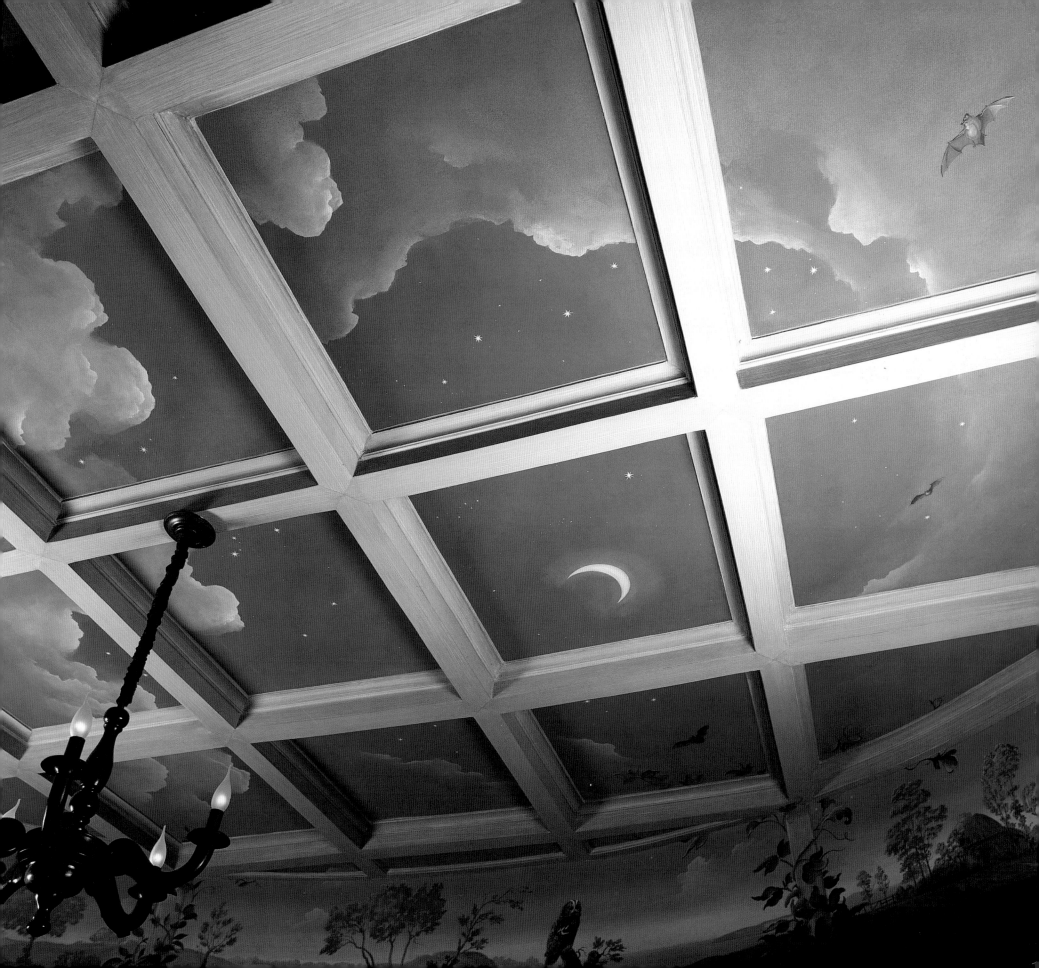

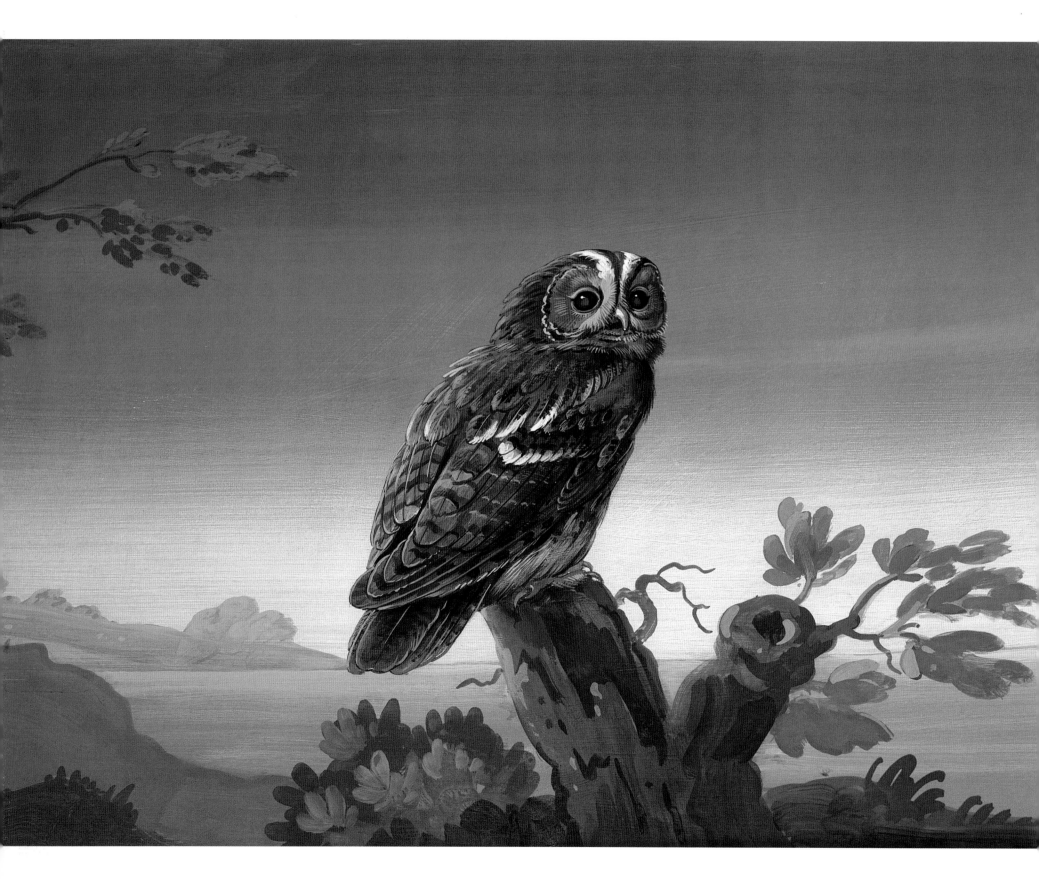

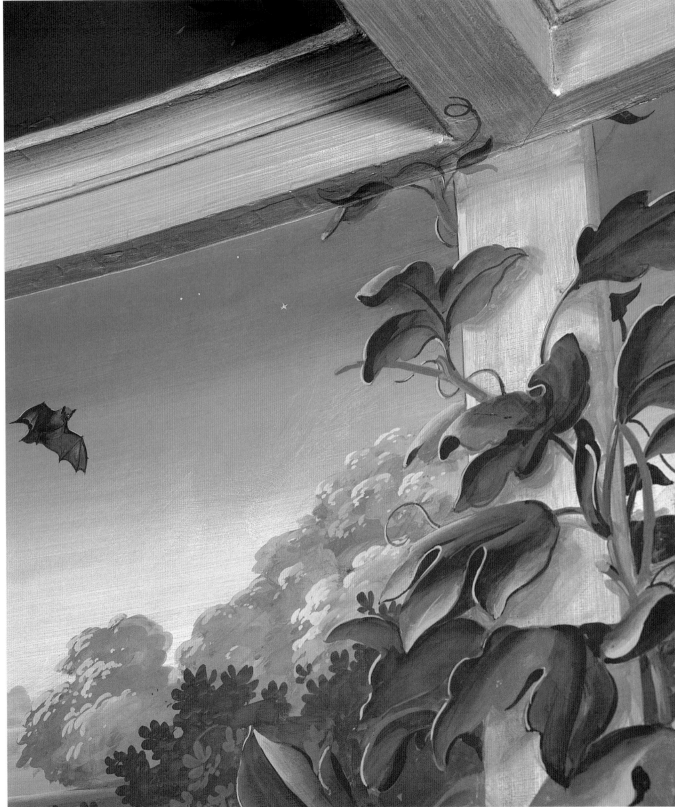

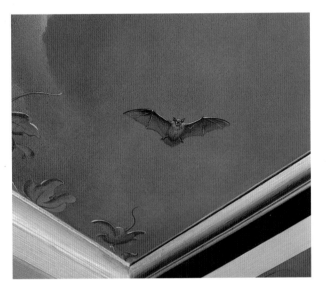

ABOVE: The owners' love of bats was reflected by those flying in the sky and hanging from the beams in repose.

RIGHT: One of the creeper-clad supports so necessary for the visual connection of panelling and ceiling.

LEFT: I painted this owl as the lynch pin of the design. It is always good to have a few surprises, and this fellow sitting above the door is one of them. His unblinking gaze locks with every guest as they turn their heads to look at the painting.

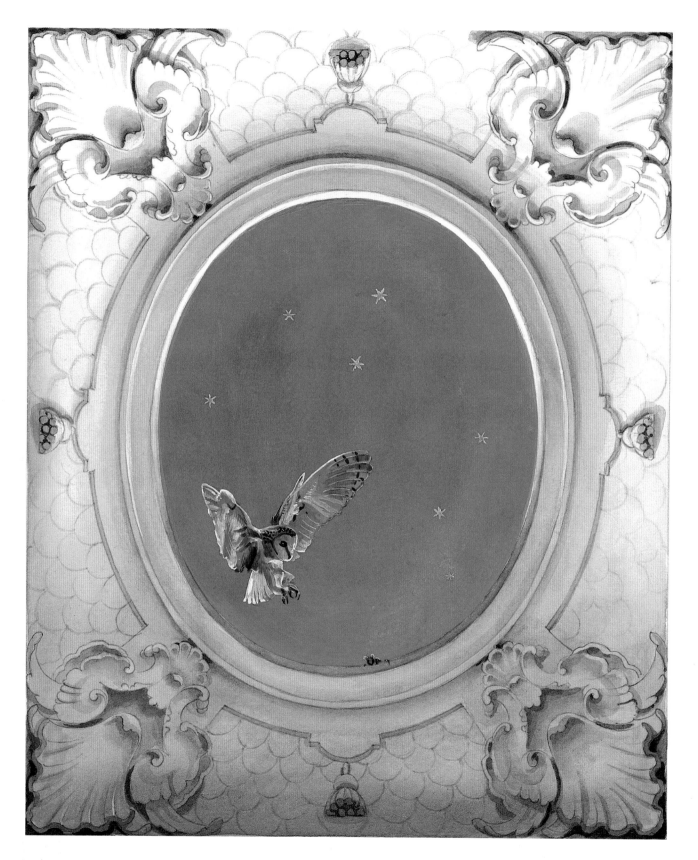

THE OWL CEILING

The hooting of owls is one of the most eery sounds to be heard in the stillness of the night. Although I love the swooping pipistrelle bats that encircle the house after dark I decided, because of its size, that the owl would be preferable in this composition.

LEFT: *The design shows, in* trompe l'oeil, *a slightly vaulted plasterwork ceiling open to the night sky. In the oval, a barn owl, with claws outstretched, is depicted about to alight on the hapless mouse overlooking the abyss. The design is for the ceiling of the small ante-chamber to the drawing room at Somerton.*

RIGHT: *This photograph shows the first stages of the work on site. The* trompe l'oeil *plasterwork has yet to be refined and built up. The stars and barn owl will be added to the central oval last of all.*

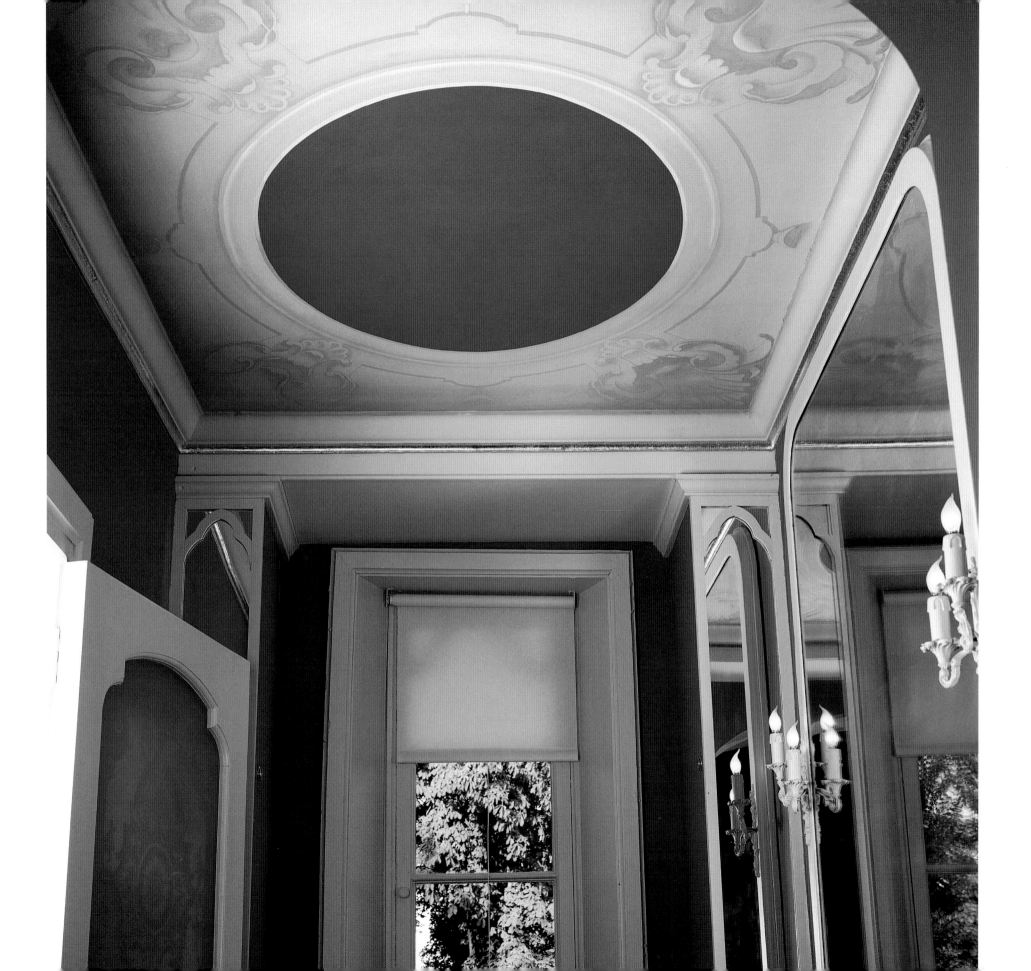

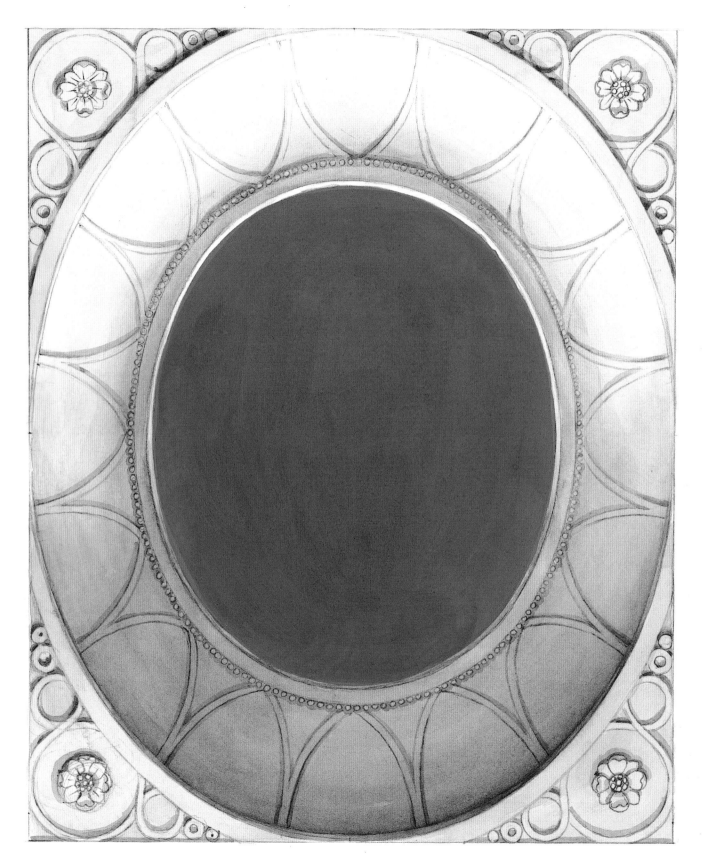

LEFT: Here is an alternative design for the owl ceiling, showing a different architectural solution, but retaining the same size oval opening to the sky.

RIGHT: Clockwise from the top right: whiskered bat; Leisters bat, pipistrelle and Bechsteins bat. All after the skilfully observed studies by Archibald Thorburn. I often use these inhabitants of the night sky in my designs. See, for example, the Hilversum ceiling on pages 28 to 31.

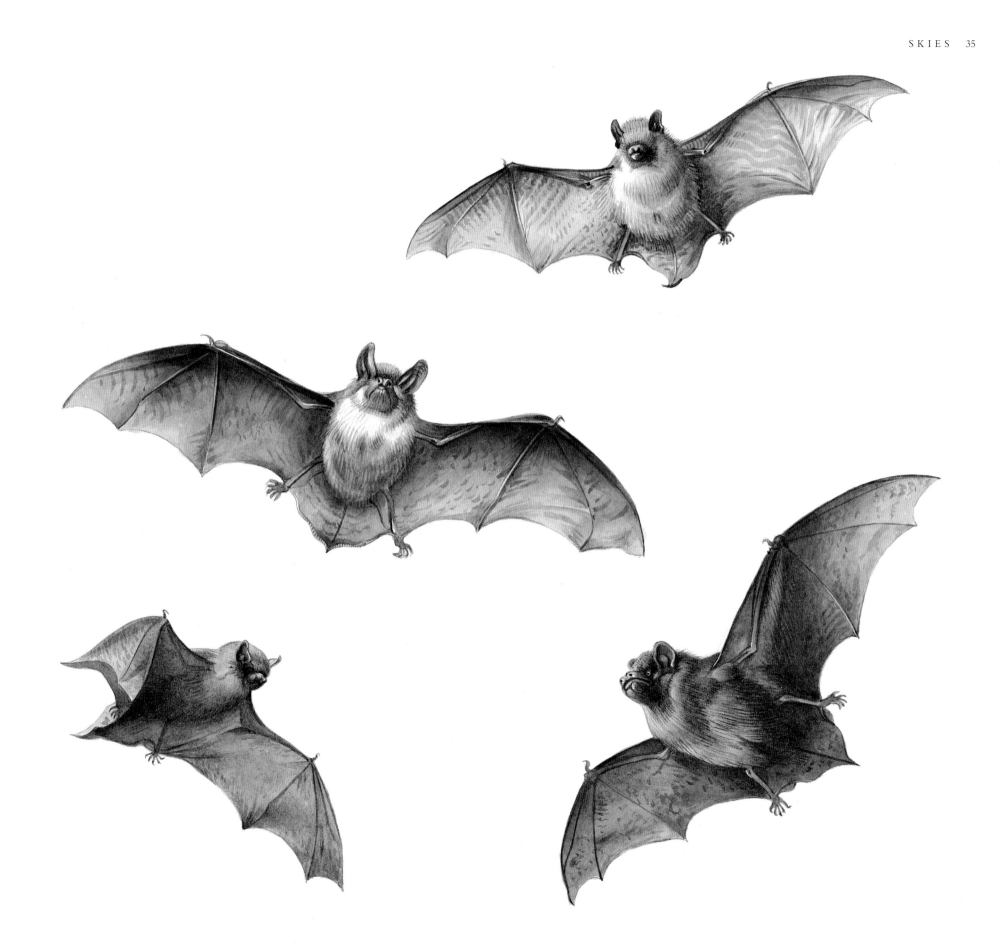

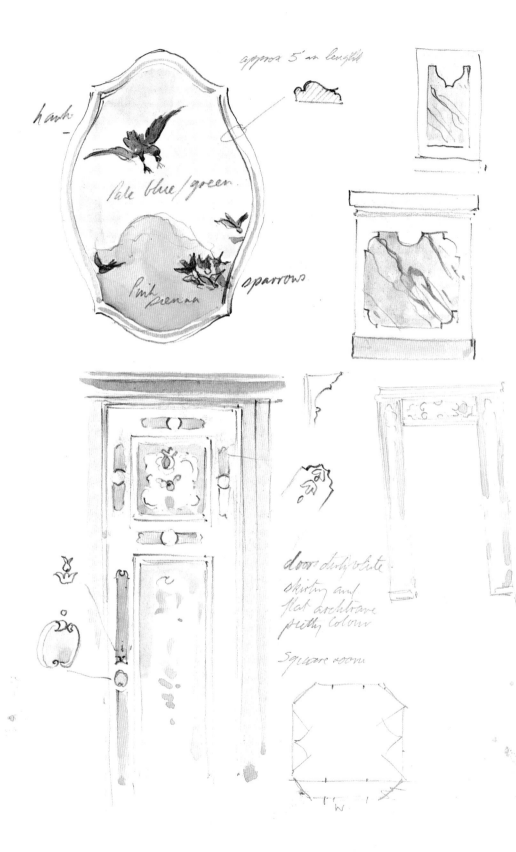

approx 5" in length

hawk

Pale blue/green

sparrows

Pink sienna

doors dirty white

skirting and flat architrave pretty colour

Square room

CA'REZZONICO

———

Over the years I have spent many happy hours in the Ca' Rezzonico, a treasure house of the decorative works of art of the eighteenth century in a splendid setting.

From the painted wall decoration and silks, to the furniture and porcelain, there is a wealth of material available for research that is both varied and intoxicating. As is so often the case, even a small detail can inspire a design or suggest the colouring for a decorative scheme. No visit to Venice is complete without some time spent in the palazzo.

LEFT: _A page from my sketchbook showing drawings of painted decoration in a closet at the Ca' Rezzonico in Venice, notably the ceiling painting of a sparrowhawk and sparrows in a panel._

RIGHT: _Two swallows and a sandmartin after Basil Ede and D. Henry. An example of the swallow can be seen on the ceiling painting at Craig-y-Bwla on page 43._

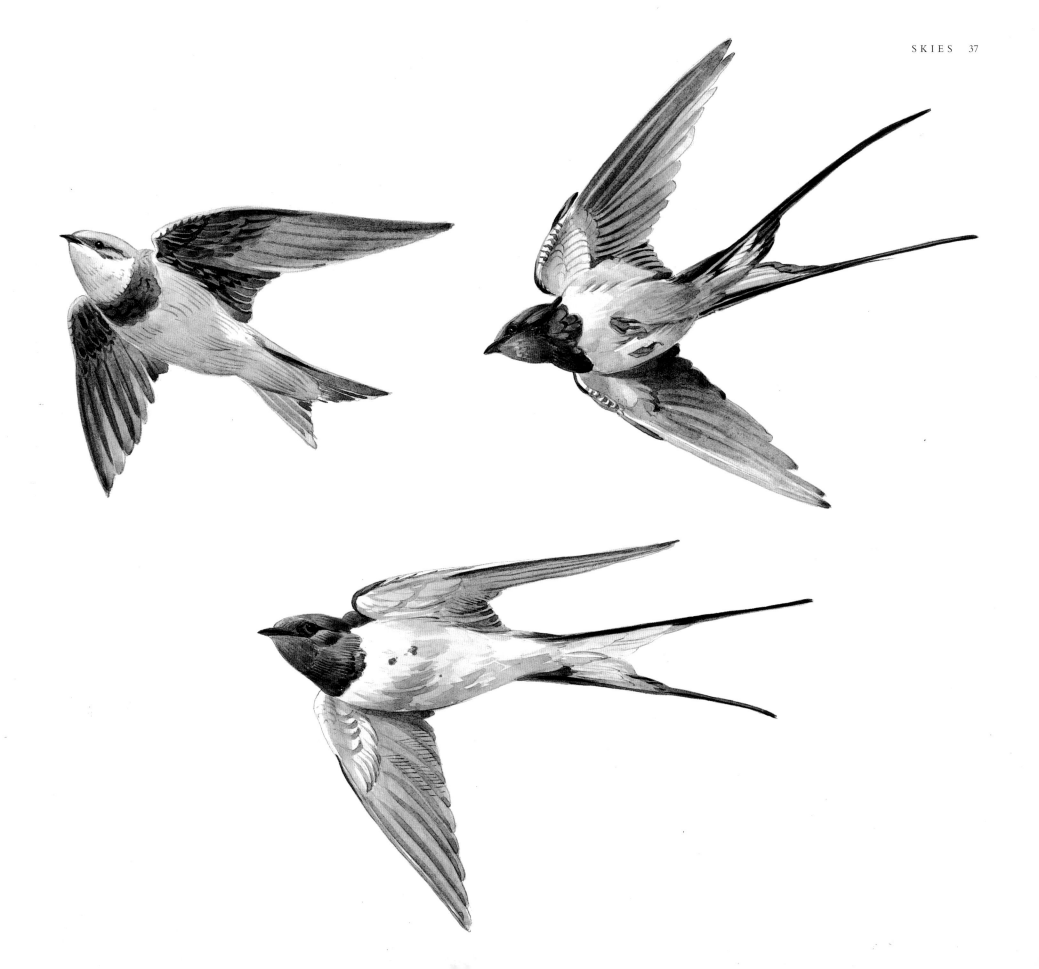

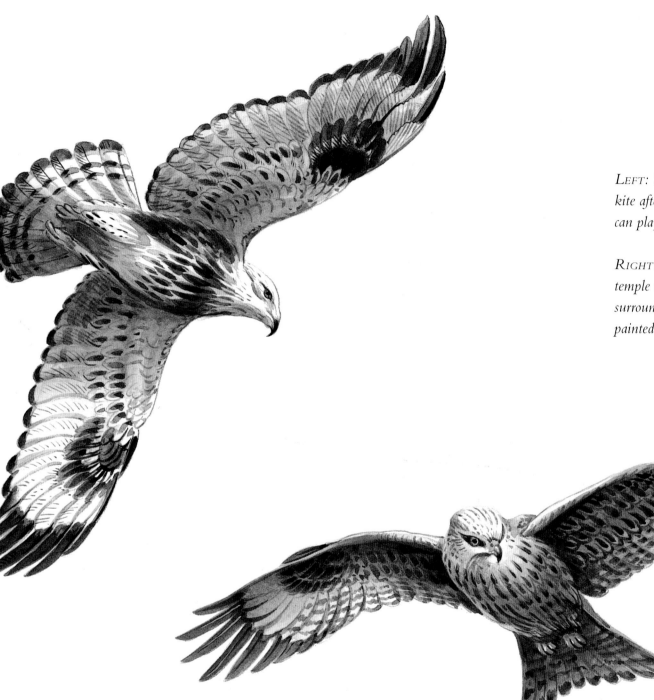

LEFT: *Studies for a rough-legged buzzard and a red kite after D. Henry. Two examples of larger birds that can play a more dominant role in the sky if needed.*

RIGHT: *A detail of the domed ceiling of the garden temple in Frankfurt showing roses entwined in the surrounding trellis against an open sky. The birds were painted by Rui Paes.*

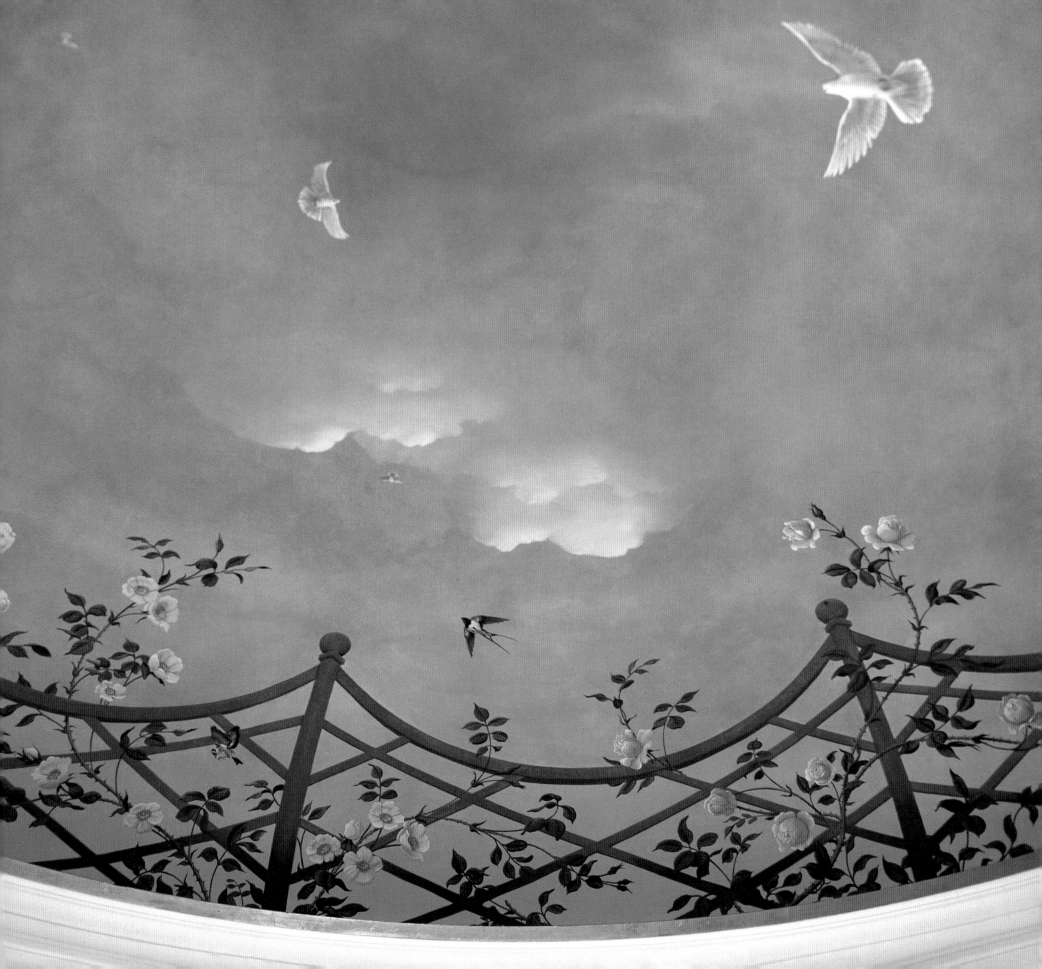

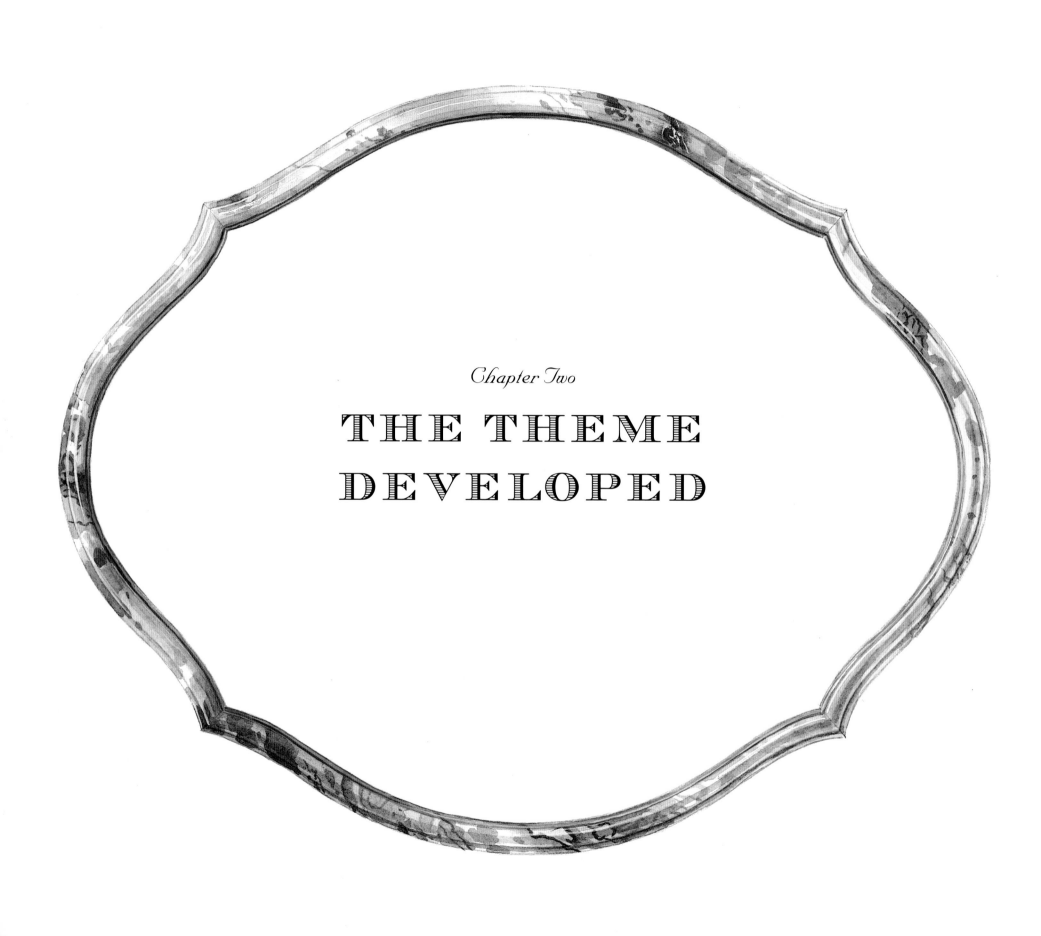

Chapter Two

THE THEME DEVELOPED

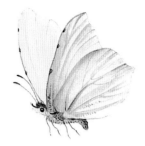

Birds, bats and insects may be the real inhabitants of the skies, but mythology and religion have provided a rich addition in the form of gods, goddesses and their offspring, angels and other heavenly forms. The manifold designs of the eighteenth-century Italian artist, Giovanni Battista Tiepolo, and a legion of other masters such as Carlone, Crosato, Piola and Veronese to name but a few, leave one not only weak with admiration but also with a vast repository of figures by which to be inspired. Much is to be gained by studying the work of Italian masters such as these. In particular, many of their compositions indicate ways to approach the myriad problems that beset the painter, such as the varying perspectives, and the devices used to help aid the design on the sloping surface of a ceiling. Also the differing tones and hues of colour used to promote the feeling of distance and proximity.

Cherubs and their secular cousins, putti, have been used endlessly in the past to add life, in a light-hearted manner, to many paintings. These enchanting, mischievous, laughing, sad or bad-tempered infants may be used in various ways to tell a story, or just amuse. Frequently one sees the welcoming smile of a cherub on arrival in an entrance hall, only to be met by the tearful countenance of another, above the door, on departure. This simple but effective device, carved in wood or in plaster, can just as easily be reproduced on a flat surface.

Rooms with low ceilings generally do not lend themselves to an architectural treatment in the form of elaborate constructions. The result of such a scheme can be a sense of oppression caused by the proximity of tons of *faux* masonry just above our heads! Perhaps the simplest architectural addition to a ceiling — after a *trompe l'oeil* moulding — is a parapet wall or balustrade. Elements such as these allow us to add flora and fauna to the ceiling. The series of four paintings executed in an apartment in Beirut is an example of work on a relatively low ceiling (see pages 60 to 67). The ceiling decoration was needed to complement the painted walls of four rooms *en filade*, which had been opened up to create one large space.

In many cases, the simplest way to create an illusion is to use a central perspective. However, there may be spaces where only one particular angle of the ceiling is visible at any given time, for example the dead end of a passageway or a room that is only appraised from one viewpoint. In this kind of situation, the perspective should be adapted accordingly.

Difficult angles can be disguised with foliage or drapery, thus helping to confuse the eye. The insertion of a bird or animal at a strategic point can help to soften a sharp angle or draw attention away from an inconvenient meeting of lines.

The sketches of plants and trees at the end of this chapter were done on a recent visit to Rio de Janeiro, in preparation for a commission for a mural painting. Studies such as these are useful reference material at those times when one needs to add a leaf or two to a composition.

In this chapter I have included examples of painted domes and vaulted ceilings. Architectural decoration on a curve can be fraught with problems and should not be undertaken unless you are confident of success.

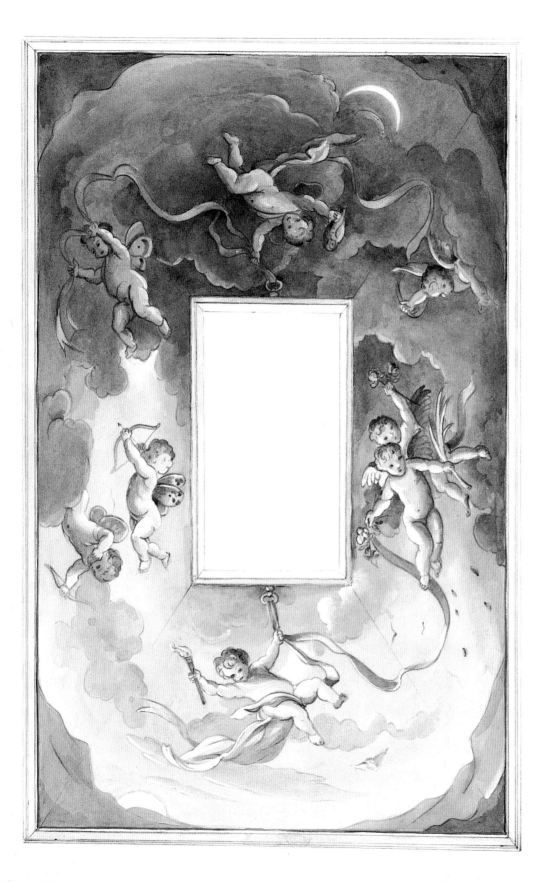

CRAIG·Y·BWLA

Set in ravishing countryside around Abergavenny in Wales, Craig-y-Bwla is a house I painted many years ago. The present owners decided that the undecorated vaulted ceiling, above the staircase, should also be painted. The theme of night and day was chosen, as one would be greeted by a vision of night on the way up to bed, and of day when descending the staircase in the morning. Also to be considered was the skylight in the ceiling. This I decided to include as a frame within the painted sky. The frame was painted as if held by a ribbon at each end, thus suspending it in the 'open' sky.

LEFT: *My design for the ceiling in* grisaille. *This is sometimes helpful to do even if the end result is to be painted in colour. One is able to work out more clearly in monochrome the interplay of light and shade, without the interference of different colours that may complicate the issue. (Right) A putto holds the ribbon with one hand; the torch in his other hand symbolises the light of day.*

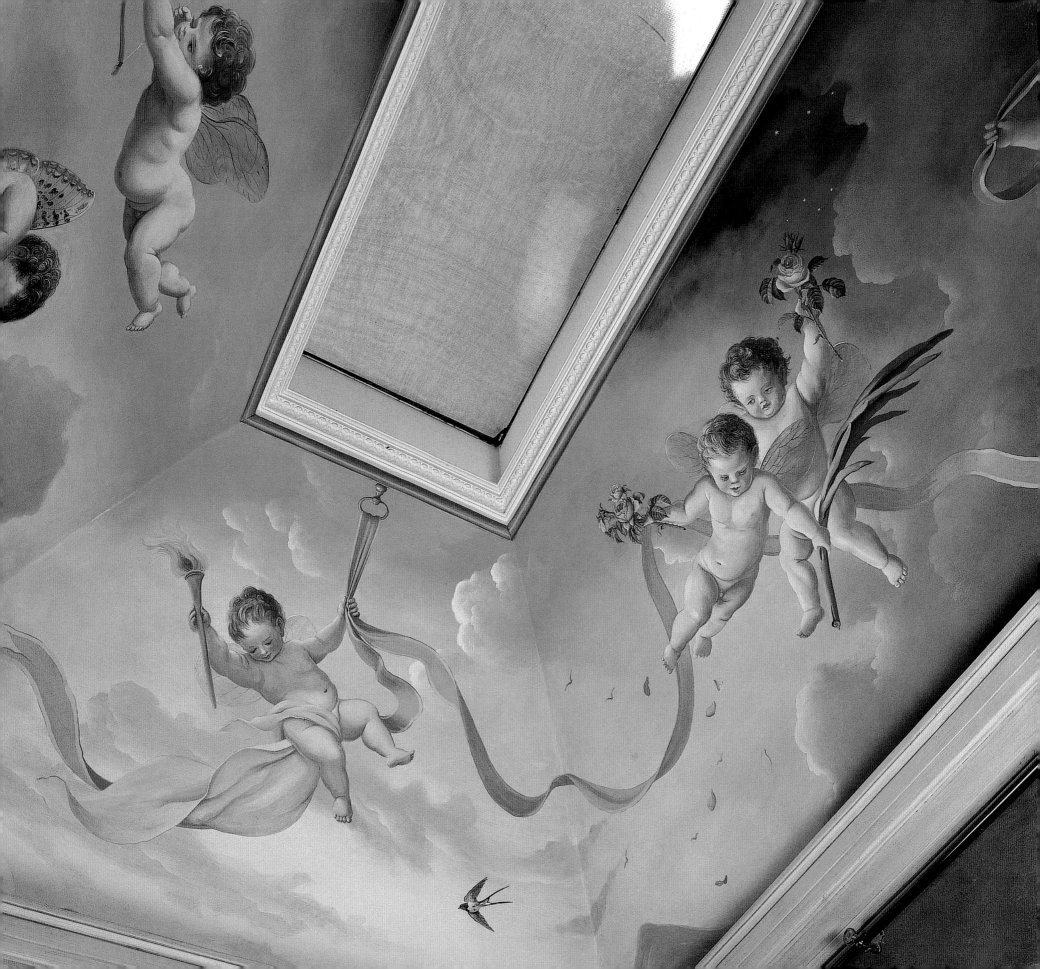

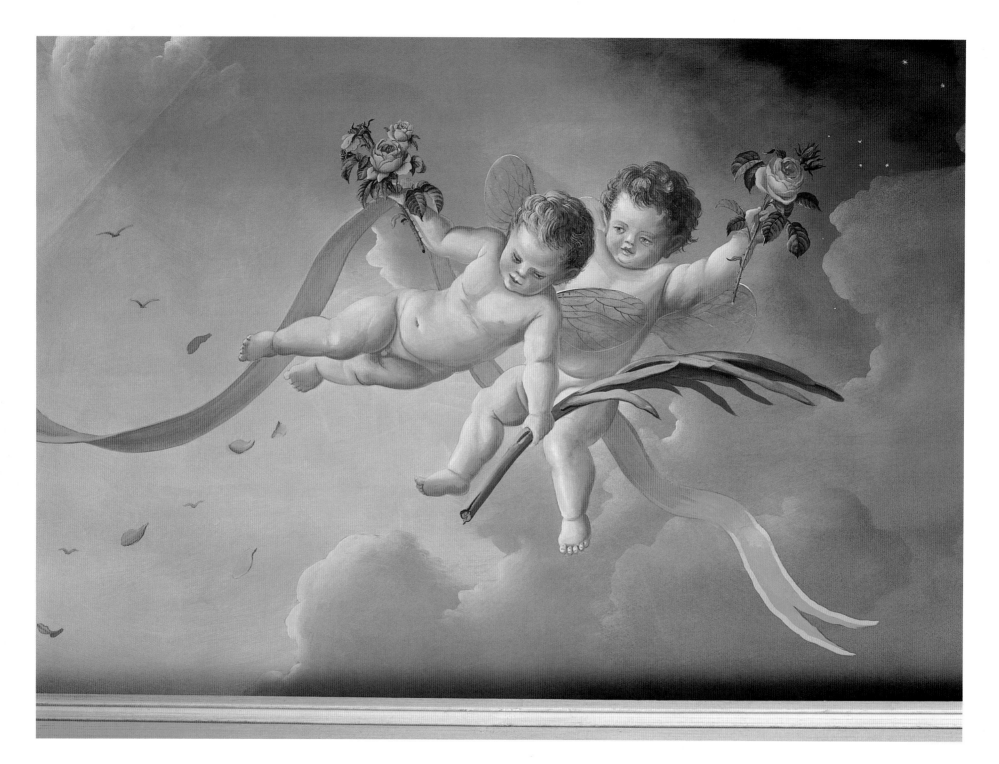

ABOVE: Two putti holding flowers help to celebrate the coming of dawn. (Right) At the other end of the skylight a putto holds the ribbon attached to the painted frame. On his right hand an owl perches to symbolise night. The crescent moon peeps through the darkening clouds and stars twinkle in the sky.

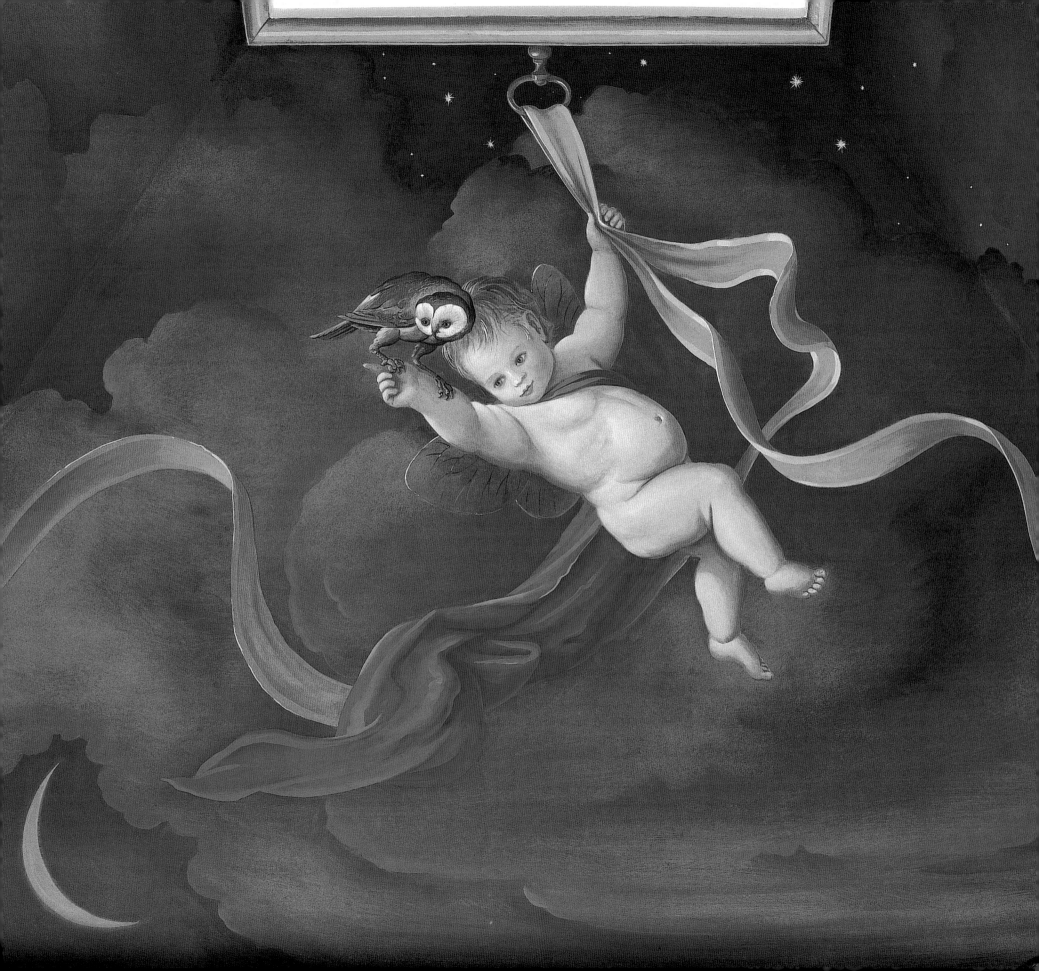

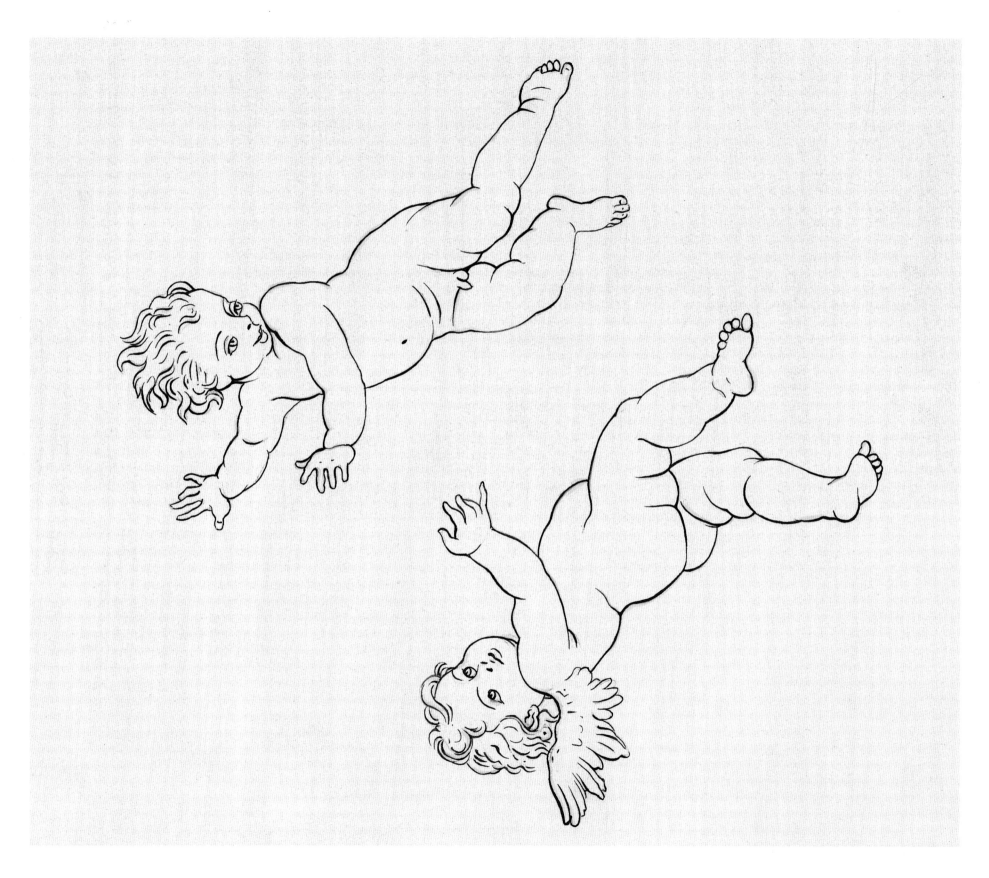

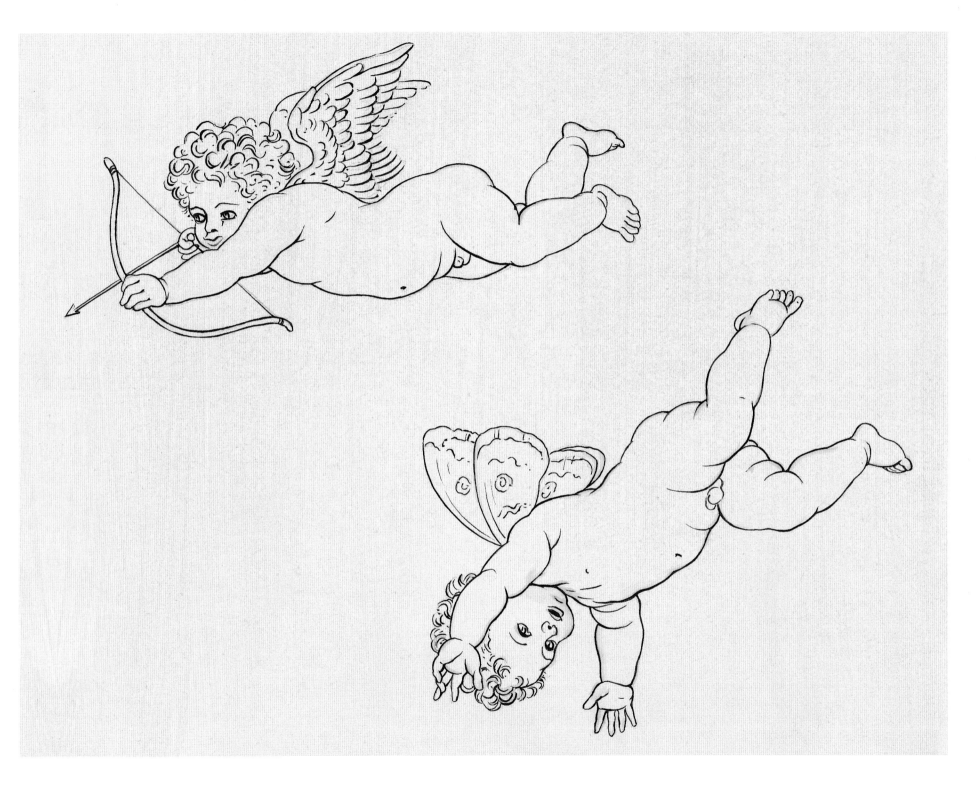

LEFT AND ABOVE: Drawings of putti cavorting in the heavens, two with feathered wings and one with butterfly wings. Great variety can be introduced by the use of different butterflies' wings.

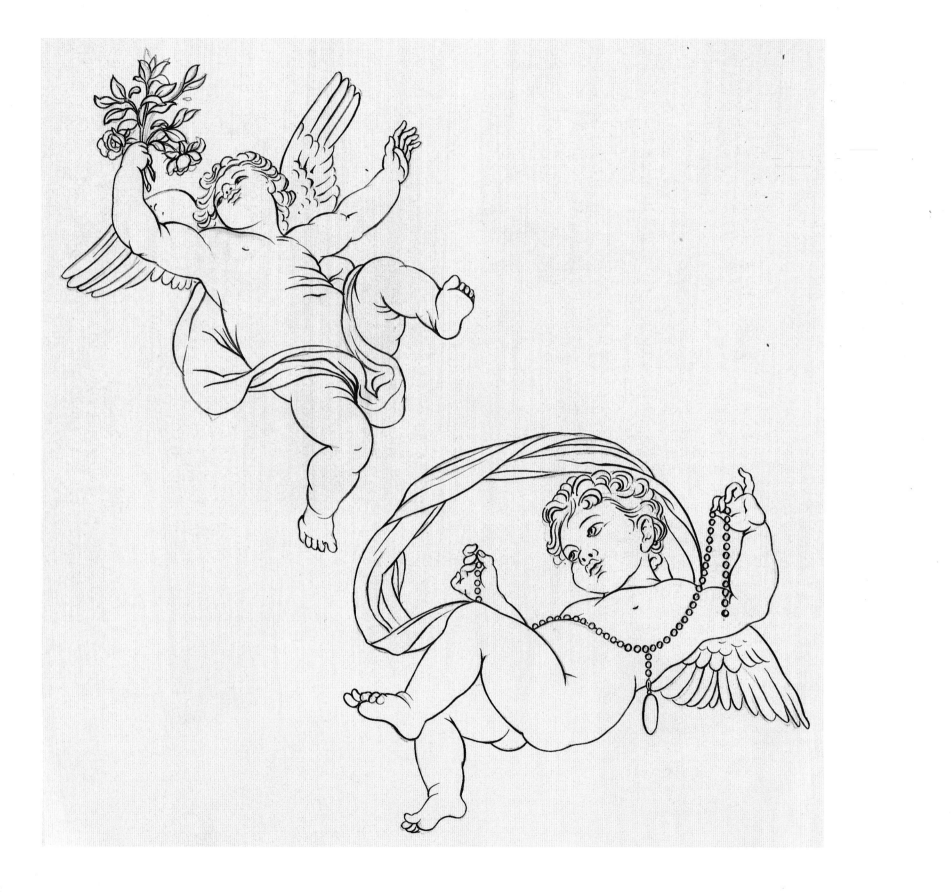

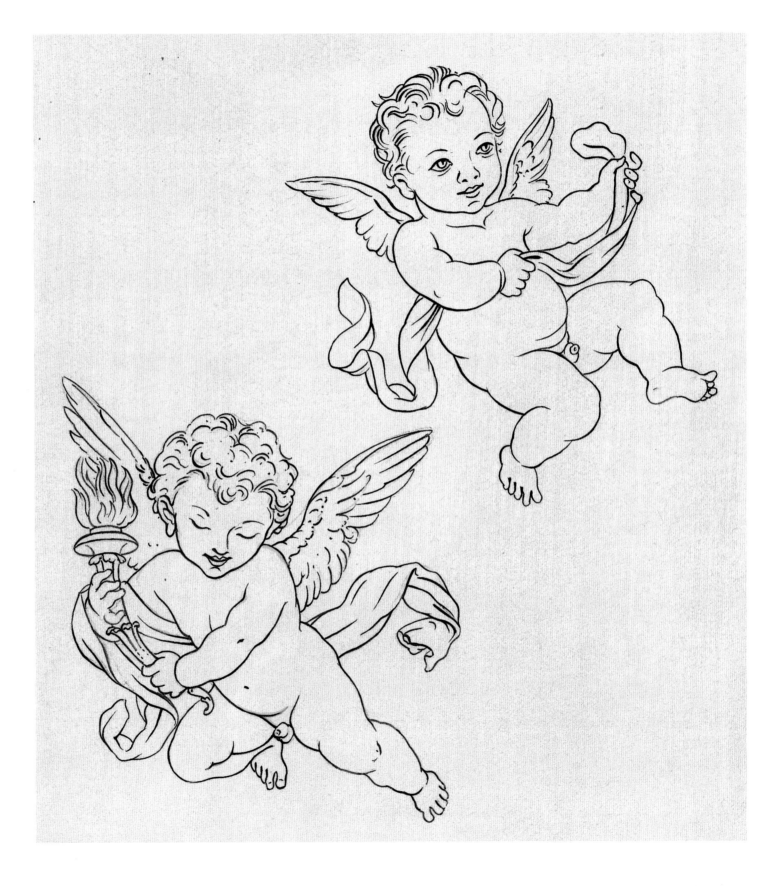

LEFT: *My drawing top left shows a putto holding flowers, while the lower one clutches a string of pearls from which dangles a miniature or timepiece.*

RIGHT: *Two drawings of putti with drapery, after Pierre-Paul Prud'hon. One holds a torch as he surveys the scene below.*

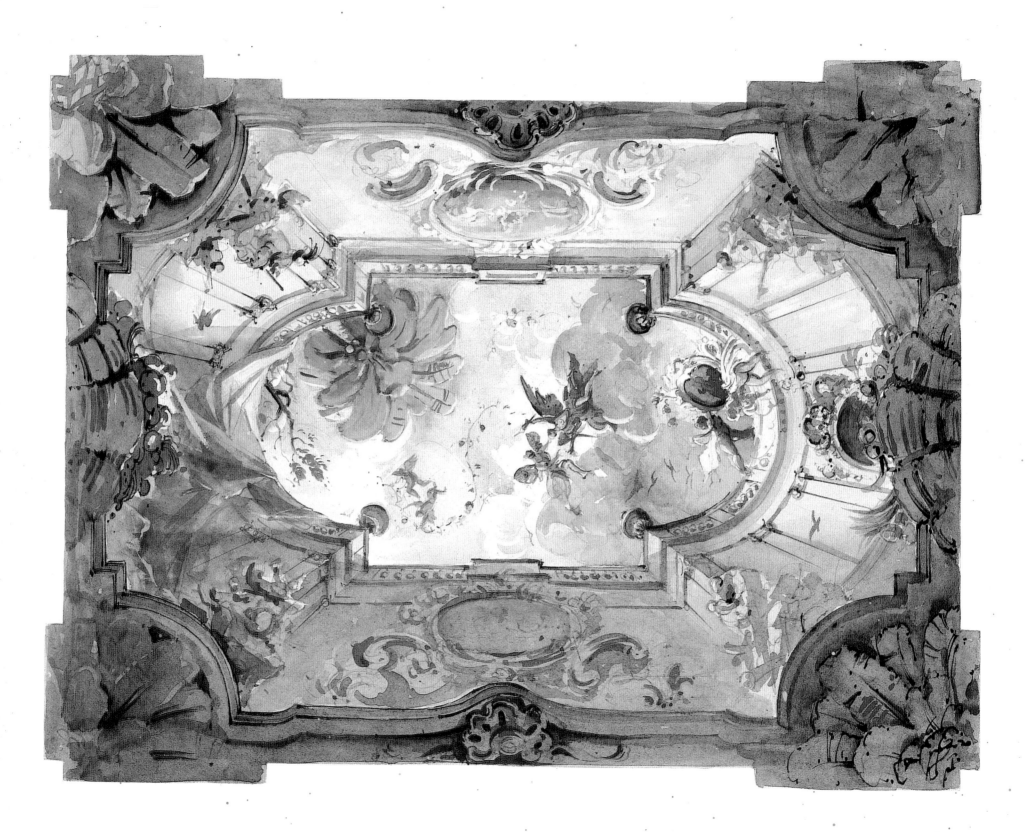

MAWLEY HALL

The subject of this painting was taken
from Milton's *Paradise Regained* – an
allusion to the salvation and restoration of
Mawley Hall by Mr and Mrs Anthony
Galliers-Pratt in the second half of the
last century.

The central figures are Adam and Eve
reunited, fêted by cherubs. *Trompe l'oeil*
stone and plasterwork were used to
increase the sense of height in the room.

*Left: My watercolour design for the ceiling of
the oak drawing room at Mawley Hall in
Shropshire.*

*Right: Milton's Tree of Life is represented by
the hybrid palm. The garlands with which the
cherubs prepare to deck Adam and Eve are
made of wild flowers collected while walking
in the park.*

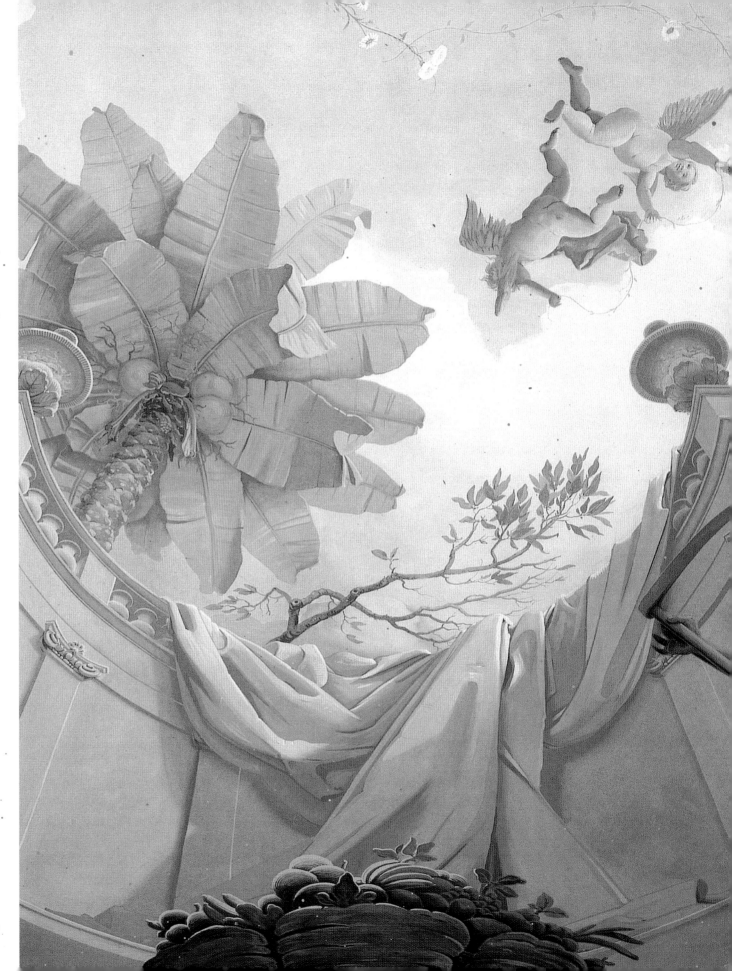

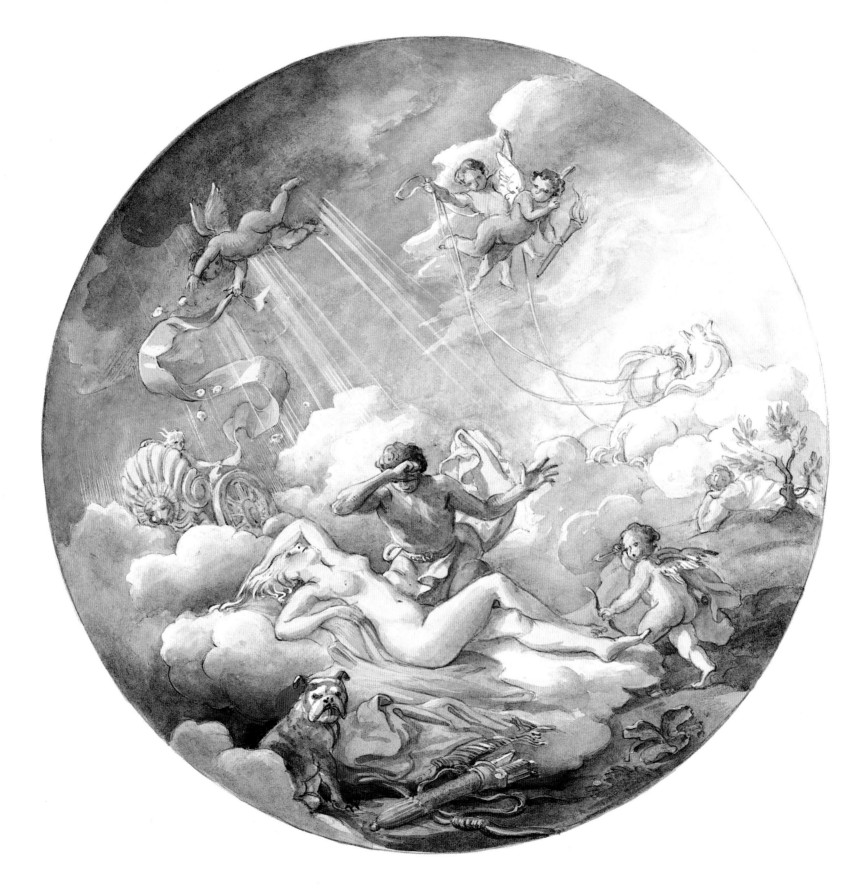

SETTRINGTON
HOUSE

This bed was designed by the late Francis Johnson for a particular bedroom at Settrington House in Yorkshire. Several years later, when the bed was finished and complete with bed hangings, I was asked to paint the interior of the dome. The decoration had, of necessity, to be done *in situ* as the bed had already been assembled and 'dressed'. It would have been an enormous amount of work to disassemble it and paint the inside of the dome in my studio, which would have been a viable alternative had time allowed. The dome is made of papier-mâché and had to be sanded to a fine finish before any painting could take place. Eventually a scaffold was erected that straddled the bed and I began to work, mainly by artificial light, amid the swags and drapes.

LEFT: My watercolour design for the dome.

RIGHT: The mahogany and parcel gilt bed with painted dome and silk hangings. The interior of the dome is much shallower than the exterior. Polychrome models of the family crest – a stork – sit above the cornice at all four corners.

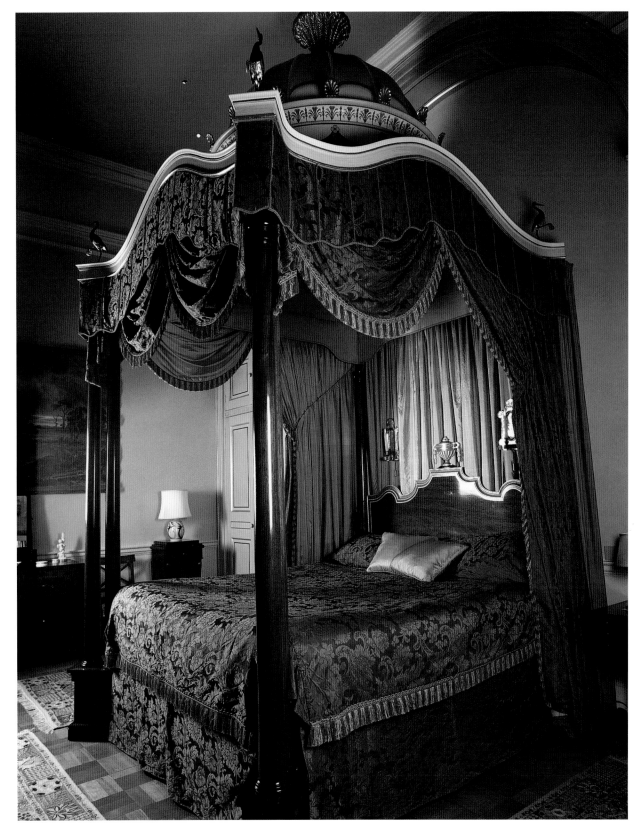

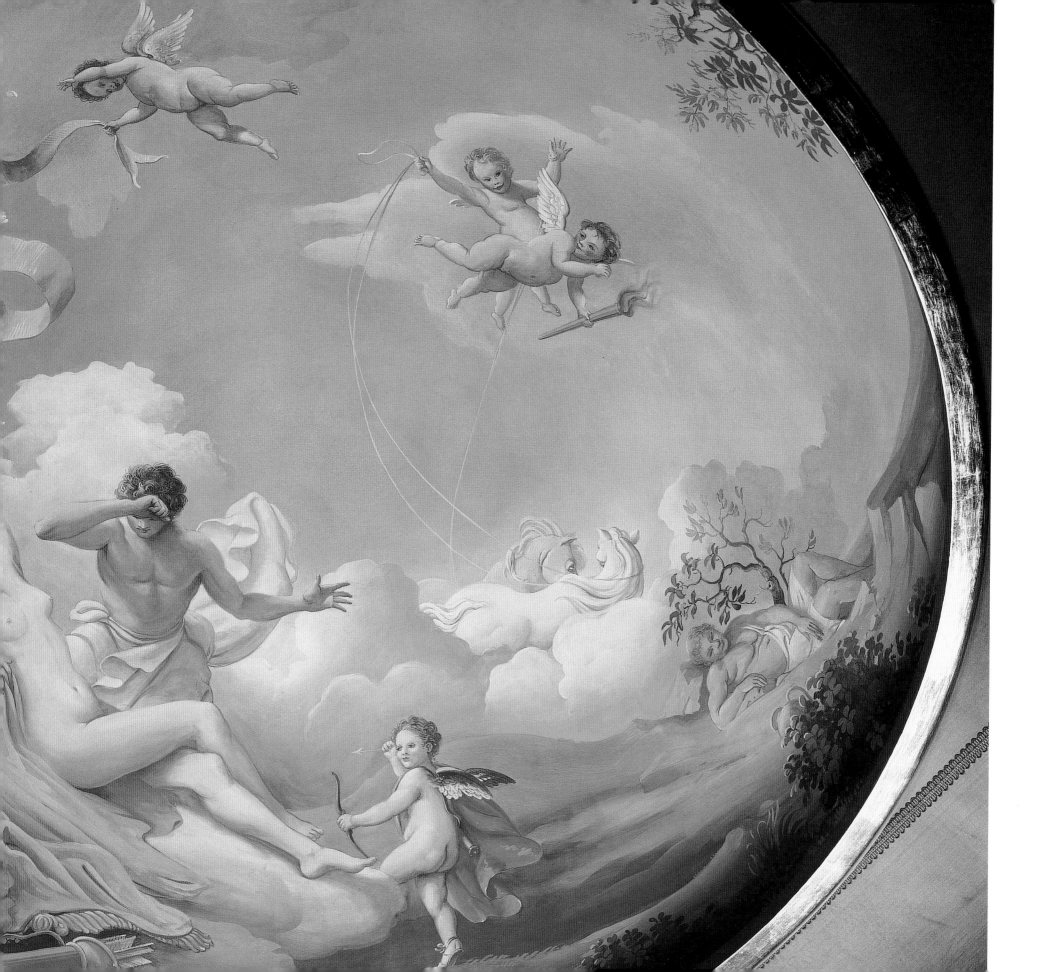

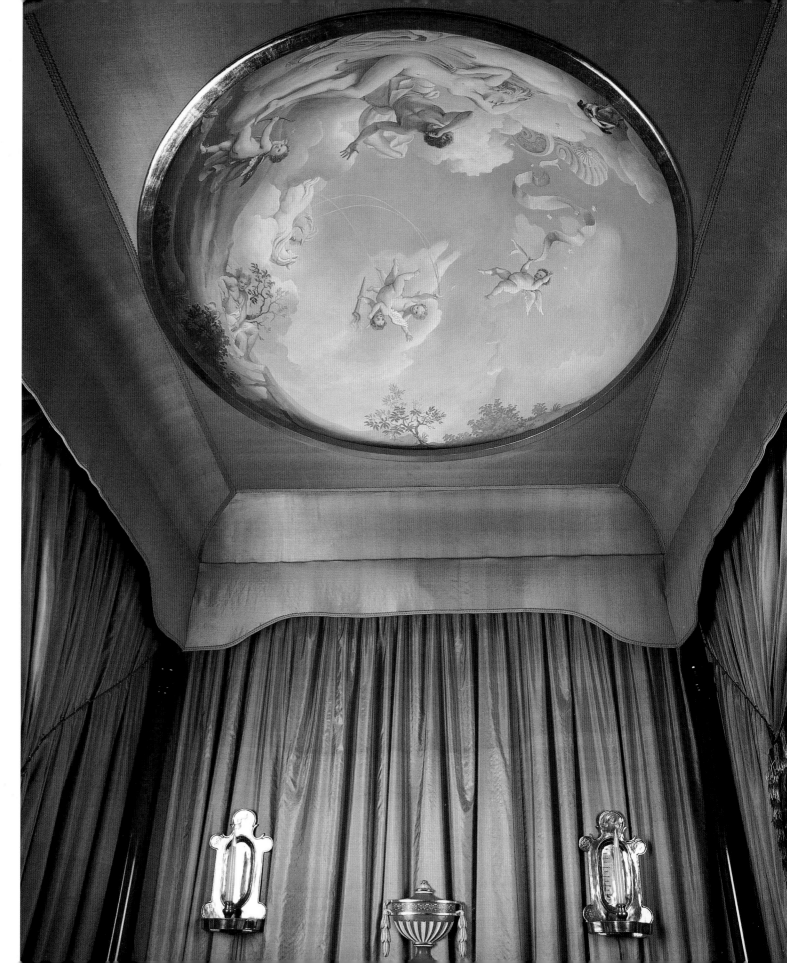

LEFT: *Part of the painted dome showing Aurora with Cupid at her feet, while Tithonus lies asleep blissfully unaware of the passionate encounter. Aurora was fated to fall in love with a succession of mortal youths and her passion for Cephalus was all the more ardent because he spurned her. Aurora's obsession led her to neglect her daily duty of leading Helios through the heavens, but Cupid saved the threatened chaos to the universe by making Cephalus return her love. She then carried him off in her chariot. This tale is a free adaptation of the Greek myth by an Italian baroque playwright, Gabriello Chiabrera, (1552-1637) which was popular in its day and widely used by artists.*

RIGHT: *Although the main viewpoint is from the head of the bed, hopefully there is enough interest in the composition for it to work from other angles.*

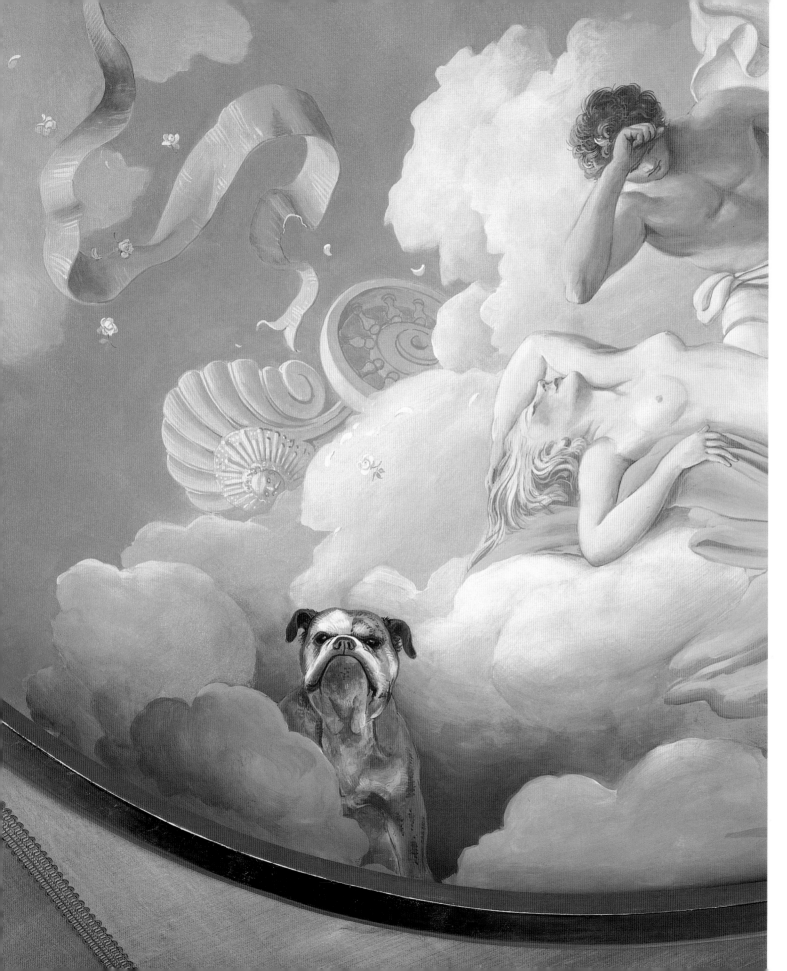

LEFT: *The abandoned chariot sits in the clouds above Aurora and Cephalus. Leticia, the family's bulldog, gazes down with an enigmatic expression; who knows what she sees or thinks?*

RIGHT: *A detail of the painted dome, in which a putto grasps a ribbon and casts flowers on the couple below. Another holds the horses' golden reins, while a third carries a burning torch.*

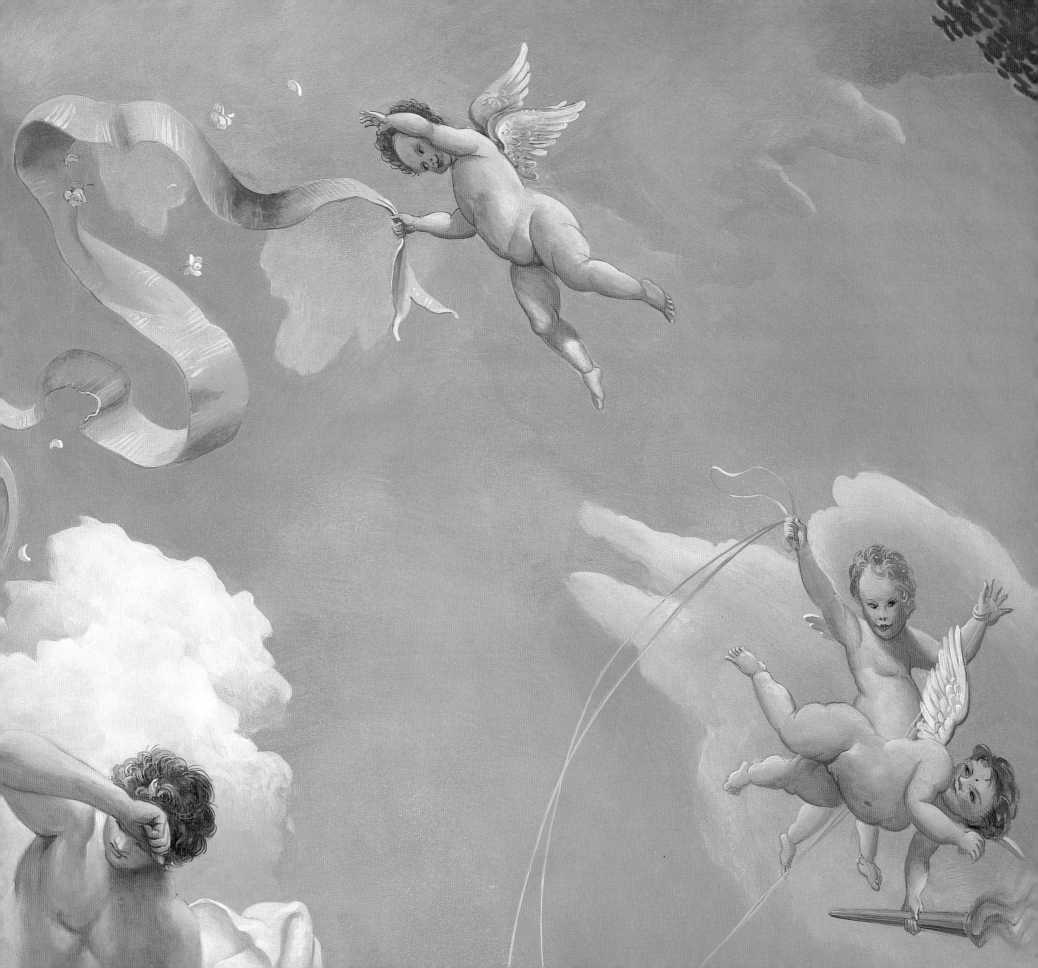

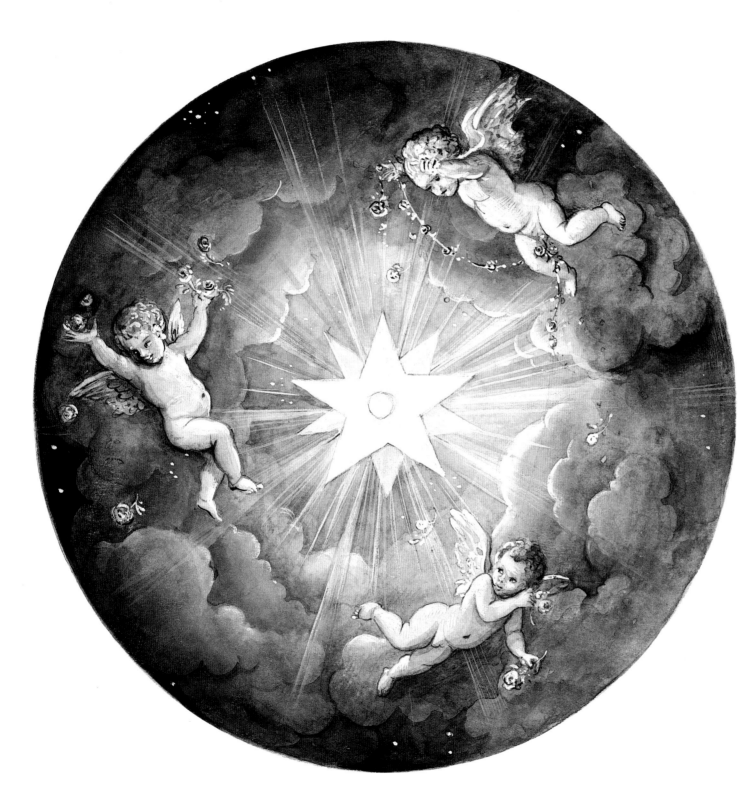

DOME DESIGNS

One of the main points to take into account when painting a dome is the changing perspective from base to apex. This can sometimes be used to advantage in a design but is not to be ignored. Fluid forms such as drapery and plants are less difficult than architecture to handle, but distortion is a possibility that we are less aware of when working close to. Therefore, consideration of the changing curve should be paramount, especially if the dome is not of a shallow gradation.

LEFT: A very simple design in grisaille for the dome of a lavatory. The design would work equally well if painted in any other monochrome, such as sanguine, indigo, or terre verte. At the centre of the star is a small downlight: a feature with which one often has to contend. The three putti in the painting appear to cast sweet-scented flowers upon the guest below.

RIGHT: Designs for a dome that I painted for a Middle Eastern client. A low landscape runs around the perimeter depicting an oasis and mosque with minaret. The other half of the design shows a string of camels and, in the foreground, a hawk. The dome is illuminated at the apex by a lantern. It was extremely hot painting this dome, as there was little ventilation. This is one of the factors to be taken into account should you find yourself in a similar situation.

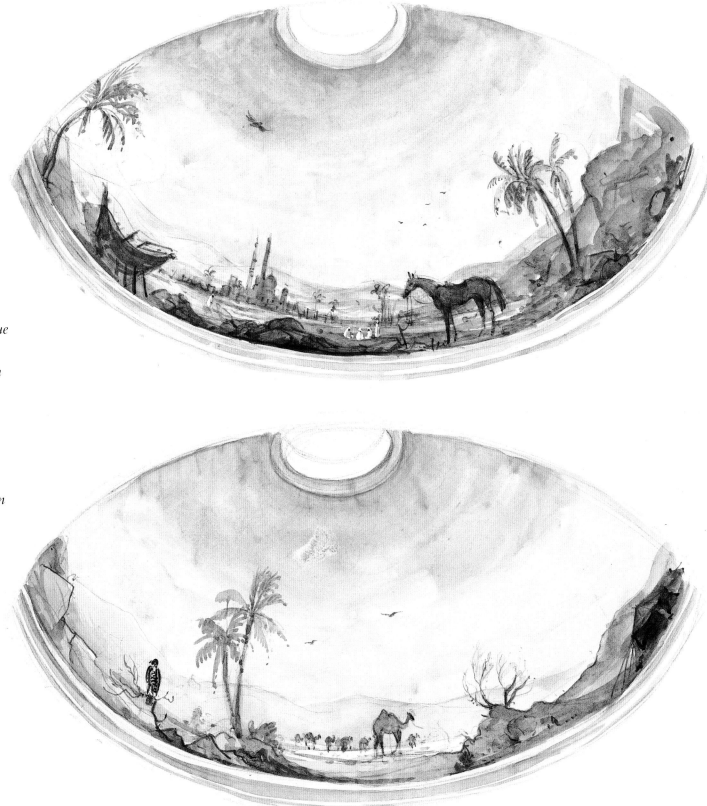

THE OURJOUAN CEILING

It is one of the great pleasures of my work that commissions take me to many different parts of the world. I spent several months in the Lebanon, with Rui Paes, painting a series of rooms in an apartment in Beirut. We also painted four ceilings to complete the scheme, as had the ceilings been left untouched, the proportion of undecorated ceiling to decorated wall would have been uncomfortable.

Working with the client, Madame Ghandour, and her interior designer, Jean Louis Mainguy, Rui and I based the scheme on the eighteenth-century decoration of various Venetian palazzi. Large areas of wall were painted in *trompe l'oeil* to look like plasterwork, and the finish was intended to recreate the patina of time.

The original layout of the apartment had four separate rooms *en filade*, however, walls were removed to create one large area, unified and supported by ten columns. The library at one end and the dining room at the other were linked by the sitting areas between.

Because of the nature of the layout, the four separate ceilings had to be harmonious when viewed together from afar.

RIGHT: In the sitting area adjoining the library I decided to paint a simple balustrade with urns. Swallows wheel beneath the scudding clouds, while doves perch on the ledge. A putto scatters roses.

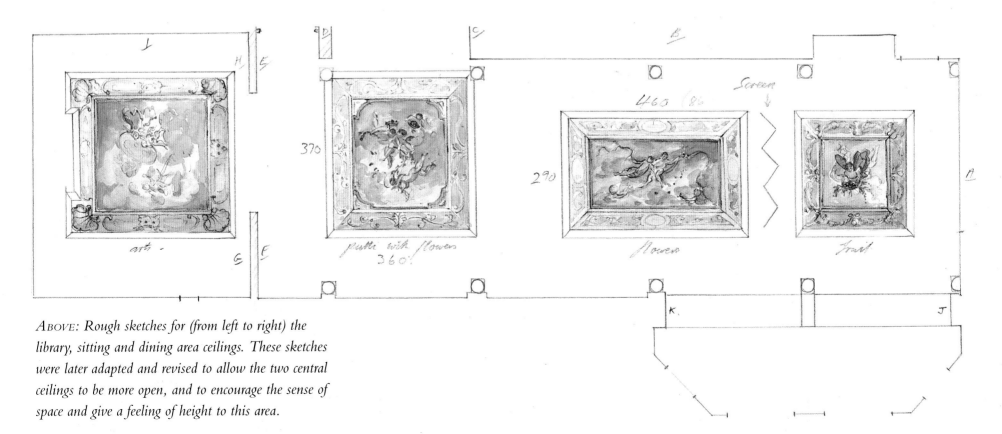

ABOVE: Rough sketches for (from left to right) the library, sitting and dining area ceilings. These sketches were later adapted and revised to allow the two central ceilings to be more open, and to encourage the sense of space and give a feeling of height to this area.

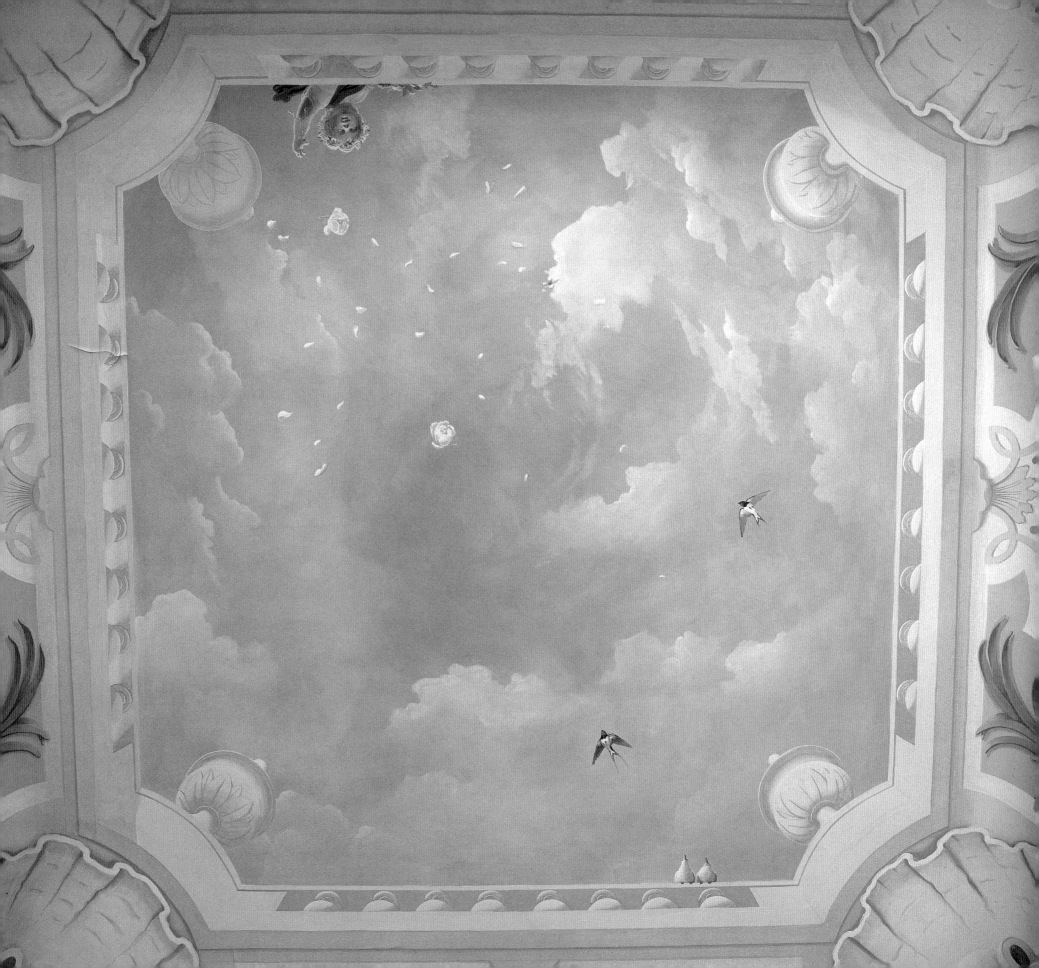

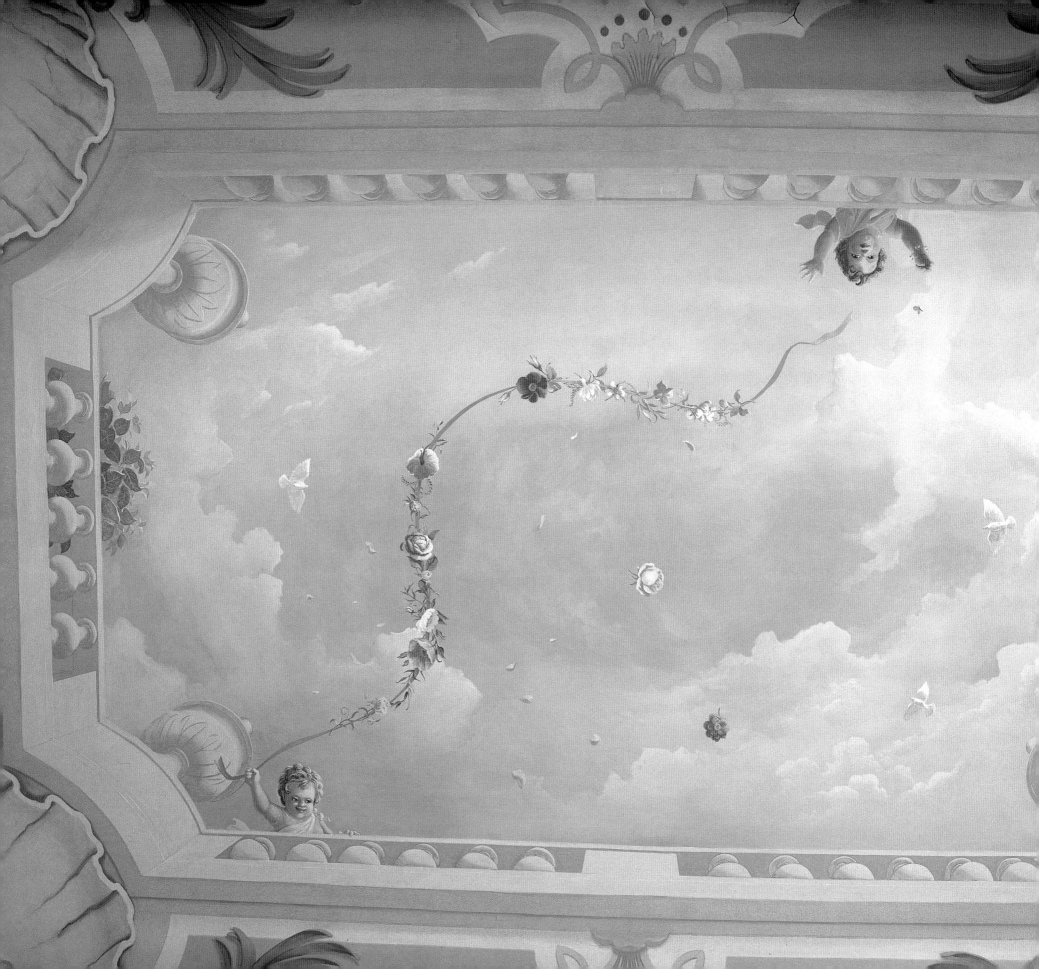

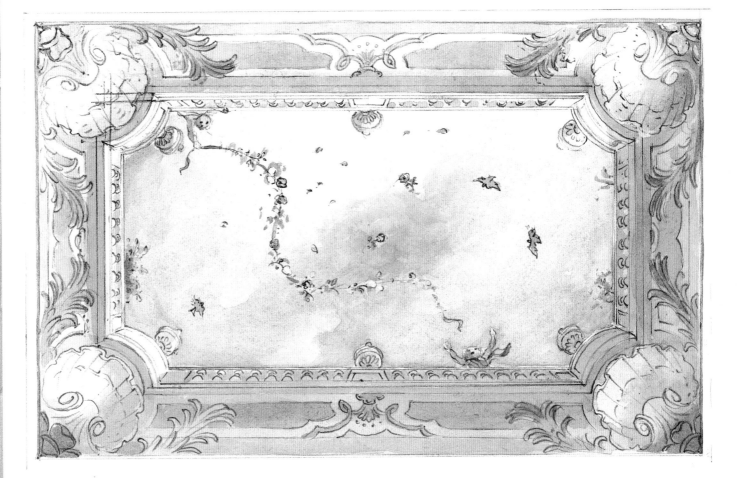

ABOVE: My design for the main ceiling of the sitting room echoed, architecturally, the square ceiling of the room shown on page 61. On the left, the painted plaster features two putti with a garland of flowers, and doves. The perspective was taken from a central point in each ceiling as this seemed the happiest solution.

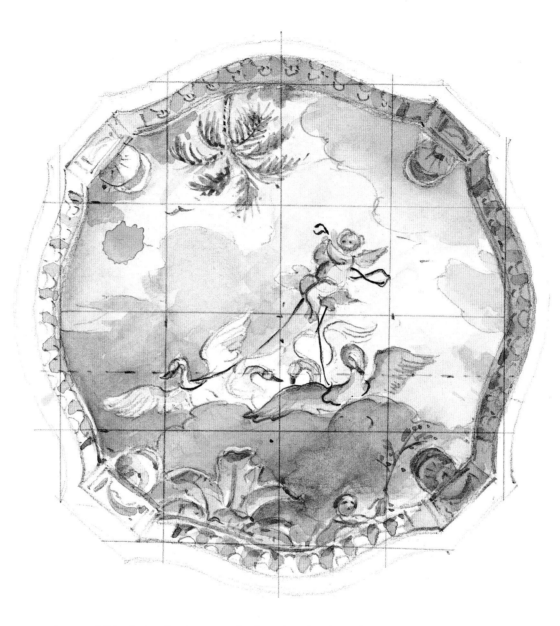

ABOVE: This design for the area of ceiling directly above the dining table depicts a putto driving two swans through the sky. A palm tree and a banana plant appear over the balustrade.

RIGHT: This photograph shows most of the ceiling structure, including shells and trellis, although the central area is obscured by a chandelier.

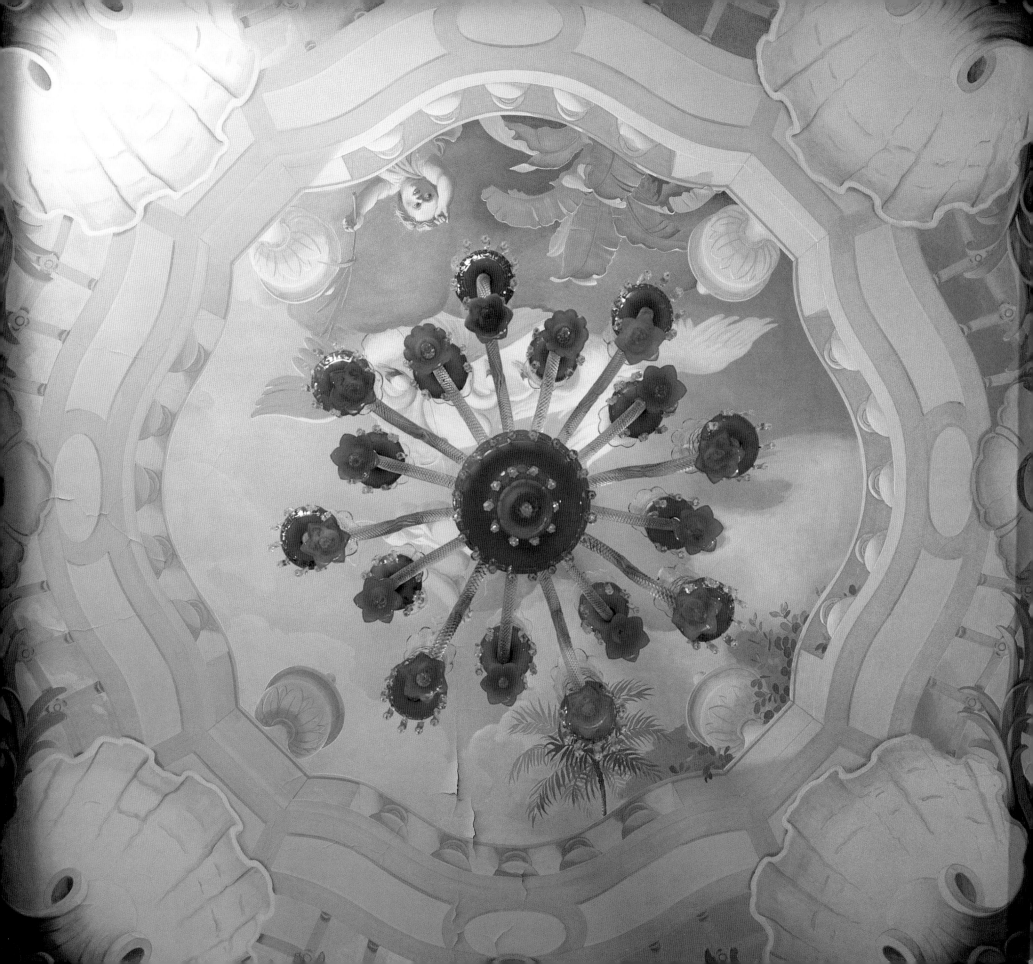

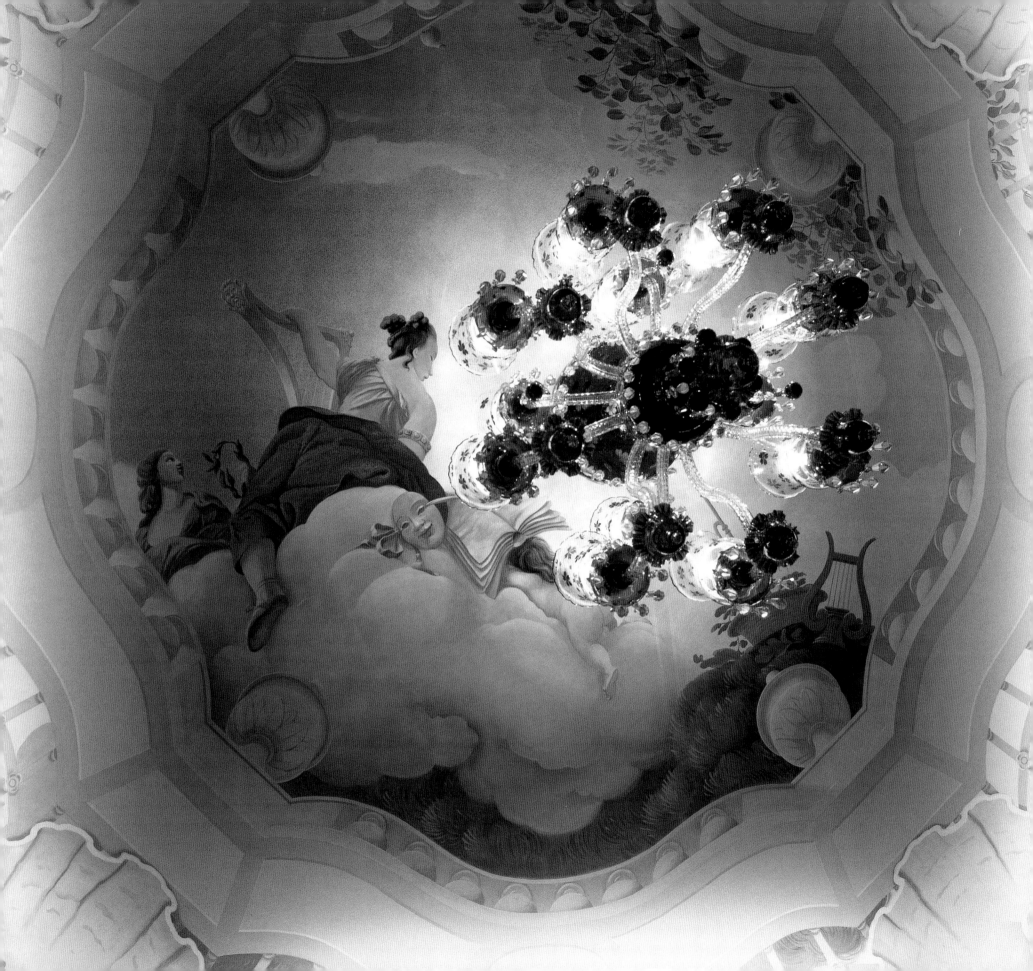

RIGHT: A general view of the library showing the recessed ceiling painting above the trompe l'oeil *bookcases. The lapis lazuli panels in the bookcases were painted by Rui Paes to echo the blue enamel plaque in the nineteenth-century oak piece in the centre. They were also intended to reflect the blue of the drapery painted on the ceiling. The large coffee table was designed in* faux bois *to complement the scheme. David Cossart grained the table to simulate oak. This was then gilded and painted with an open gothic design taken from a medieval illuminated manuscript.*

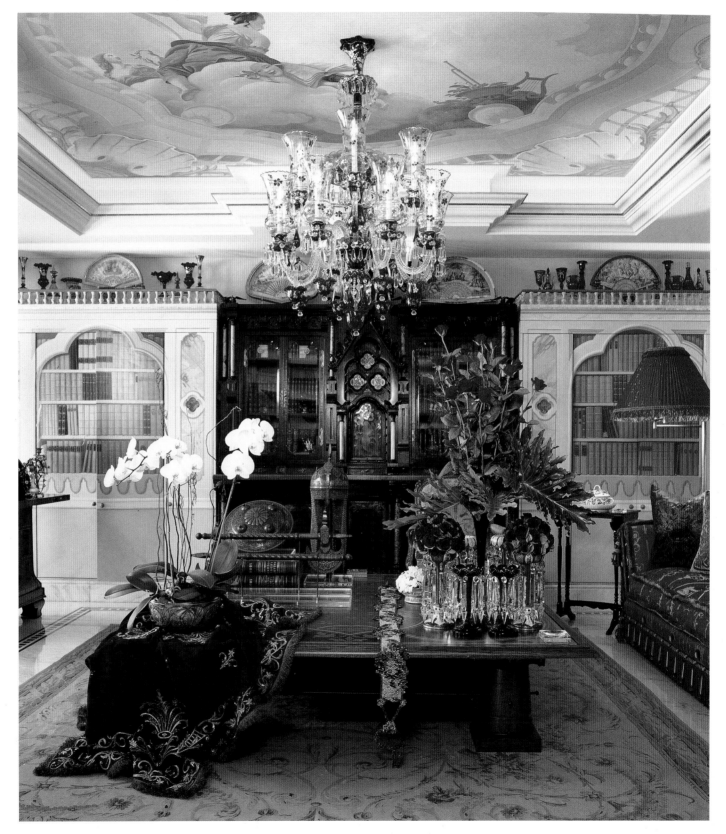

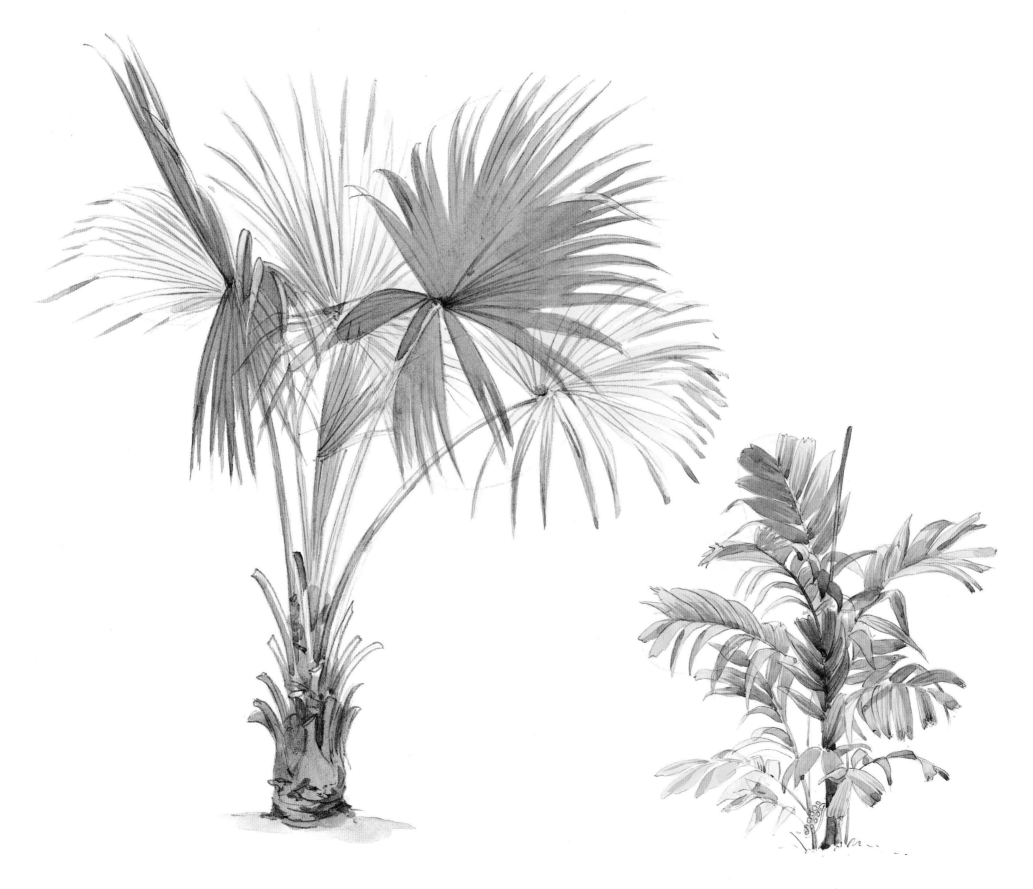

PLANT STUDIES

The only prize I ever won at art school, at the age of seventeen, was for plant drawing. Under the eagle eye of my aptly named tutor, Miss Flora Ogilvy, I was made to observe every detail of each specimen. It has stood me in good stead. Since that time I have always painted plants of every description, both at home and on my travels. It is one of my greatest joys, and when I was invited to visit Brazil recently, to make studies of plants for a mural painting, I accepted with alacrity. Albeit these sketches were not drawn from below, they are nevertheless an *aide memoire* and a guide.

LEFT: *Two types of palm tree. Palms – whether young or fully grown specimens – frequently appear in my designs. I find the interplay of light on their leaves gives movement to a landscape: one has the white light on the leaf, the leaf in shade, and the wonderful luminous light that shines through the leaf. In a breeze, these areas of light are continually changing.*

RIGHT: *An* agave attenuata.

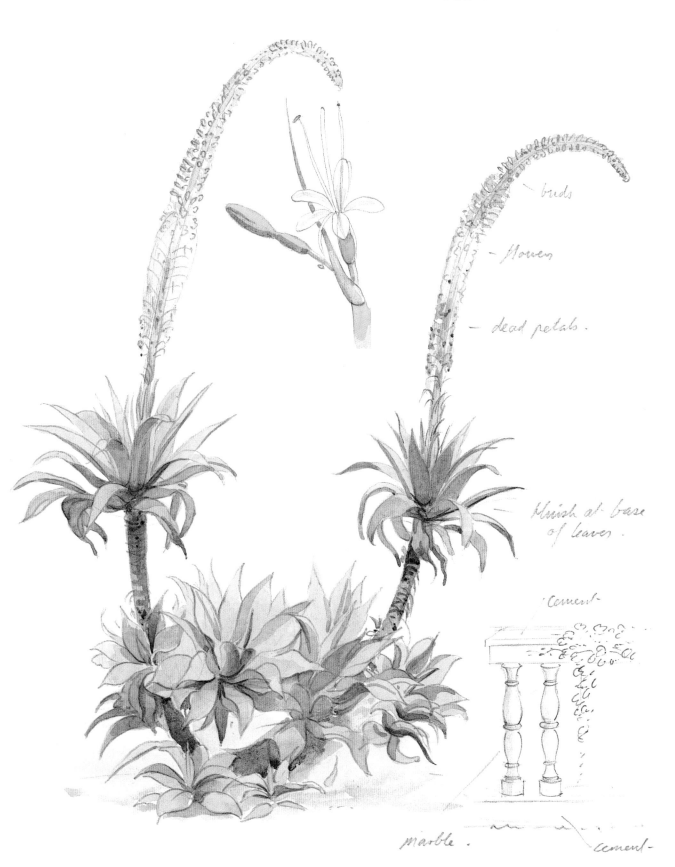

buds

flowers

dead petals.

bluish at base of leaves.

cement

marble.

cement

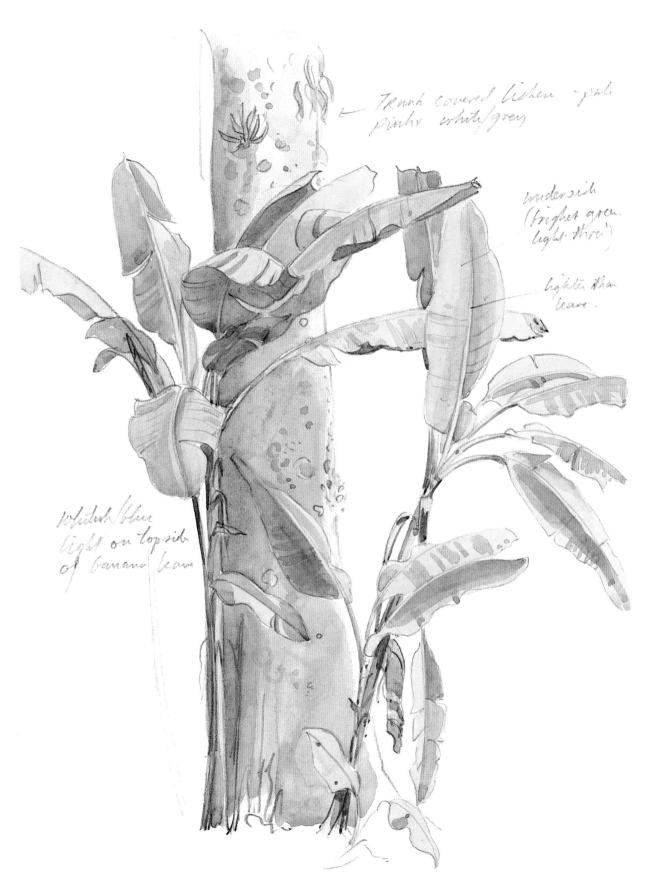

Trunk covered lichen - pale pinks white/grey

underside (brighter green, light thro')

lighter than leaves.

whitish/blue light on topside of banana leaves

LEFT: *The banana plant is one of my favourites. The play of light on and through the leaves is a joy and the various flowers and fruit are, from a decorative point of view, superb.*

BELOW: *An* Artocarpus heterphyllus, *otherwise known as a jackfruit.*

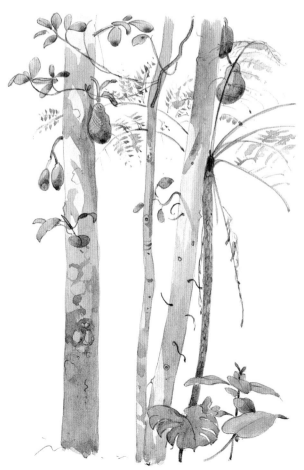

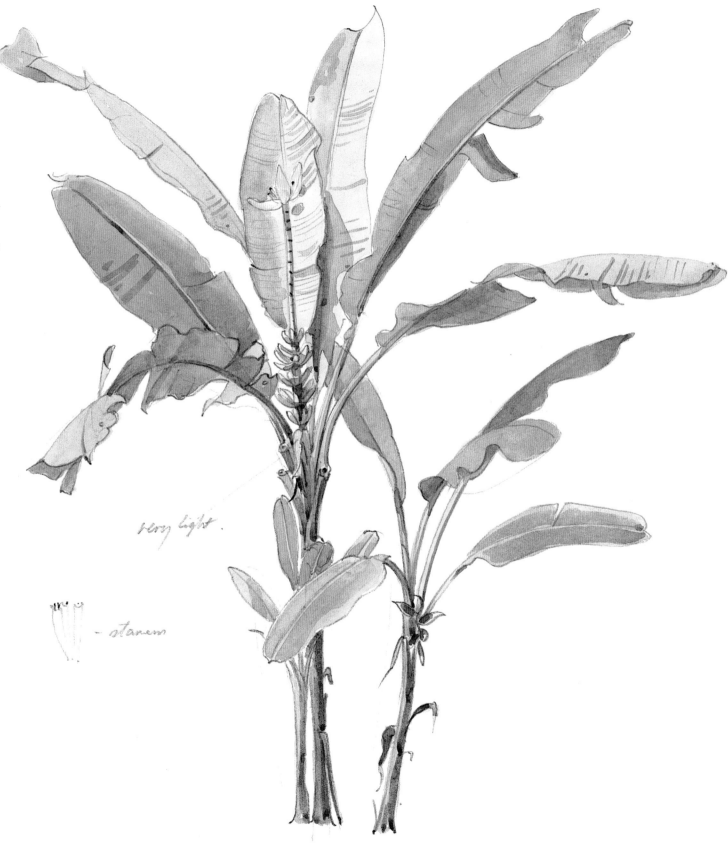

RIGHT: Another banana plant. Banana leaves were used to great effect by the architect John Nash on the drawing room ceiling of the Prince Regent's Pavilion at Brighton. A confection of Indian and Chinese inspired architecture, the pavilion was a triumph of the exotic.

very light.

— stamens

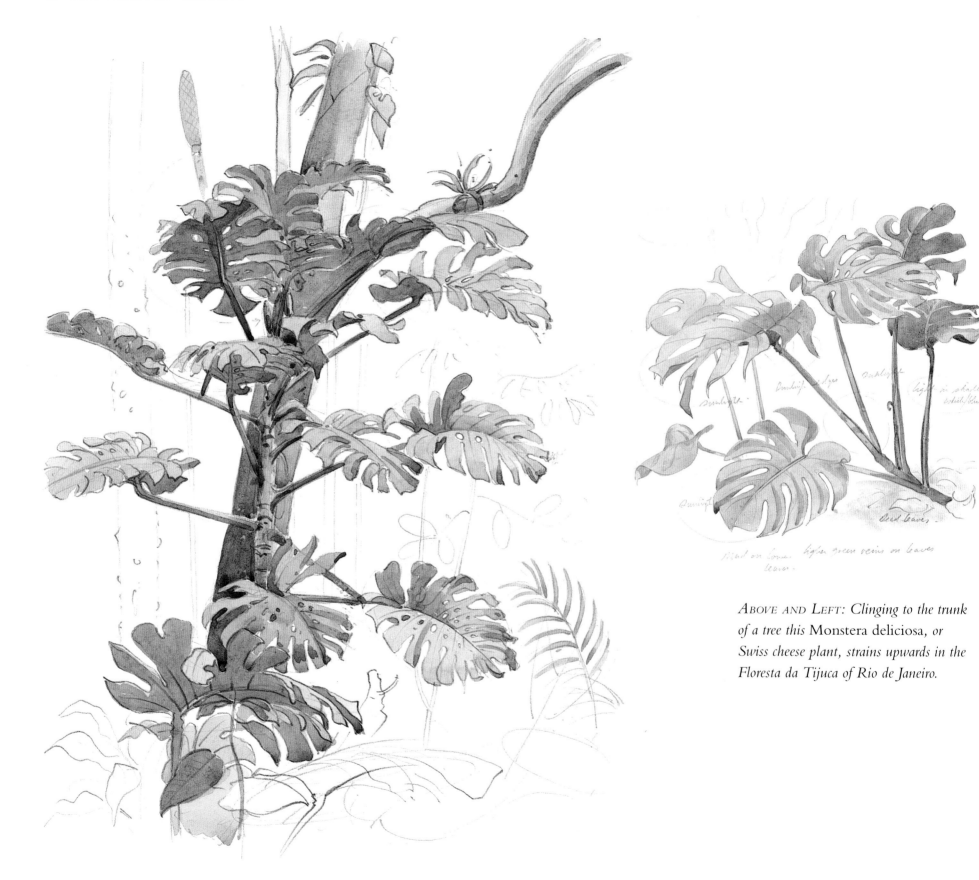

ABOVE AND LEFT: Clinging to the trunk of a tree this Monstera deliciosa, *or Swiss cheese plant, strains upwards in the Floresta da Tijuca of Rio de Janeiro.*

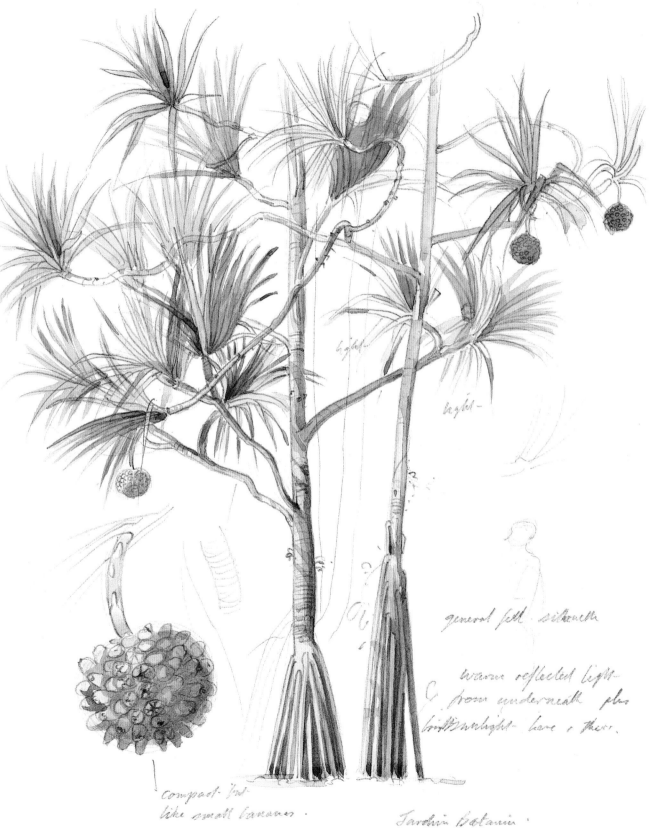

RIGHT: This bizarre-looking plant, which I sketched in the botanical gardens in Rio de Janeiro, benefits from having large fruit as well as spiky grey-green leaves.

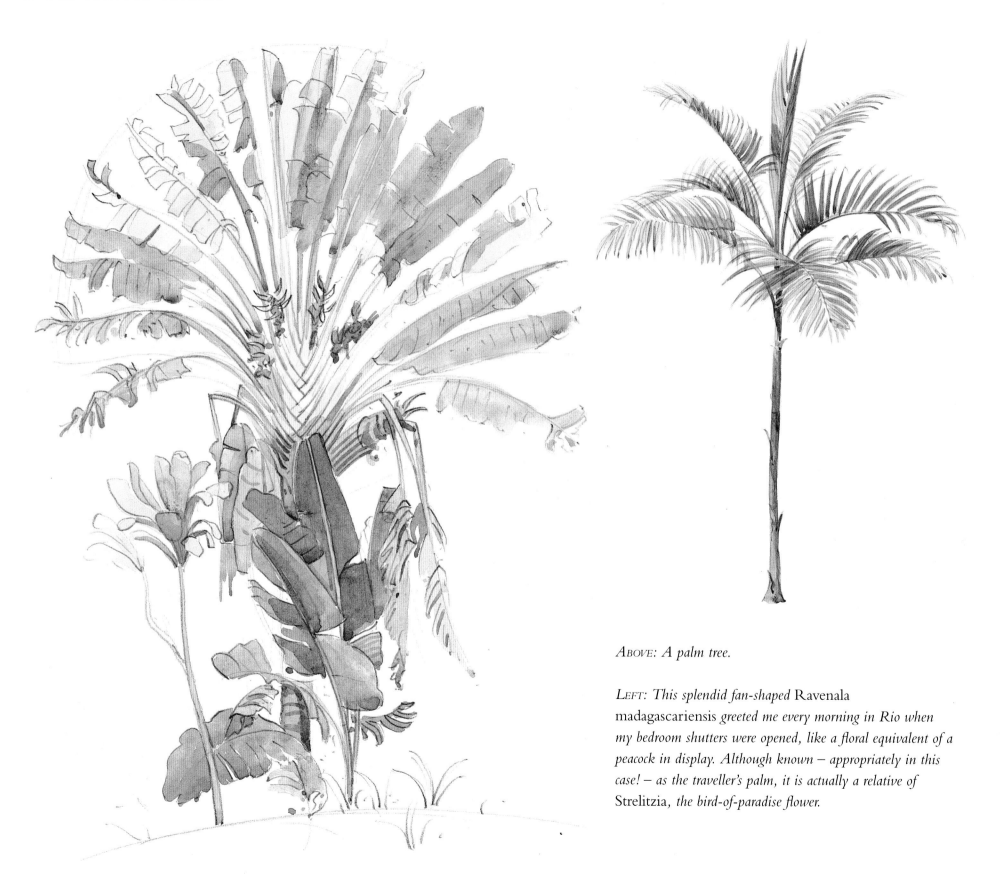

ABOVE: A palm tree.

LEFT: This splendid fan-shaped Ravenala madagascariensis *greeted me every morning in Rio when my bedroom shutters were opened, like a floral equivalent of a peacock in display. Although known – appropriately in this case! – as the traveller's palm, it is actually a relative of* Strelitzia, *the bird-of-paradise flower.*

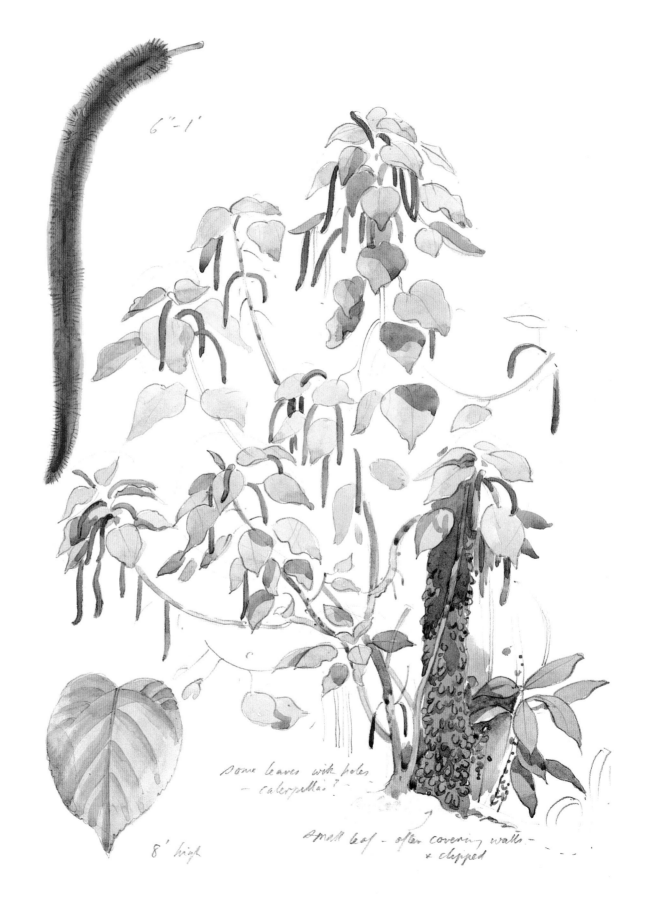

RIGHT: Acalypha hispida *or the chenille plant is arresting in any company thanks to its carmine furry tails. It is an exotic plant to paint, sprouting from a wall or through balusters high above one's head.*

6"–1'

some leaves with holes
— caterpillars?

8' high

small leaf – often covering walls –
+ clipped

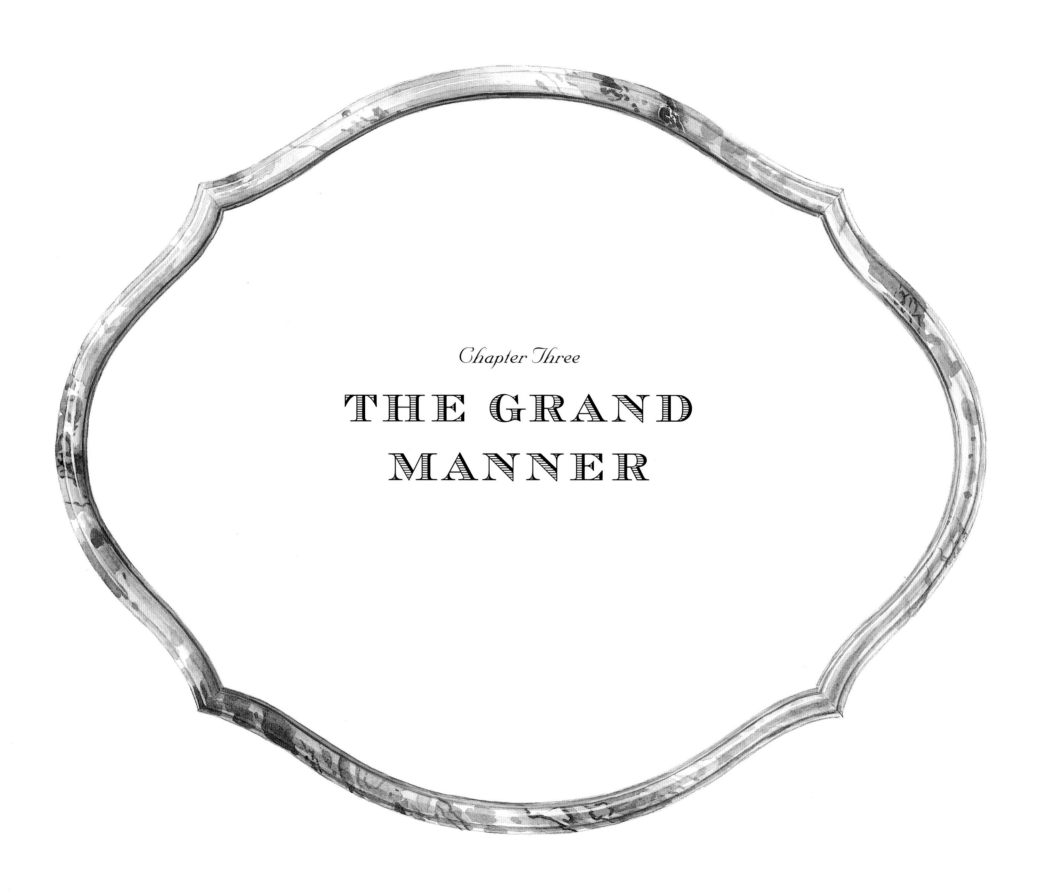

Chapter Three

THE GRAND MANNER

The opportunities to work on a large scale and to produce a ceiling painting in the grand manner are few and far between for several reasons. Firstly, the client has to be prepared to accept that the space to be decorated will be out of action for some considerable time. Unfortunately there are no quick solutions for applying the design and bringing it to a satisfactory finish, and in my experience hitches and delays are inevitable. Many times I have arrived on site with the promise that all will be prepared and ready for me to begin, only to find the place swarming with workmen. There is little alternative but to hang around for several days or leave and return when the essential preparation is finished. Both options are frustrating and time wasting.

Another reason that large works are less frequently commissioned is, of course, the cost. The painter is well advised to think through carefully the amount of work and time involved before committing him or herself to a price. As a young man, in my middle twenties, I most certainly underestimated how long it would take me to paint the walls and ceiling of the south staircase at Ragley Hall. With the plan of working one week a month, I calculated that it would take approximately five years. After fourteen years I eventually

finished. Had it not been for the generosity of my long-suffering hosts, one wonders what would have happened. It is difficult to know what to do with a half-finished painting! I can now appreciate the relief they must have felt, at the splendid celebratory luncheon party they gave for a hundred guests, when the decoration was finally completed.

Perhaps the most important aesthetic factor governing the commission of a ceiling painting in the grand manner is where it is to be painted. If the house or building does not support such a design, then it will only look awkward and out of place. The other side of the coin also has to be considered. An important building or house of architectural merit must be treated with care: one does not want to produce a scheme that is at variance with the spirit of the place.

The wealth of myth and allegory for subject matter can sometimes make it hard to know where to begin. However, the germ of an idea can often develop by discussing with a client their interests.

Indeed, the history of a house or family may spark the starting point for the design. Once the main theme has been decided, it is much easier to organise the peripheral images you may wish to include.

If the design for the painting is architectural, then of course the structure must work. Figures, animals, plants and drapery can be added to the basic design. Sub-plots can also be introduced once the central theme has been organised.

Many years ago I painted a staircase for a client that was to include portraits of friends and acquaintances. As these became too numerous to fit into the design, we decided to represent many individuals by other means: the chief of a Scottish clan was represented by a feather; a well made-up actress by a Painted Lady butterfly; two impecunious princelings, who were always on the scrounge, were depicted as caterpillars eating a banknote. Others had their initials carved (in *trompe l'oeil*) into the stone columns and architraves. Eventually everyone was included and much fun was had devising the varying representations.

On the following pages are a few examples of some of the more complex projects with which I have been involved.

RAGLEY HALL

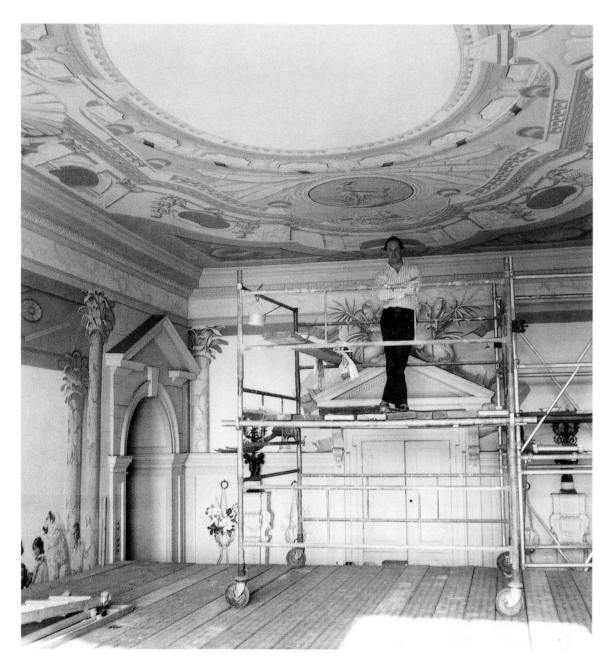

The south staircase hall at Ragley, in Warwickshire, took more than a decade to paint. Because of my inexperience I decided to leave the ceiling until last, contrary to the way I prefer to work, which is from the top downwards. I have the late Sir Osbert Lancaster to thank for saving me from potential disaster. He strongly recommended that I work directly on to the plaster rather than have the ceiling papered before painting. As he rightly pointed out, should a strip of paper (the shortest length of which would have been 22 feet/7 metres) 'lift', it would require major scaffolding to restore it. A crack or peeling paint, on the other hand, could be repaired much more simply.

There is only a slate roof above this ceiling and, at that time, several hip baths had been strategically placed to prevent rain seeping through.

LEFT: *A false floor was erected over the entire area of the south staircase hall and a moveable scaffold tower was placed on top. The photograph shows me standing on the tower, which could be wheeled around as necessary.*

RIGHT: *The theme of the ceiling painting was the temptation of Christ. In the centre Christ and the Devil are pictured on the Mount of Temptation at the moment when the Devil offers Christ all the riches of the world.*

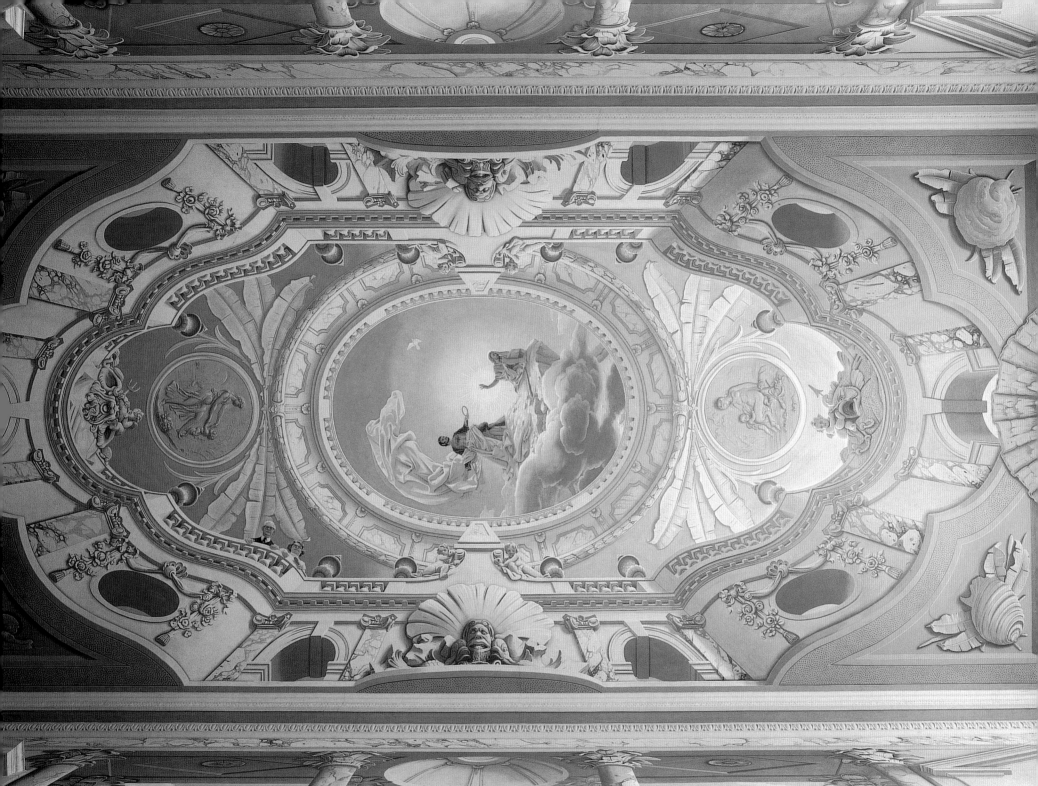

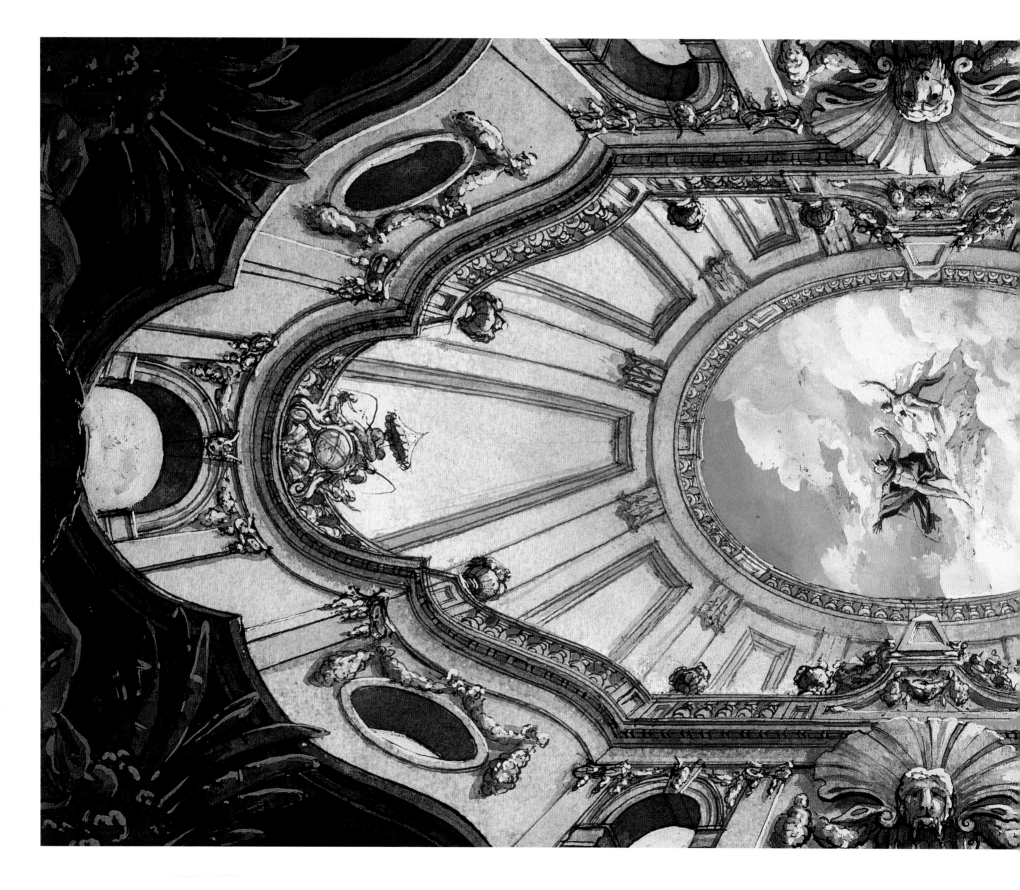

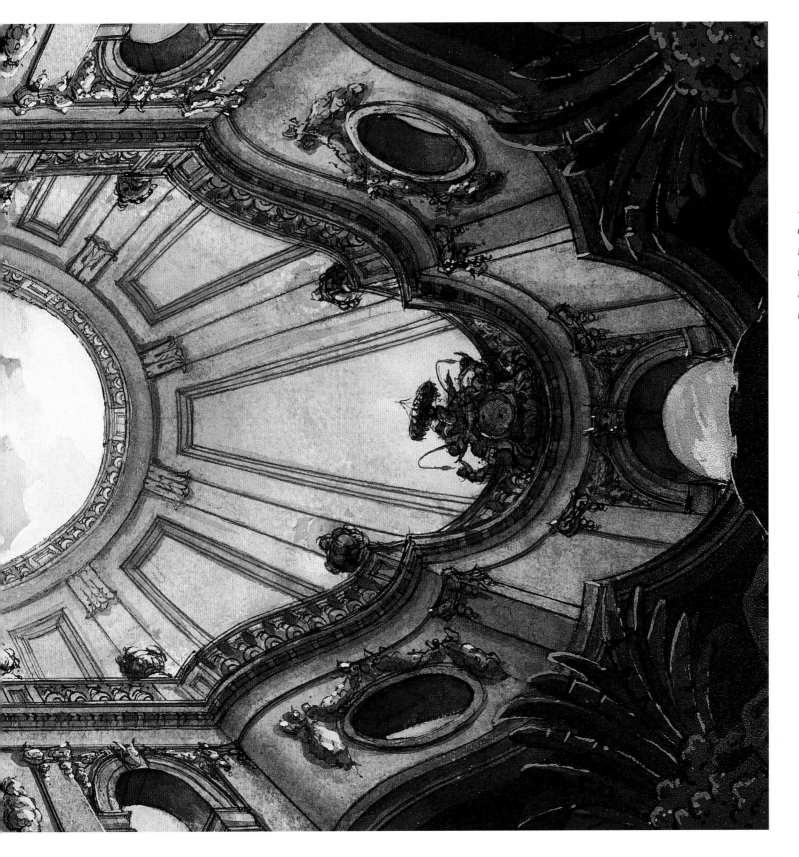

LEFT: My first design for the ceiling executed in 1968. I later revised and altered the design when I realised that 'support' for the dome would be needed beyond the walls I had painted.

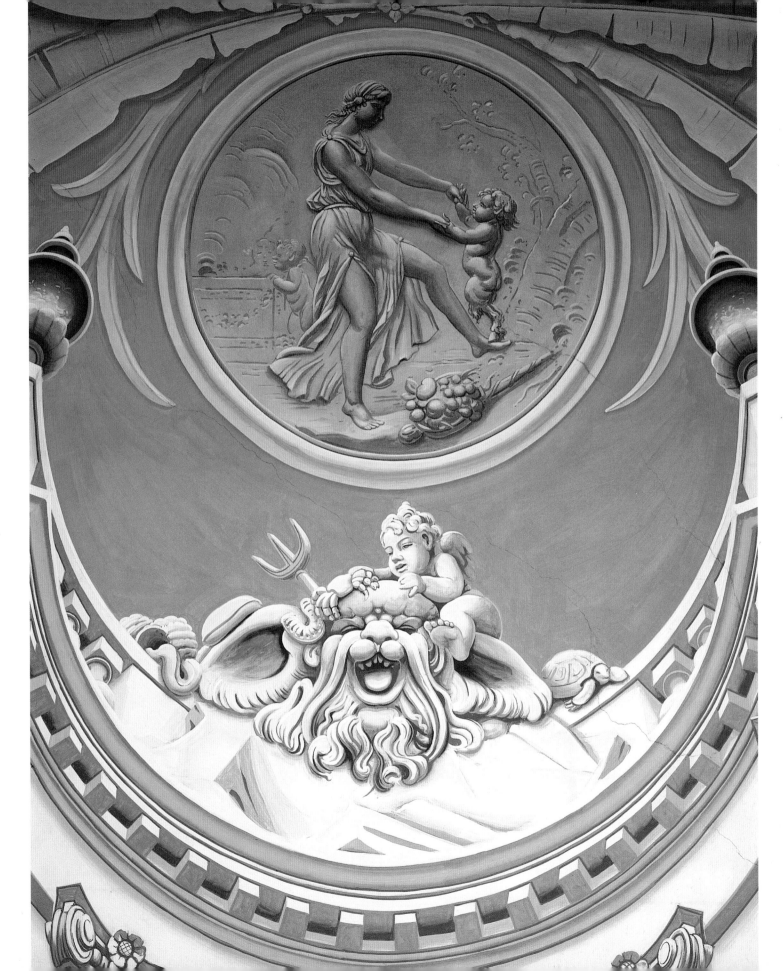

Left: A detail showing the shell and banana leaf decoration in the north-east corner, immediately above the 'real' cornice and painted marbled frieze.

Right: The south end of the upper balustrade culminates in this sculptural group taken from a study I made of one of the marble fountains in the Piazza Navona in Rome. The roundel is after a bronze relief by the French sculptor Clodion, which I found, also in Rome, on a visit to the flea market. It now hangs in my study. The original terracotta is in the Fitzwilliam Museum, Cambridge.

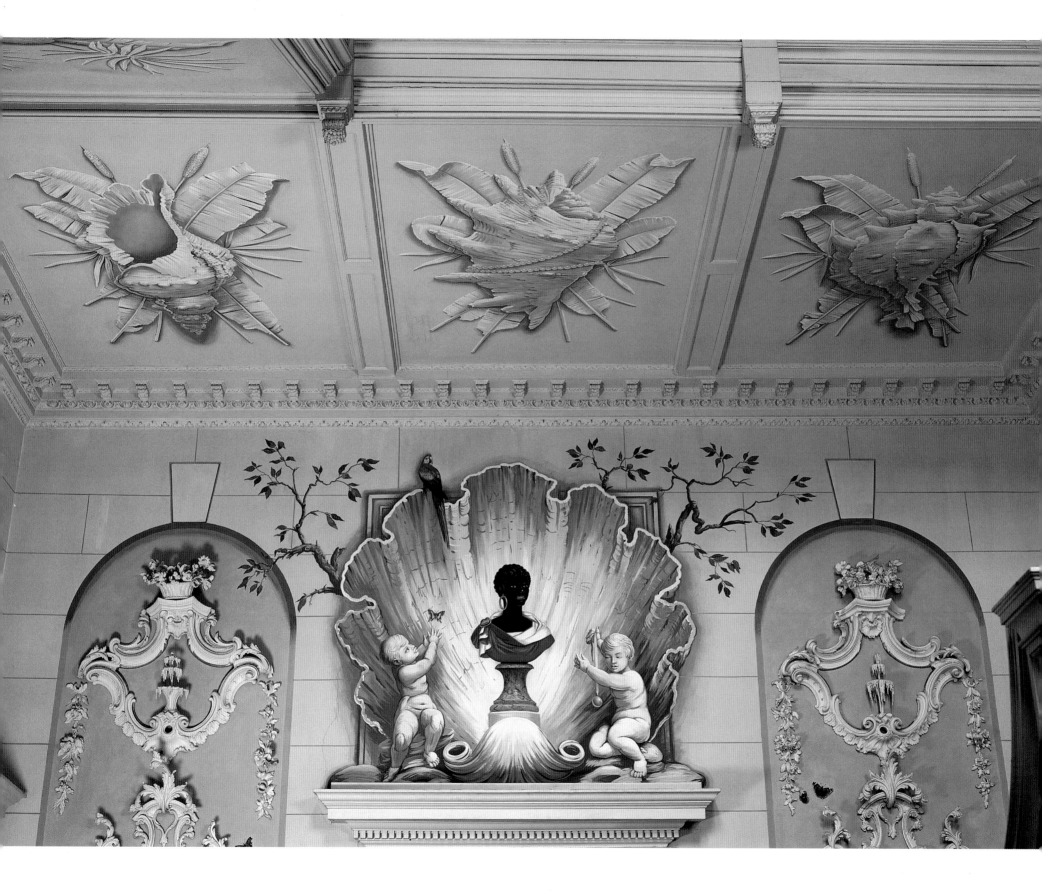

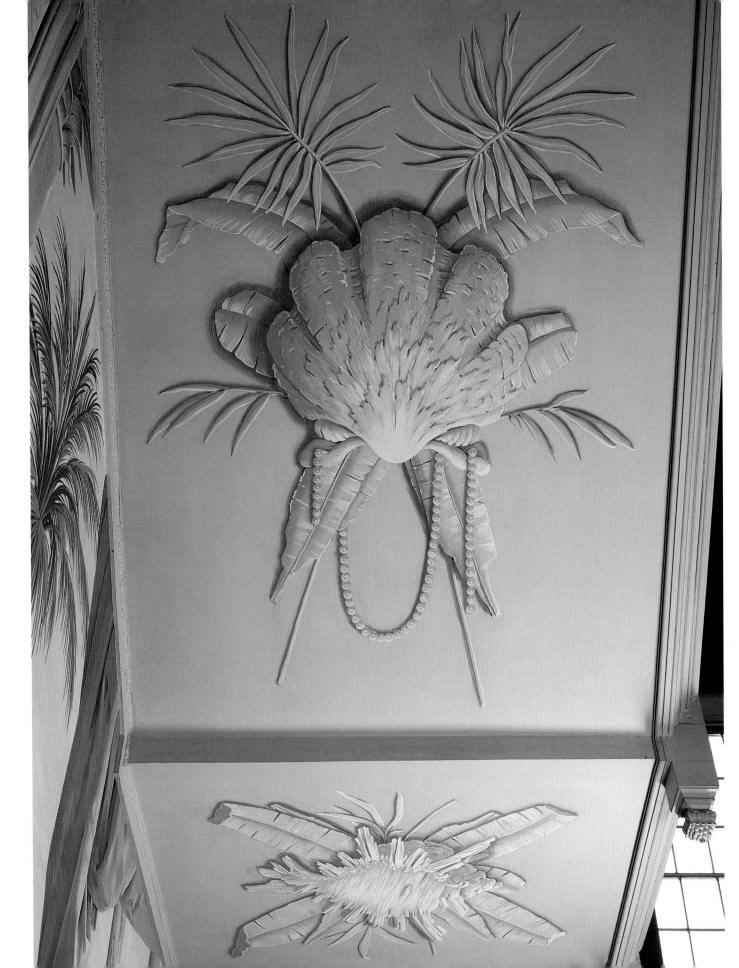

LEFT: *Three shell trophies sit in panels under the landing. Painted in* grisaille, *they continue the shell element present in the overdoor below. A macaw perches on the top edge of the large shell within which is a blackamoor, one of the Seymour crests. The name derived from St Maur during the Crusades. The family have lived at Ragley for over three hundred years. The shell was the very first thing I painted in the staircase hall; these were to be the first brushstrokes on over five thousand square feet of blank white wall.*

RIGHT: *Two of the three shell trophies under the landing: a medley of palm and banana leaves with a different shell on each as a centrepiece, held together with a string of pearls, one of the many symbols relating to the sea and the underworld.*

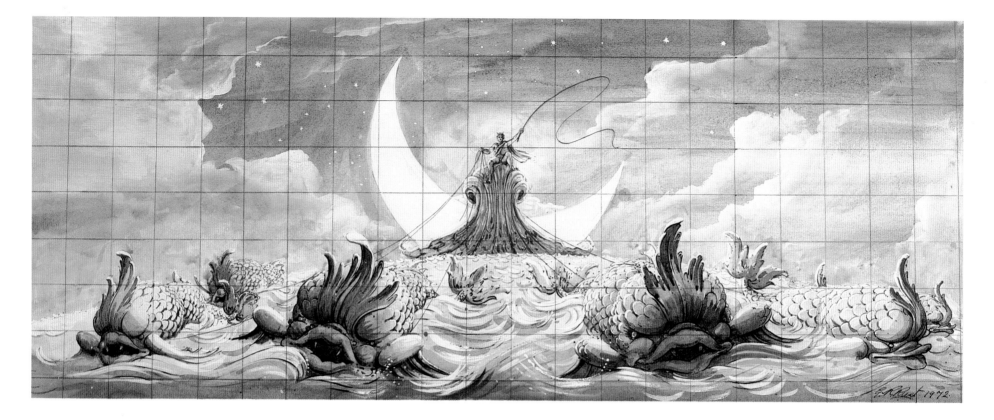

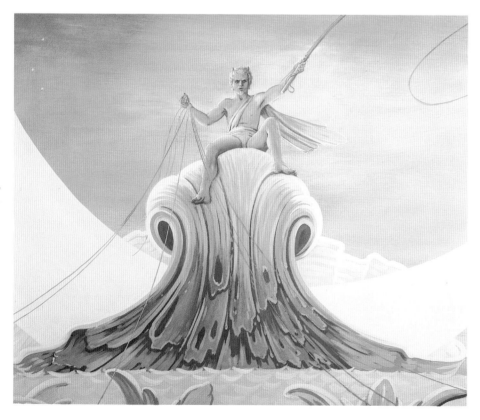

ABOVE: This is my sketch for the ceiling of the half landing. Neptune rides the waves in a shell, carrying the crescent moon, drawn by dolphins.

LEFT: Lord Hertford posed for me to draw the figure of Neptune by sitting on top of the log box in the south staircase hall. As his wife captured this unusual scene on camera the doors opened from the great hall to reveal Joe, the handyman, with a basket of logs. His mouth fell open at the sight of his lordship in his underpants and the logs fell to the floor. I don't think he ever fully recovered.

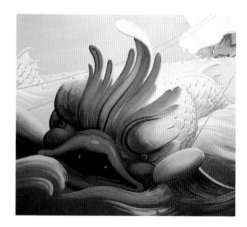

ABOVE: One of the dolphins pulling Neptune. This is an example of a figure that should, ideally, have been painted on a higher ceiling. Greater distance is needed for it to 'read' convincingly.

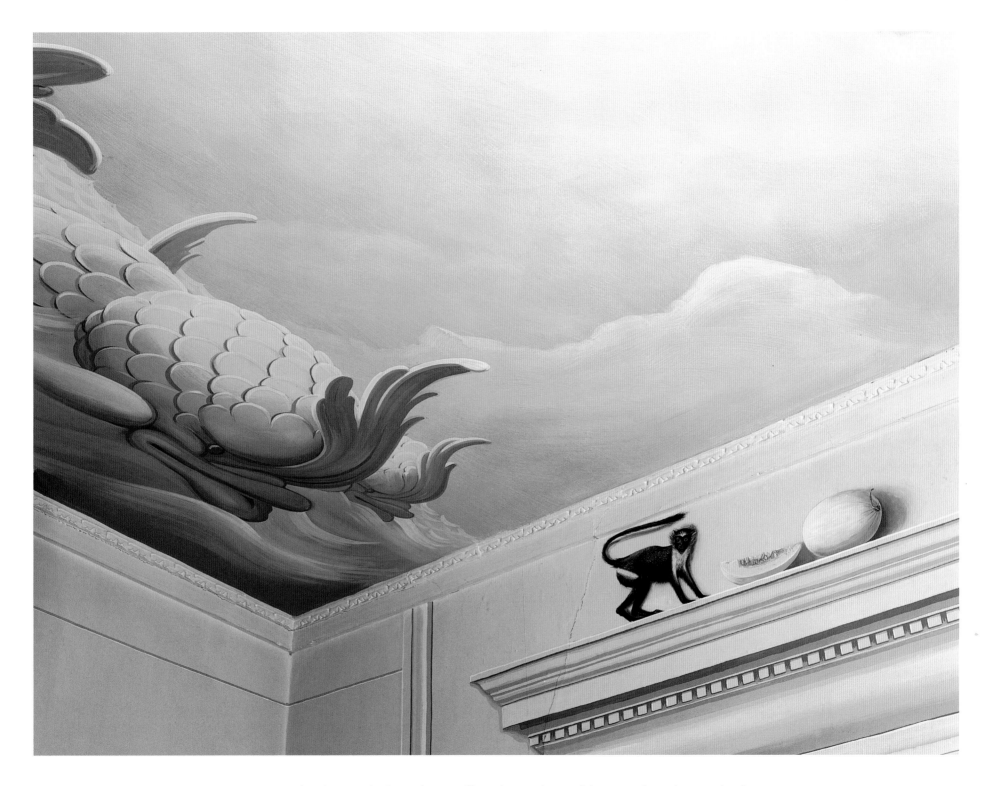

Above: The photograph shows the grisaille *ceiling and one of the painted overdoors under the half landing. The Diana monkey alludes to one of the daughters of the house, her namesake and, at the time of painting, a little girl of four years old.*

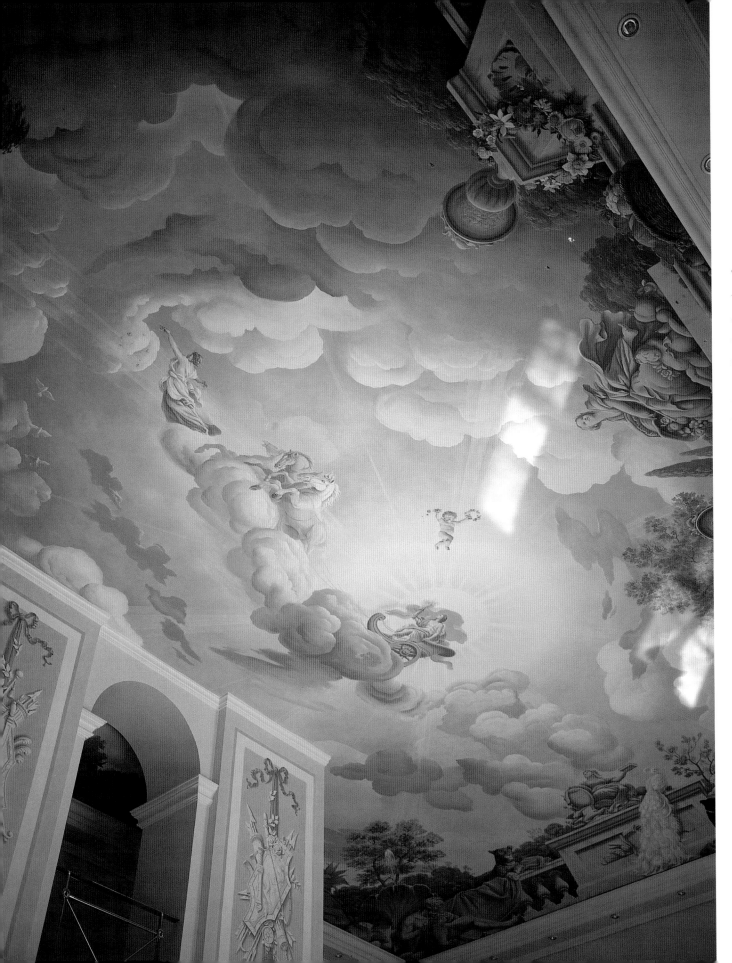

FRANKFURT

The owners of this neo-classical inspired
villa in Frankfurt decided to have several
of its rooms painted, including the
ceiling of the saloon on the *piano nobile*,
shown here.

Inspired by the dramatic Tiepolo
frescos at the not so distant palace at
Wurzburg, I decided on a design of an
open sky. This would include a depiction
of Aurora bringing the dawn and, above
the cornice, a landscape and balustrade
supporting various forms of flora and
fauna. Rui Paes worked tirelessly with
me on this project and was responsible
for painting all the birds and animals.

The ceiling was squared up before the
main area of sky was blocked in, then
work began on the process of finishing
the sky before starting in earnest on the
surrounding structure.

As the room has a gallery running
around three walls, consideration had to
be given to the fact that the decoration
would be viewed at close quarters as well
as from the floor below.

*Left: A view of the slightly vaulted ceiling
showing the two* trompe l'oeil *panels of
arms above the chimney piece.*

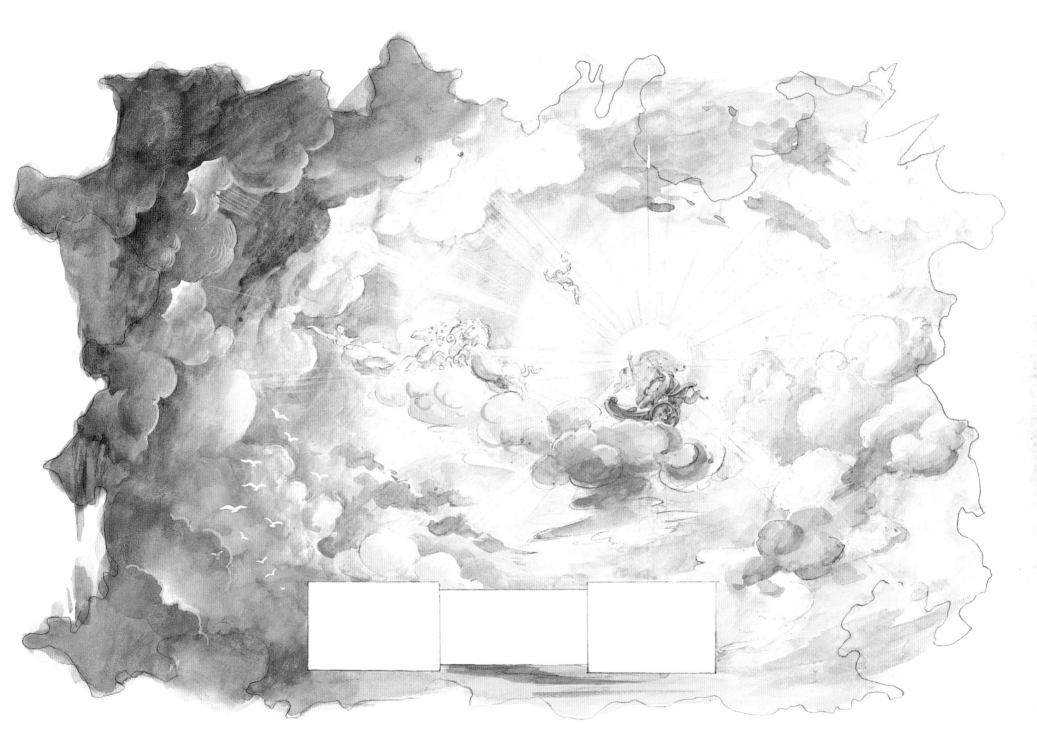

ABOVE: My sketch for the sky showing Aurora bringing the sun to illuminate the world of shadow and darkness.

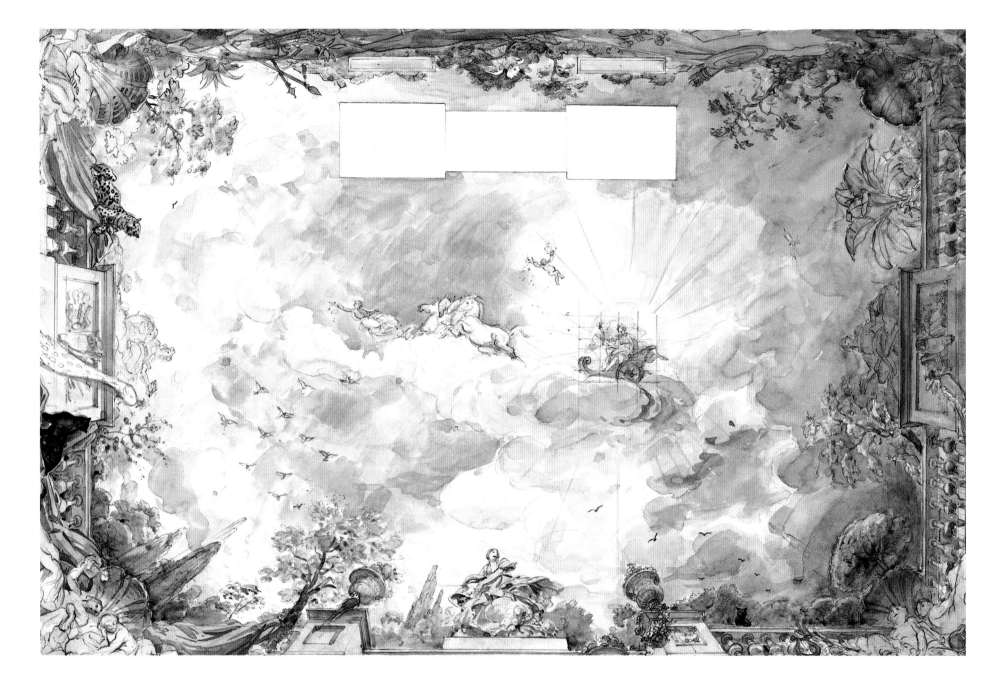

*ABOVE: This sketch shows an earlier version of the design with the figure of Aurora reversed.
Although it 'read' well on entering the saloon, it did not work so well once one was in the room.
The sculpture of 'abundance' sits in the centre, above the window.*

*RIGHT: As the painted balustrade turns the corner of the plaster vaulted ceiling, the perspective
could look uncomfortable. The draped figures under the shell fountains either side of the central
sculpture help to disguise this and deceive the eye into seeing a more harmonious 'join'.*

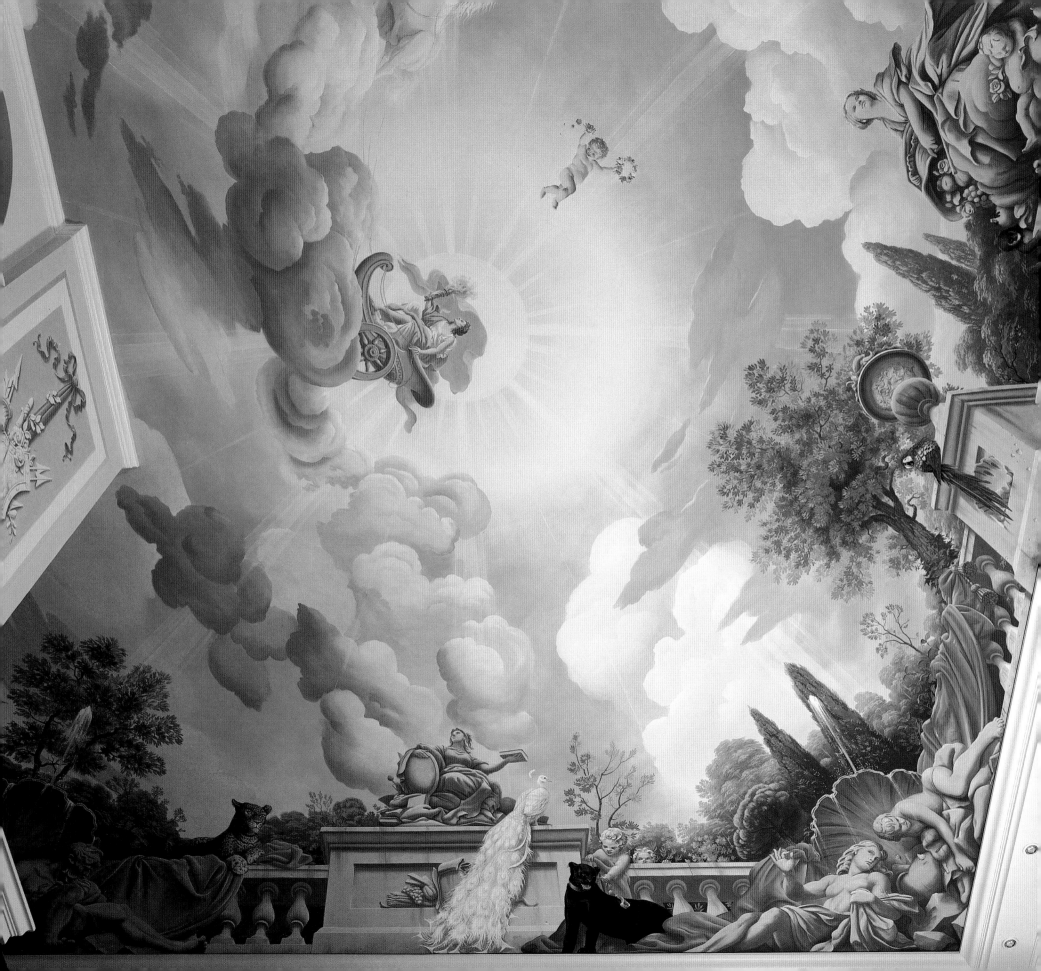

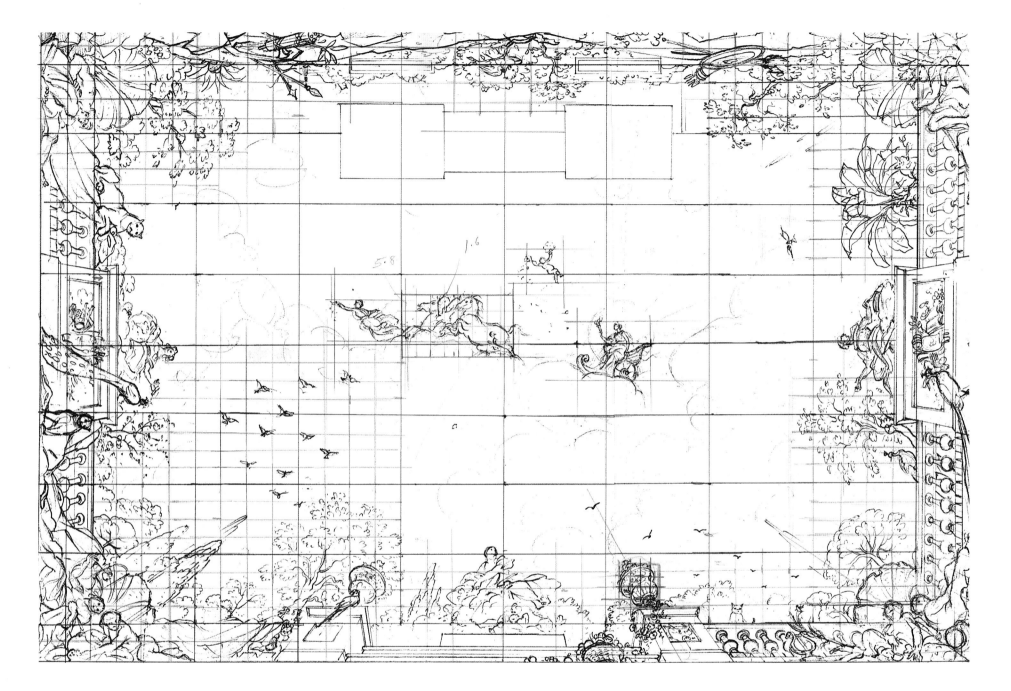

ABOVE: Working drawing showing the various areas squared up for translation to the ceiling. The grid is divided into smaller sections only where needed. Where there are symmetrical objects, such as the urn, they are drawn out once, then reversed.

RIGHT: As Aurora makes her way across the sky, Joy strews rose petals in her path through the billowing clouds.

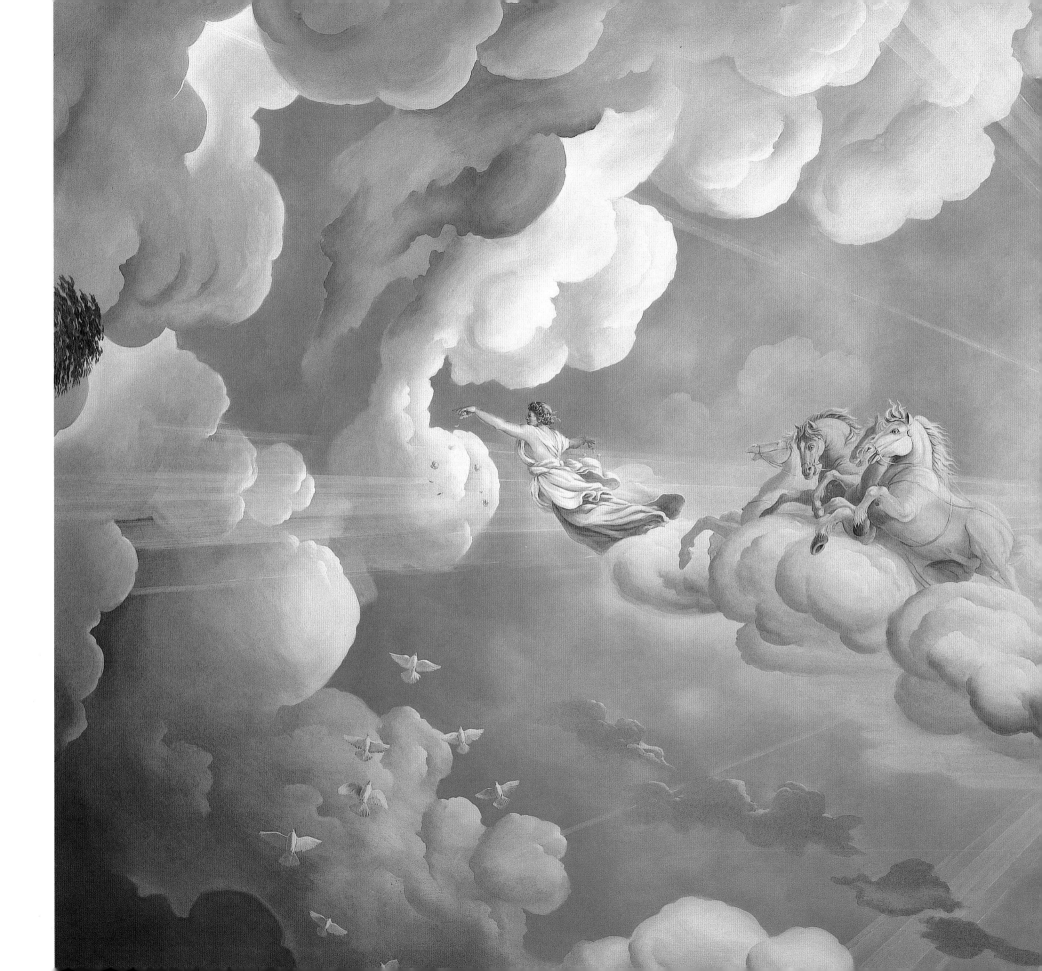

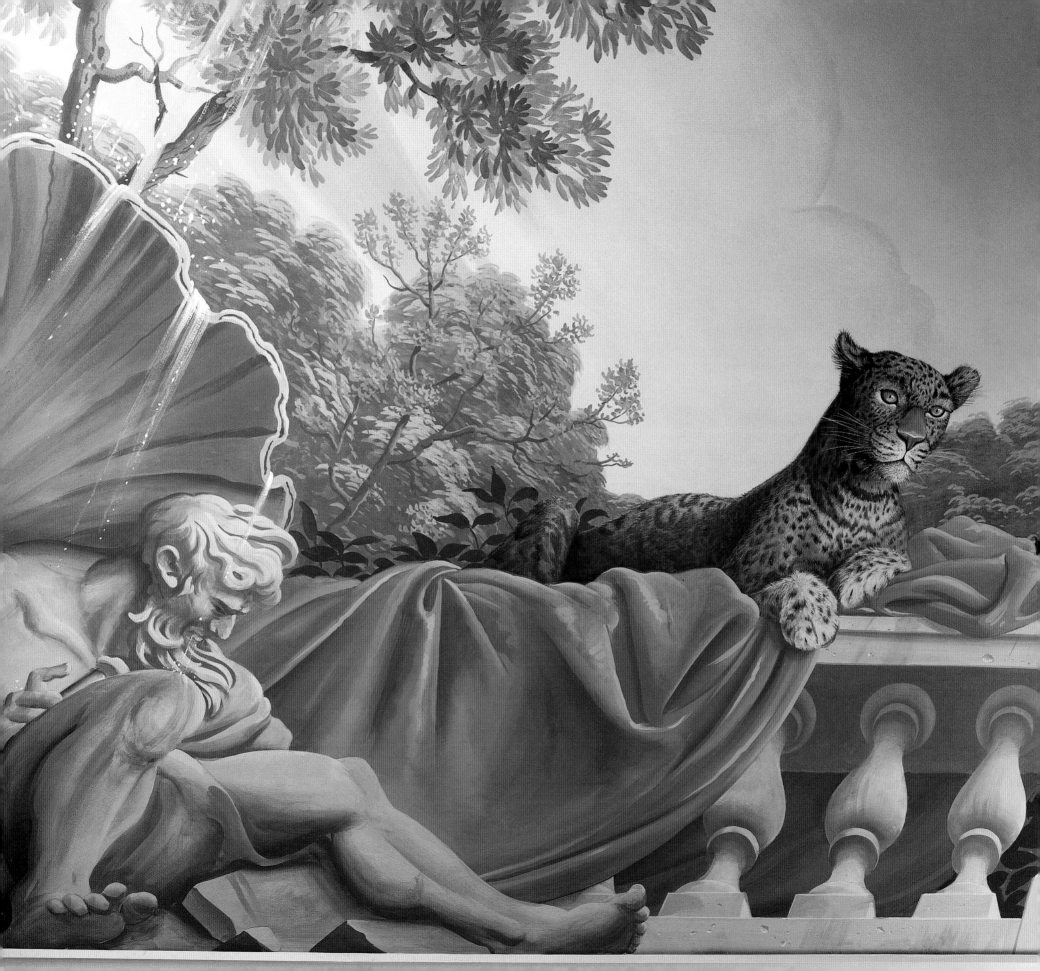

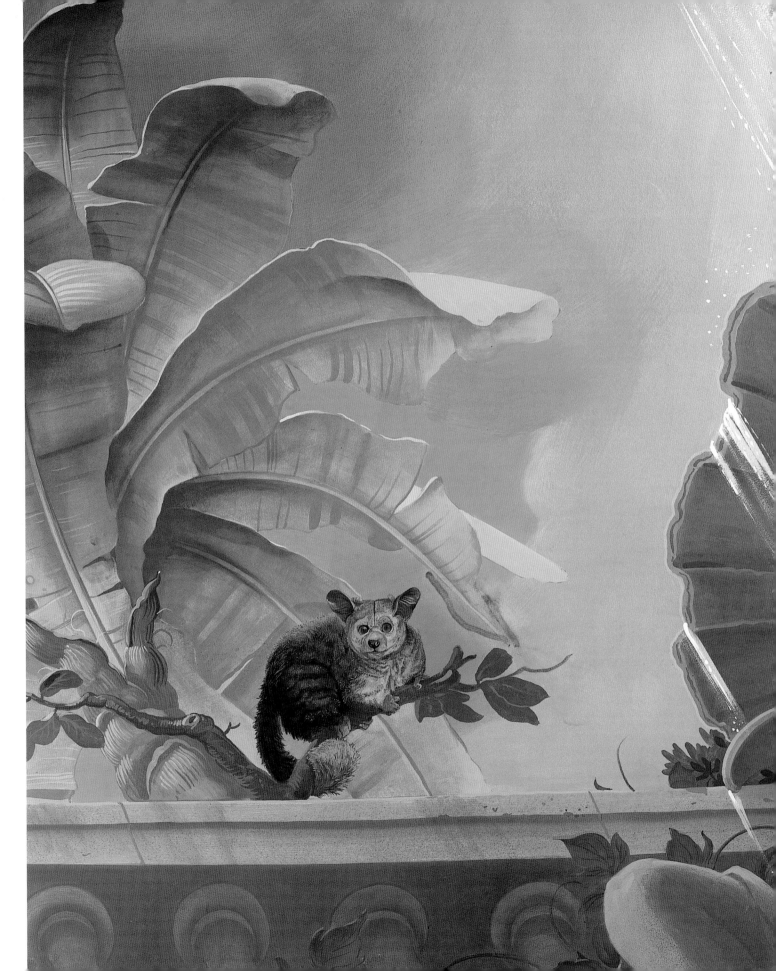

LEFT: *One of the larger animals painted by Rui Paes, this leopard rests contentedly on the balustrade overlooking the scene below. The red drapery is a good foil for the fur and helps to link the animal to the figure below the fountain.*

RIGHT: *A bush baby nestles on a branch above the balustrade.*

ABOVE: A peacock butterfly rests on a sprig of oak leaves, adding a small accent of colour to the detail.

RIGHT: A sulphur-crested cockatoo perches on a branch. It is important to place the bird or animal in the correct position before painting in the support.

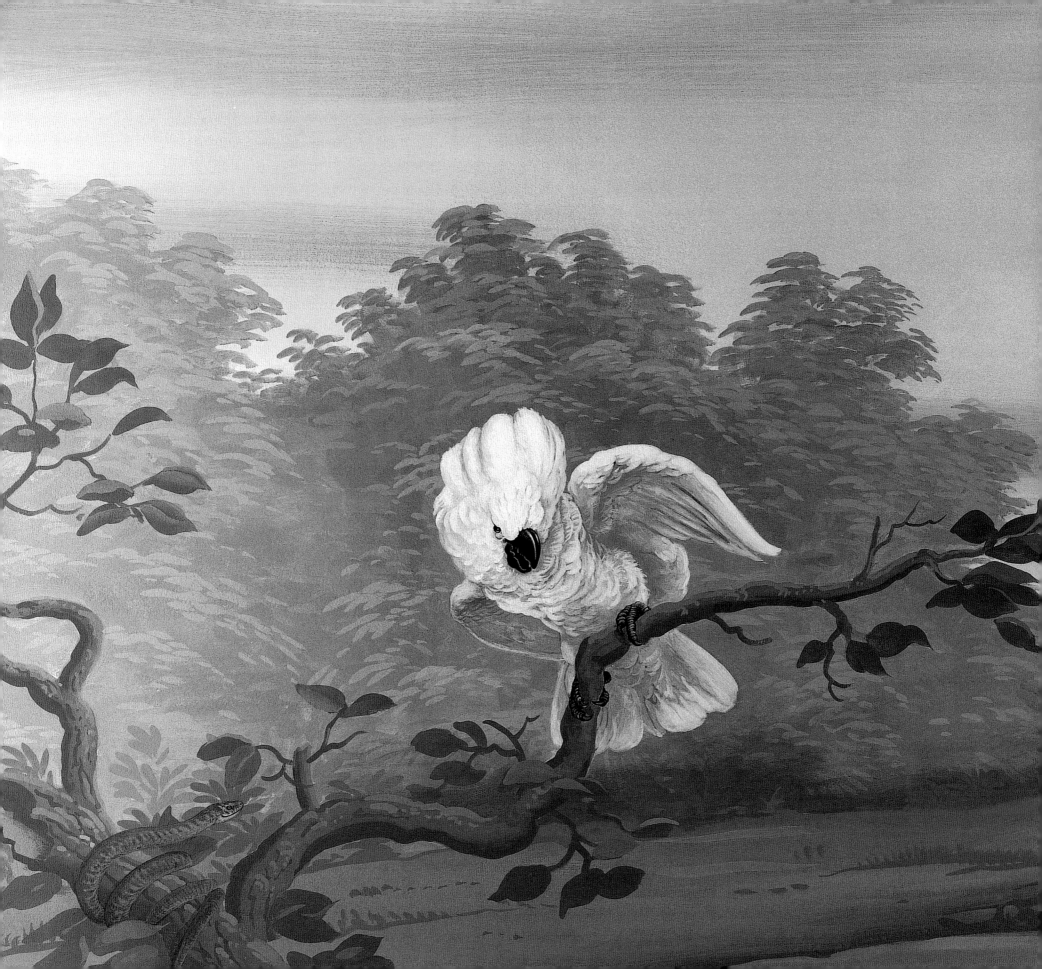

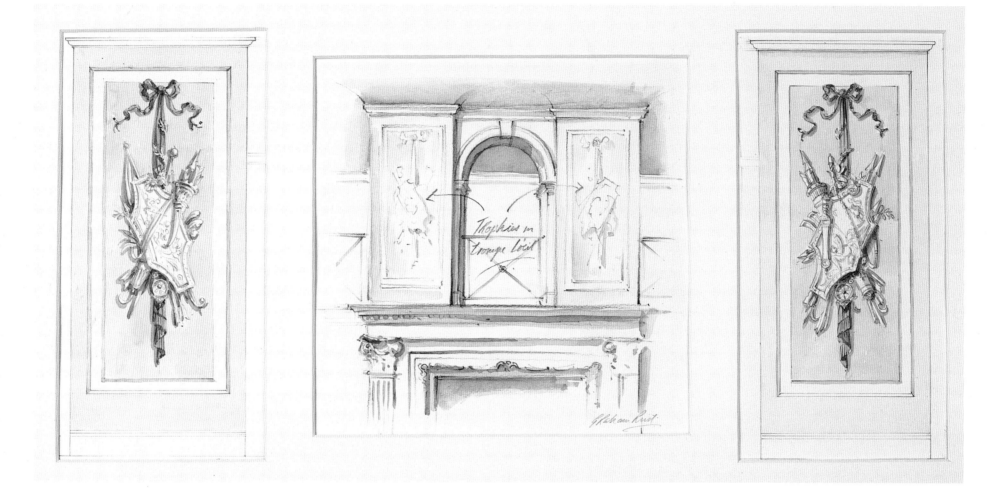

ABOVE: My sketch of the chimney piece showing the two panels featuring trophies of arms.

RIGHT: This photograph of the ceiling shows the chimney piece superstructure where it meets the ceiling. Often one has to work with the existing colour scheme in a room, but in this case the colours for the walls and soft furnishing were chosen to complement the ceiling. Colour constraints, however, can help to focus one's ideas when working on a scheme or design.

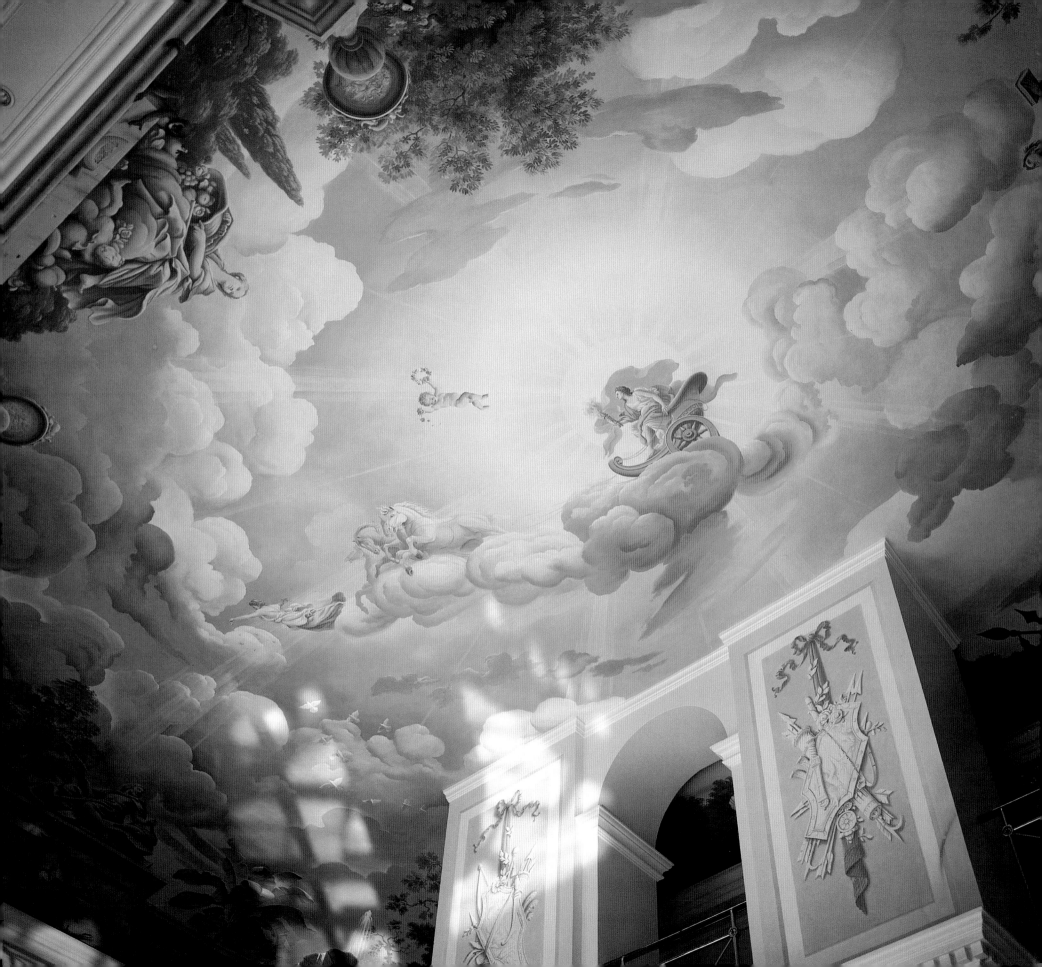

THE SPRING CEILING

The structure of this architectural ceiling with a large opening to the sky is one that can be adapted and used in several ways.

Extra subject matter can be introduced should you wish to give a different theme to the painting. Instead of spring, it could be a game of 'hide and seek' or a festival of flowers, or indeed be the setting for a tale in *singerie*. Perhaps even the bones of an aviary with a glorious collection of parrots and macaws. The perspective is central, but the light source can be adapted if natural light plays a part in the illumination of the room.

BELOW: The elegant figure of Mercury, messenger of the gods, after Domenico Piola, the eighteenth-century Genoese painter. This design could form the centre piece of a ceiling similar to the one opposite.

RIGHT: Inspired by a ceiling design by the French architect and designer Daniel Marot, I took the theme of spring for this ceiling. On the lower level, servants unveil the shrouded statues and prepare for celebration, bringing plants and flowers to decorate the hall. The sky area above awaits a design. This could be enlivened by a few winged creatures or a meeting of the gods in a more dramatic sky, depending on the theme chosen for the painting.

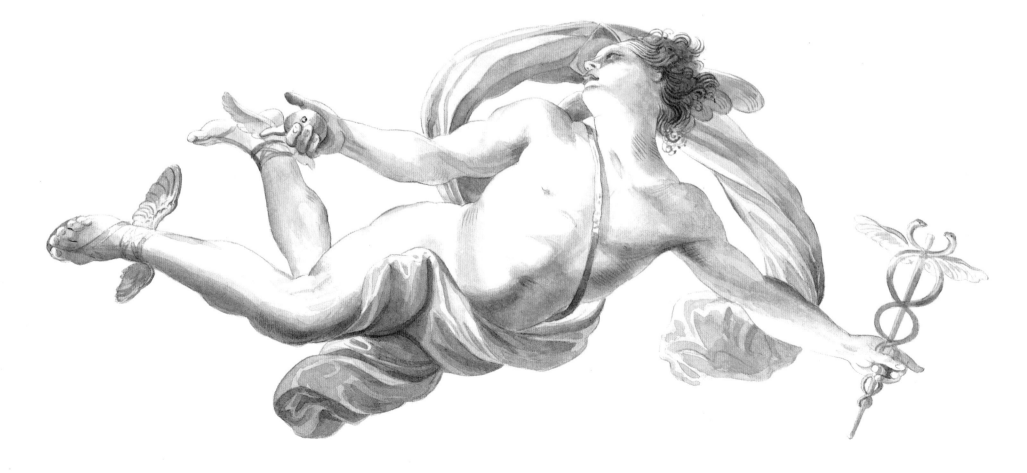

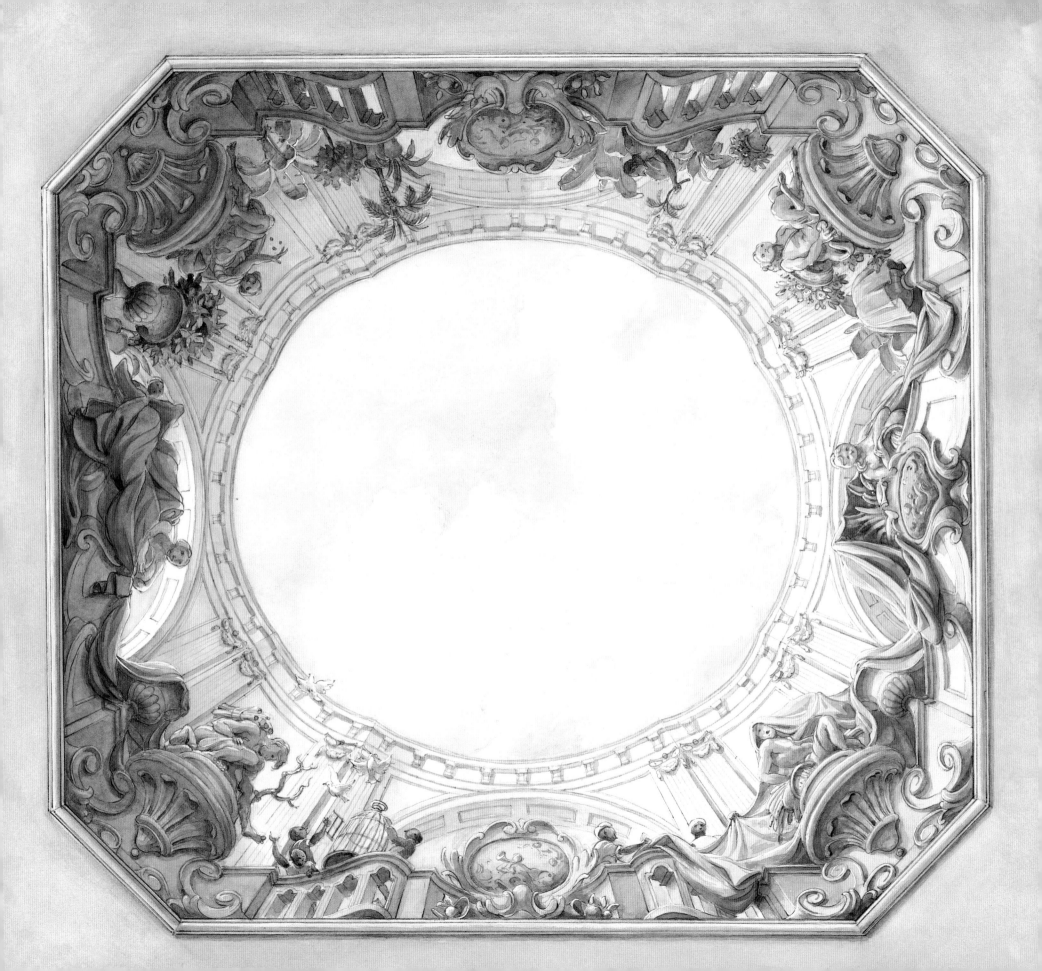

A ROMAN BATH

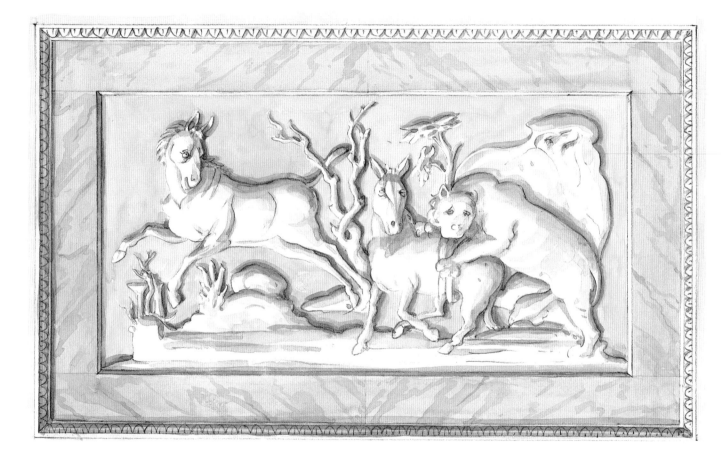

The bathroom is an ideal place to employ painted marble to embellish, or add to, any real marble used in the room. Bearing in mind that at some point one will be lying in the bath tub, the ceiling will become a focal point to be decorated and painted. Although in the scheme shown here I have chosen a design painted as a *trompe l'oeil* relief, a *trompe l'oeil* mosaic would be eminently suitable, if you have the patience to complete it.

ABOVE: This design for a trompe l'oeil *plaster relief was taken from a Roman mosaic at El Djem in North Africa. It is one of a pair designed for the ceilings of bath and shower areas in a palace in Ryadh.*

RIGHT: Two marble samples showing alternative inlays for the outer frames. These are but two examples of many painted marbles that could be used, depending on the general scheme for the room.

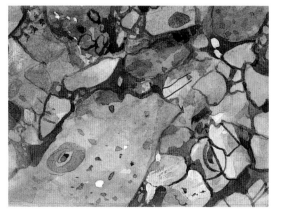

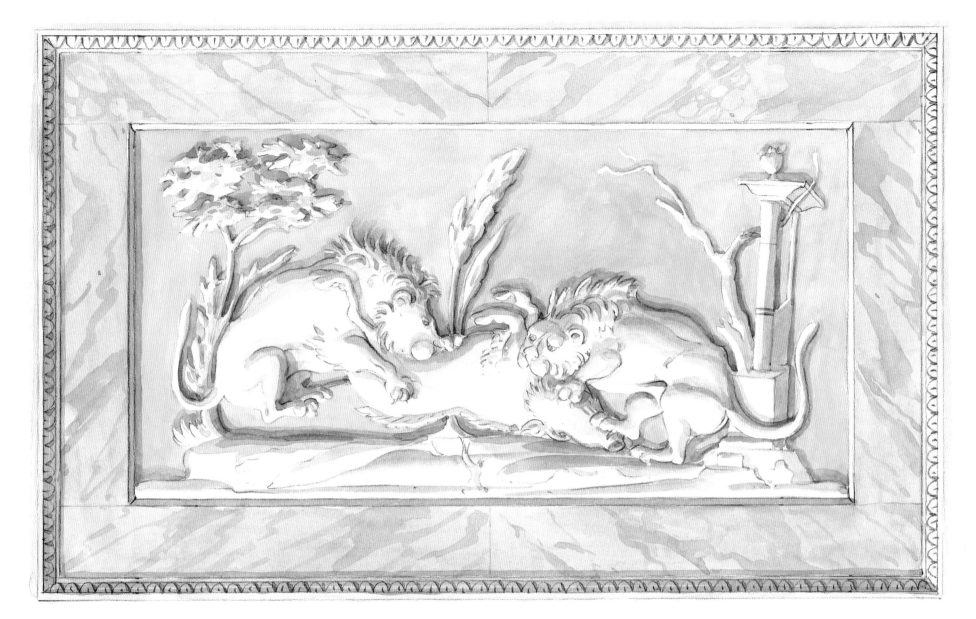

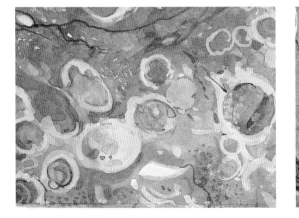

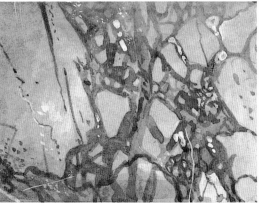

ABOVE: Two lions attack a boar, one of the interpretations, in trompe l'oeil *plasterwork, from the original Roman mosaic. Although the ground is a pink made from burnt sienna and white, it would work well in any other earth colour.*

LEFT: Two more marble samples show alternative colourings for the room. One of the problems with any painted room and particularly a bathroom, is humidity, which can affect the paint and cause it to lift or peel. Make sure this will not happen before embarking on a lavish scheme in faux *marble.*

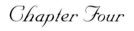

Chapter Four

DESIGNS
FOR SMALL
CEILINGS

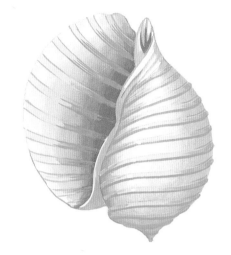

Few of us have vast ceilings to paint or indeed feel that it would be appropriate to embark on a large project within the context of the rest of the house. However, a small ceiling painting can both surprise and delight just because it is unexpected. I have tried in this chapter to suggest ideas for areas to be painted and designs that might easily be adapted to a particular situation. The ceiling of a small lobby or landing can be a good starting point, as can a guest lavatory. The varying ceilings of bay windows also afford space for decoration. With some of these smaller projects, such as the interior of the half tester of a bed, the painting can be done on a panel or canvas and applied to the ceiling later.

To lie in bed and look up at a painting is a great pleasure. The subject matter can vary from the sublime to the erotic. One of the advantages of a painting above one's head, when lying down, is that it can be viewed in the same way as a painting on the wall: it is not necessary to create the illusion of a perspective viewed from below. One of the simplest ways to create a canopy to be painted above the bed, is to fix a moulding directly

on to the ceiling. This rectangle will then enclose the painting and allow fixings for hangings. You can see an example of this on page 124.

The pelmet or drapery hanging from the moulding will in most cases partly obscure the painting from a distance, thus creating a surprise for the guest when they approach the bed and look up. For this reason the subject matter must be chosen with care. One does not want one's prospects curtailed by shocking the maiden aunt. If titillation is required, mythological themes have traditionally been used as a camouflage for more human desires.

In many instances little more than a pattern on a small ceiling will complete the decoration of a room or closet. Recently, while visiting the Picolomini Library in the duomo at Siena, I was reminded how successful the varying sizes and

arrangements of eight pointed gold stars on a deep blue ground can be.

Gold dots or dashes can be equally effective and the spacing and size can vary enormously. As I write, looking up at the ceiling of the Celestial Gallery in the Palazzo Durazzo Pallavicini, I am presented with three different arrangements of this device. Gold dots are lightly spaced on the cobalt blue panels and more densely on the raw sienna and parma violet areas. They create interest and movement and are enhanced by the curve of the slightly vaulted ceiling as light plays on the surface. It is worth remembering that light is reflected by gold. Therefore if the light is behind you, the gold in front of you on a flat ceiling can appear black. Of course, moving around, light and dark interchange.

Another point to consider is how natural light behaves in the room, and the difference created by artificial light. The photographs of the Gothic Ceiling on the following pages clearly show the varying reflections in the gold dots. This, and several of the other ceilings in this chapter, are in my house at Somerton, Suffolk.

THE GOTHIC CEILING

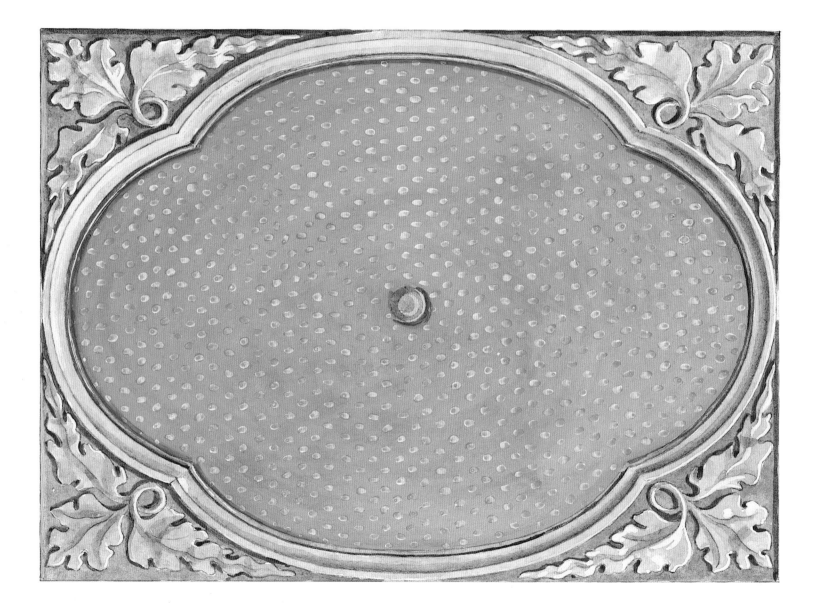

ABOVE AND RIGHT:This ceiling in a small lobby in my house at Somerton was designed to complement the gilded gothic screen on one of the walls. In the photograph, the partially finished painting of the trompe l'oeil *plasterwork can be seen.*

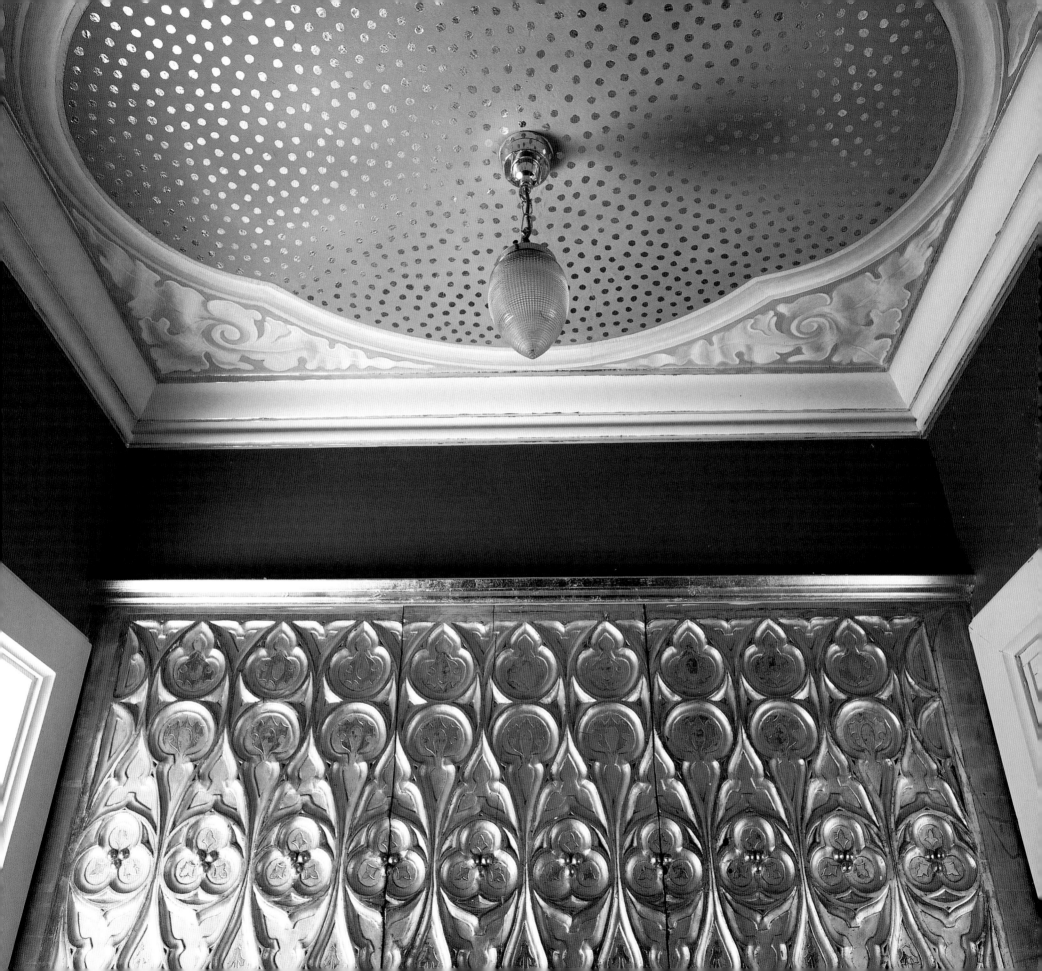

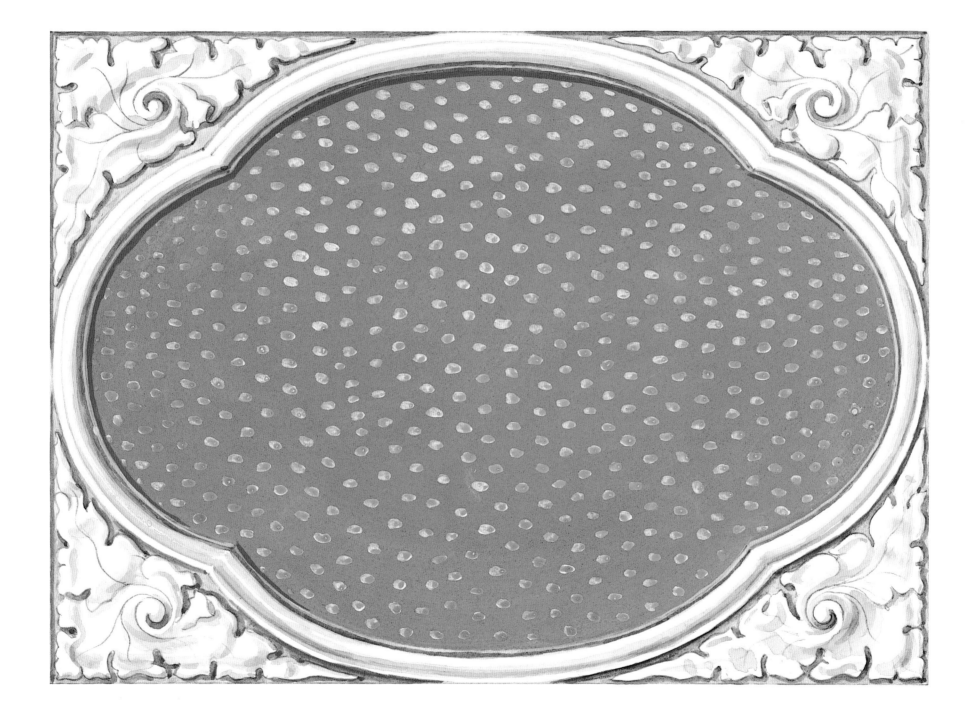

LEFT: One of my designs for the trompe l'oeil *plasterwork of the Gothic Ceiling, showing an alternative background colour.*

RIGHT: A photograph of the gold leaf dots, actual size, on a plain ground. The spacing and size of these dots can vary according to the design. Over a large area, a unity will evolve even if the dots are not precisely the same distance apart. After painting a plain ground, I then paint the dots in a light yellow ochre before applying the size and gold leaf.

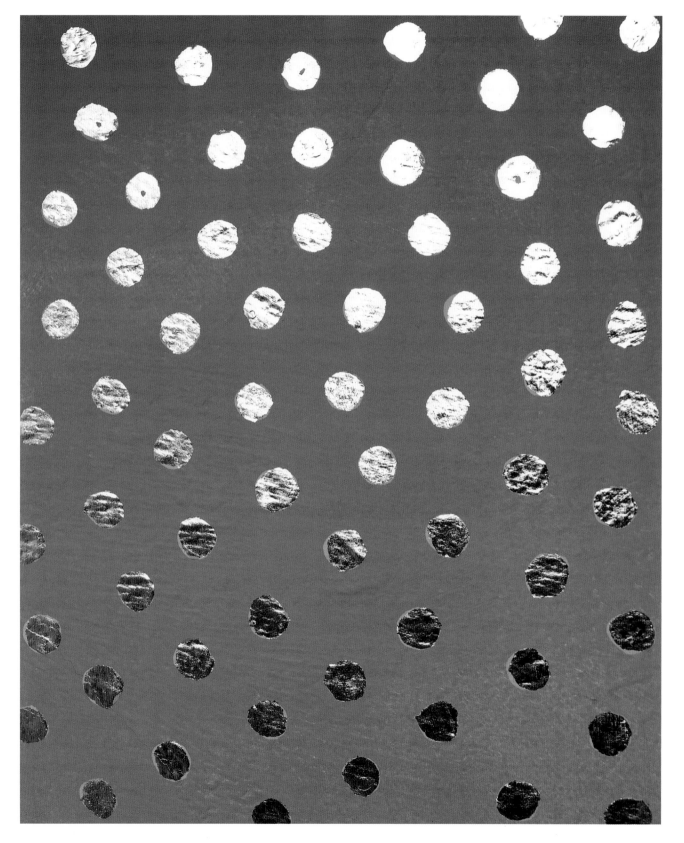

THE SHELL CEILING

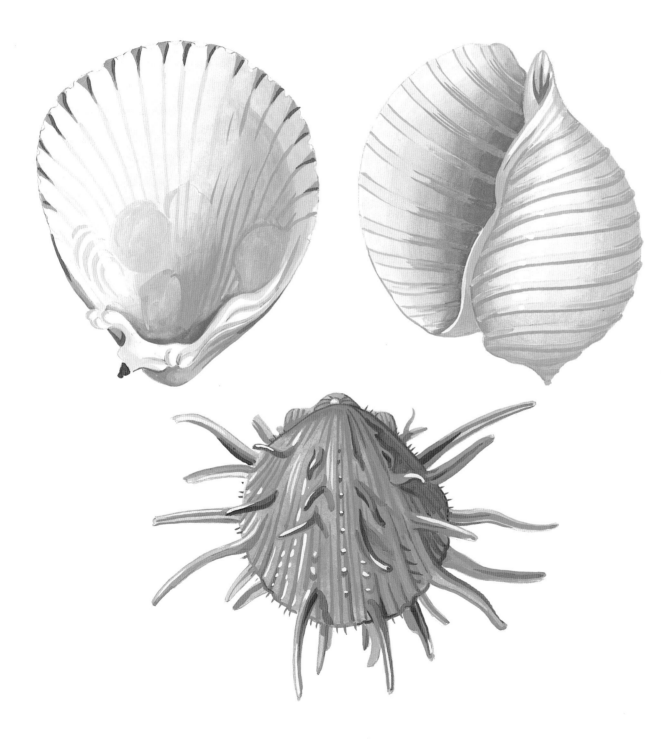

The theme for this small ceiling was suggested by a shell-shaped basin in the adjacent flower room, the ceiling of which was also to be painted. The juxtaposition and proximity of these two ceilings, one square and one rectangular, necessitated a design that could be adapted for both. With a lantern hanging from the centre of the square ceiling, and two small downlights in the large ceiling, I was obliged to work around these central points. As you can see from the design on the page opposite, I decided to reflect the shell motif in the corners using a variety of shells from my collection.

The olive leaves encircling the lights help to emphasise the garden aspect of the entrance and are a symbol of peace to my visitor. As the design is symmetrical, the work involved in transposing it onto the ceiling is greatly reduced. It is only necessary for one corner to be drawn out, as this can then be traced and repeated in the other three. When choosing shells it is best to select ones of a similar size and ones that work well together.

RIGHT: The design, to scale, for the shell ceiling. The ceiling is approximately five feet (1.5 metres) square and has direct natural light from the garden on two sides.

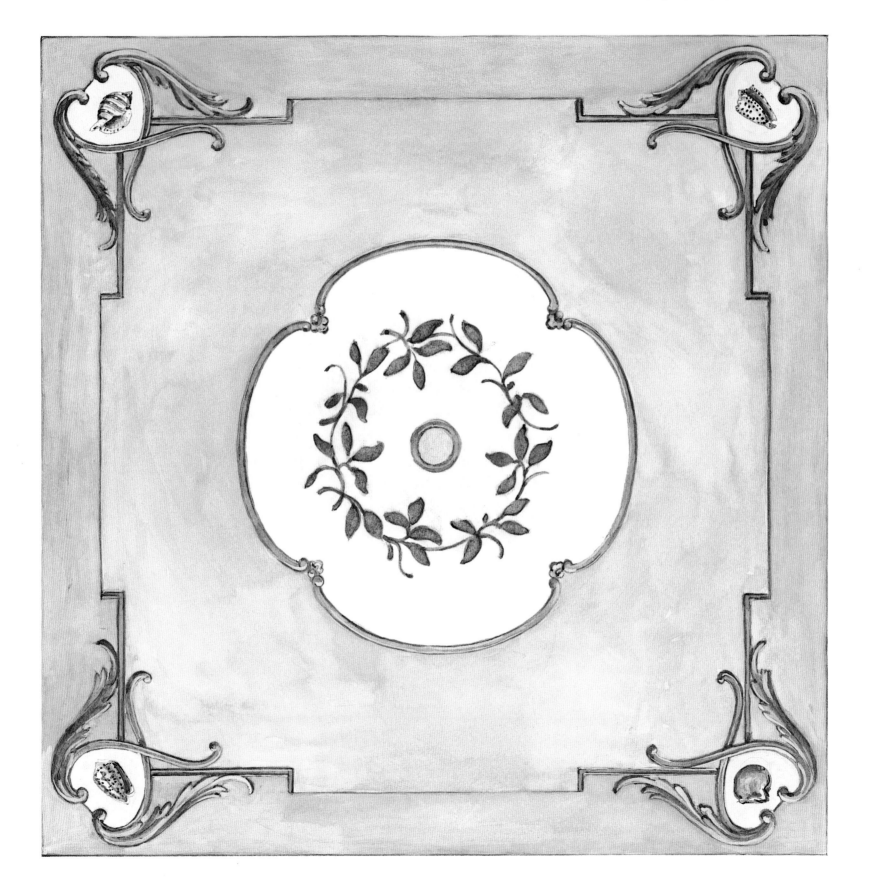

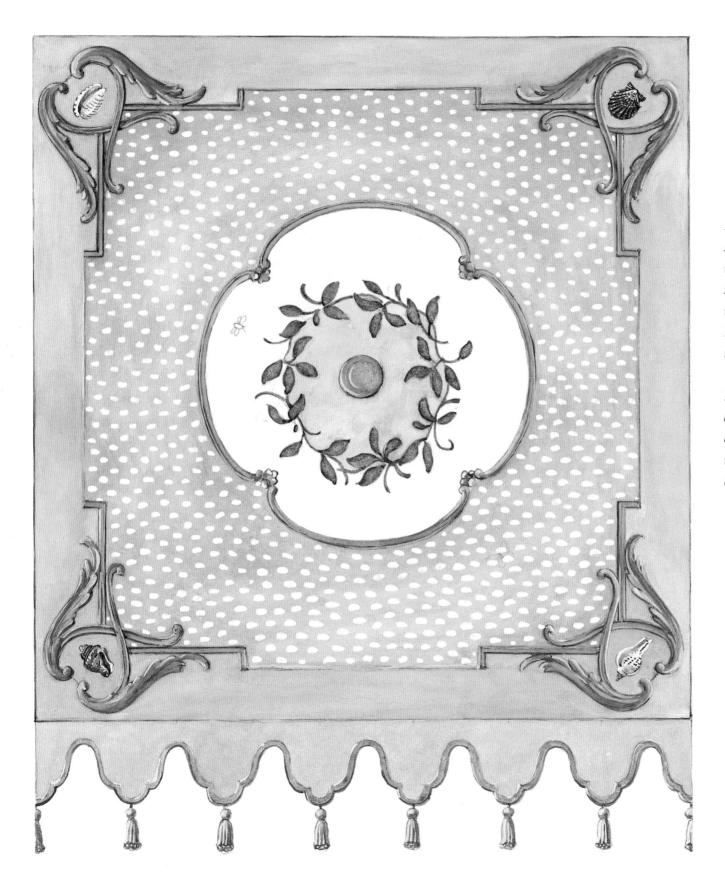

LEFT: *An alternative interpretation of the same design with the addition of a pelmet with tassels. Difficulties can occur with the spacing of the cut-out shapes of the pelmet when the lengths of the walls vary. However, there would be no problem in this instance as the ceiling is square.*

RIGHT: *A photograph of the partially completed shell ceiling of the garden entrance at Somerton. Eventually the walls will be painted to tie in with the ceiling decoration.*

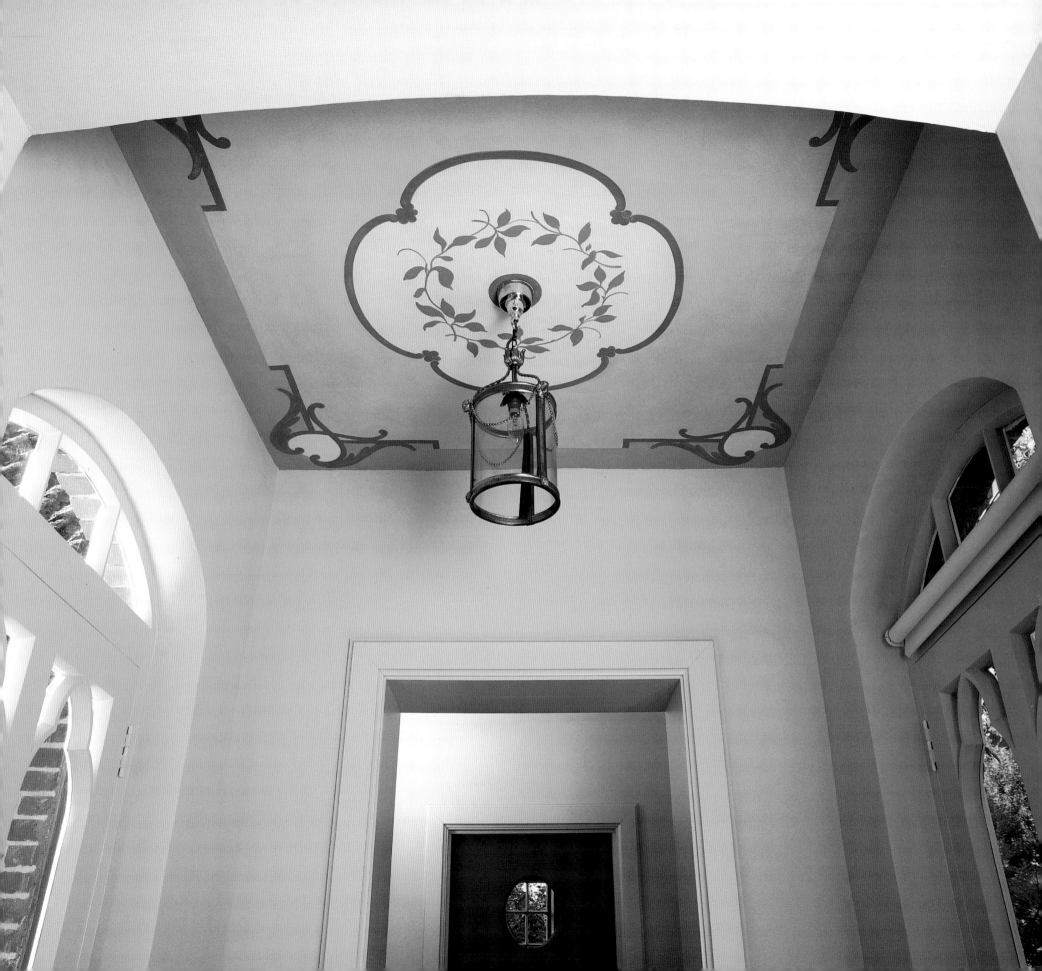

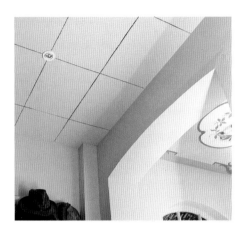

ABOVE: *The adjoining ceiling of the flower room. The ubiquitous downlights have to be incorporated in the design in a satisfactory manner. On the ceiling are the charcoal lines of the initial squaring-up stage (see page 154).*

LEFT: The working drawing for the flower-room ceiling, repeating the same motifs as used on the shell ceiling, and joined by trellis in the middle. The long sides are expanded and interrupted by shells and foliage to balance the design.

BAY WINDOW

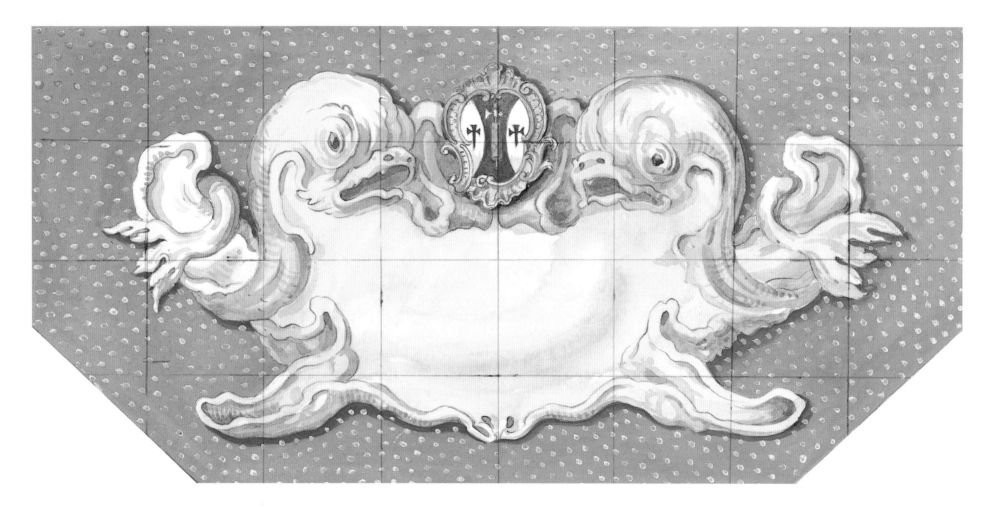

A key consideration when painting a design over a bay window, is which way round you wish the design to 'read' best: either from sitting in the window or from a position in the room. I attempted several solutions before settling for the dolphin design.

ABOVE: The design for the bay window ceiling uses an auricular cartouche of dolphins supporting the shield of my arms, in a rococo frame. The whole design is painted to look as if in stucco on a spot-gilded field.

RIGHT: The finished painting in the morning room at Somerton with an inscription in the centre of the cartouche:

> *Painting is silent poetry,*
> *Poetry is eloquent painting.*
> SIMONIDES C.556–468 BC

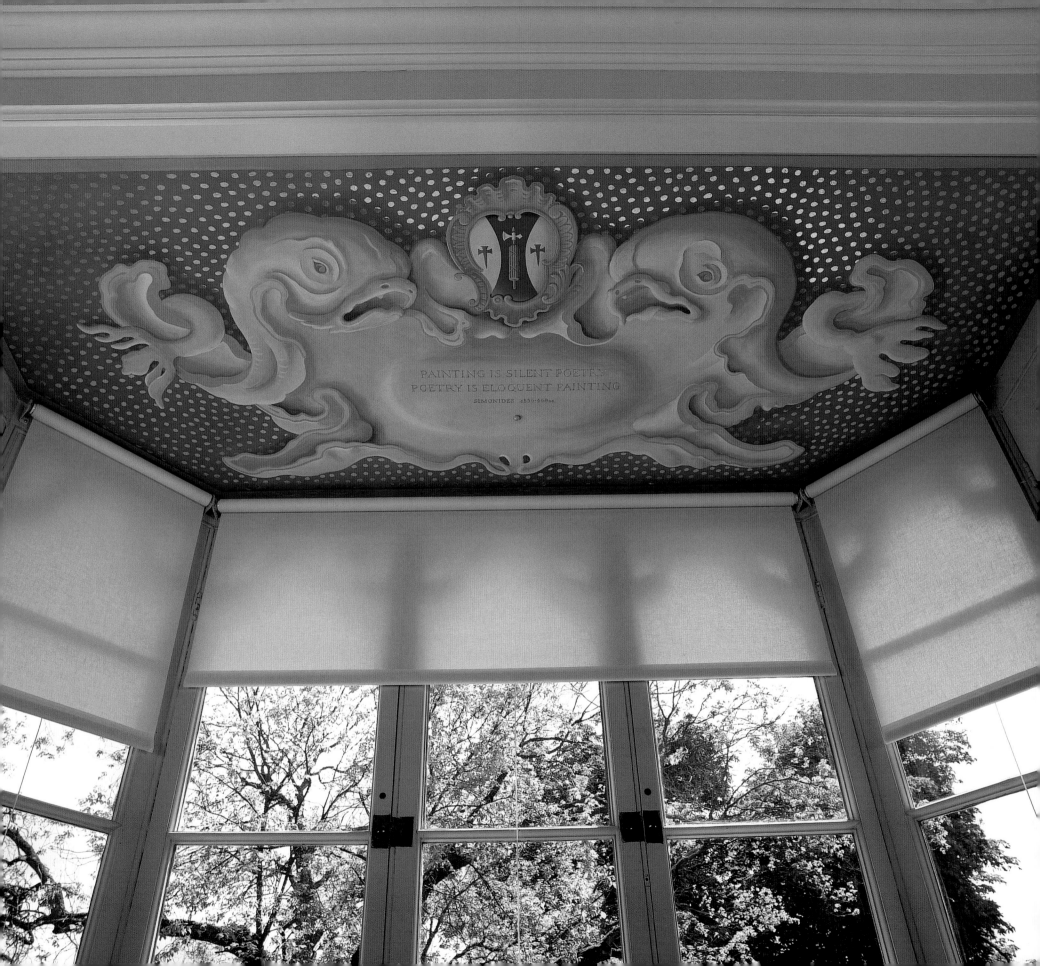

PAINTING IS SILENT POETRY
POETRY IS ELOQUENT PAINTING

SIMONIDES c556-468BC

RIGHT: This was one of several designs that I embarked upon for the ceiling of the bay window. The effect of a panel is created by trompe l'oeil *stiles and rails. The central image is of a Turk smoking a pipe while holding an armorial shield. The reason for choosing this subject is that the tobacco leaf is a memento of a very happy year that I spent as Artist-in-Residence at Woodberry Forest School in Virginia in the 1960s. The tobacco design was adapted from a drawing by Johann Esaias Nilson, which I happened upon in Frankfurt. Two leaves, one viewed from above and one of the underside, were planned to sit on either side of the central motif. In this instance, the design was not carried out and I opted instead for the dolphin* cartouche *on the previous pages.*

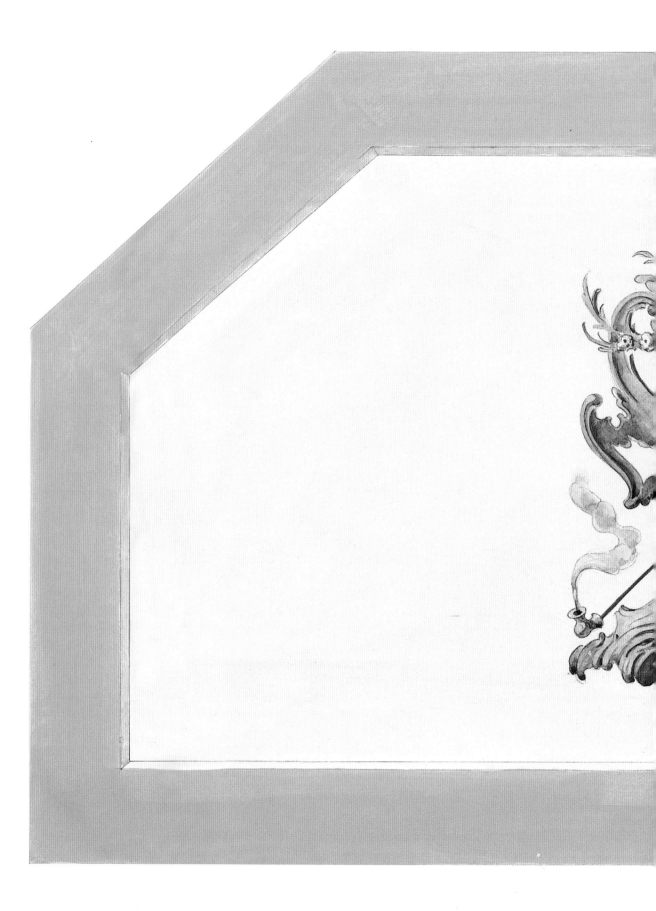

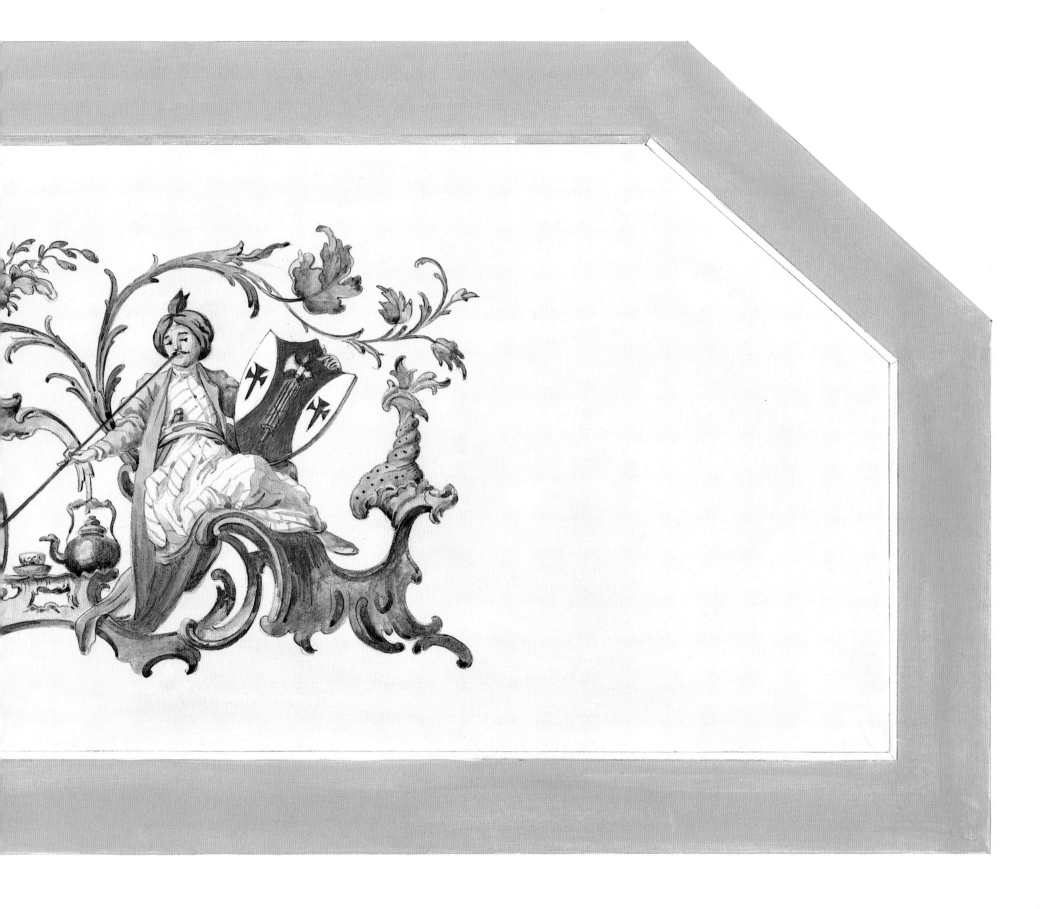

ABOVE: An alternative design for a bay window ceiling. This could equally well be adapted to a semi-circular shape for a different location, with the green ground changed to another colour sympathetic to the room. The central baroque relief is best viewed from a window seat rather than from within the room and this would apply if incorporated with the design opposite.

ABOVE: This pencil sketch indicates a different emphasis for the ceiling with the decoration confined to the border. My intention here was to paint trompe l'oeil *mouldings to contain a border composed of flowers and vegetables painted in polychrome. Any additional decoration to the central panel, as in the addition of the central baroque motif opposite, would be in shades of white, or white and gold.*

BED CANOPY

—

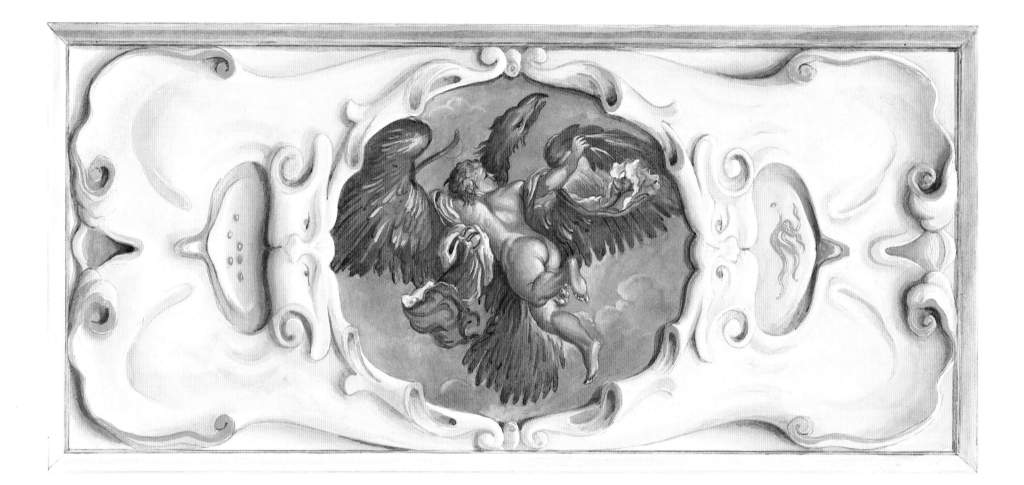

I based the design for the central roundel in this canopy on an engraving after Titian's drawing of Zeus and Ganymede. This was painted in a monochrome of magenta and framed using an auricular device to look as if in a stucco and parcel gilt setting. The underlying theme of 'life' is represented by the gilded seed on the left and the withered pod on the right.

RIGHT: *The painting in progress showing the initial stages of work on the 'stucco' framed by a gilded filet and offset by the striped yellow silk.*

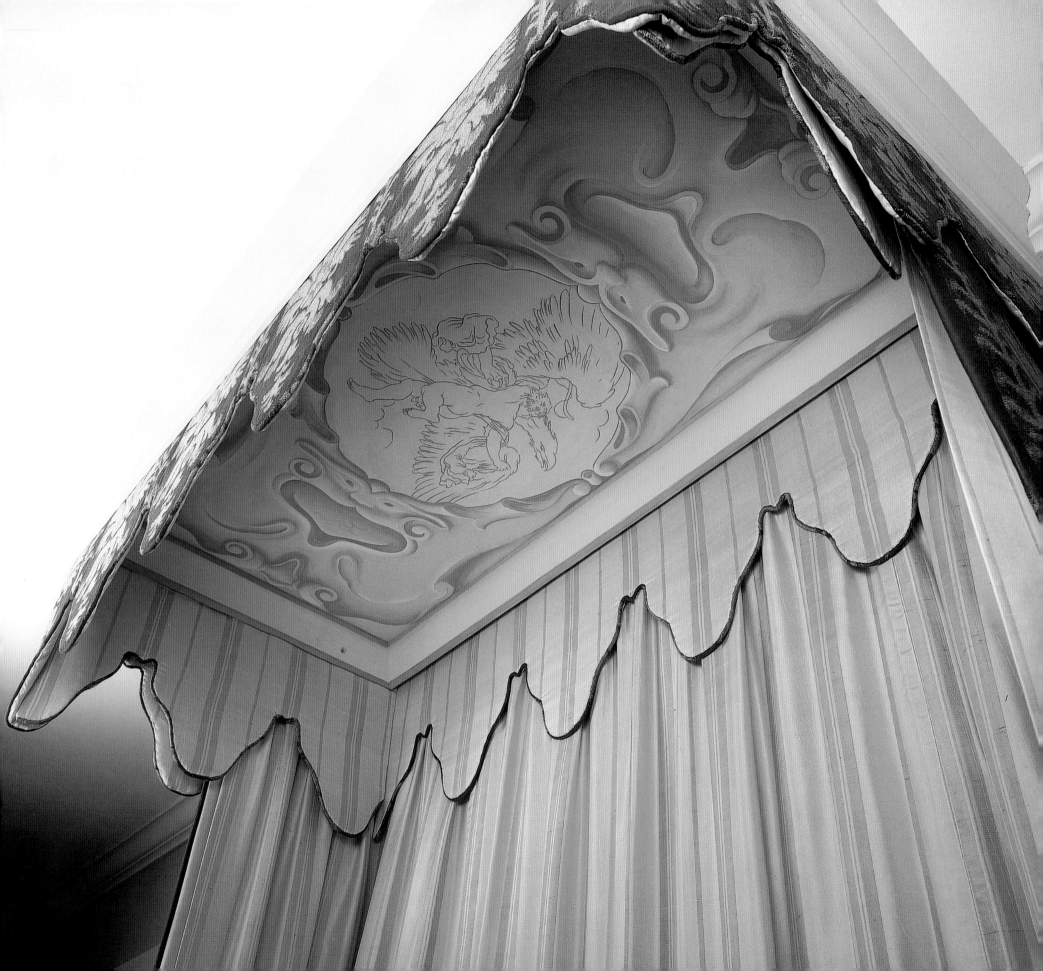

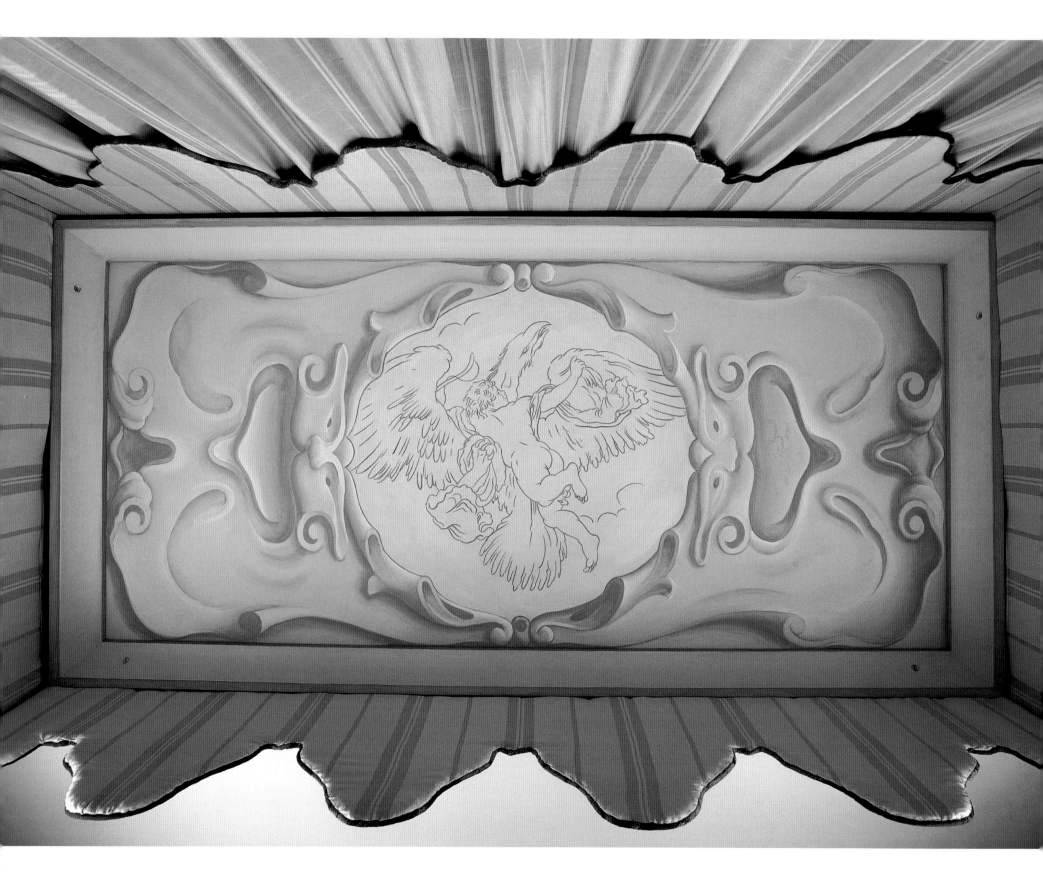

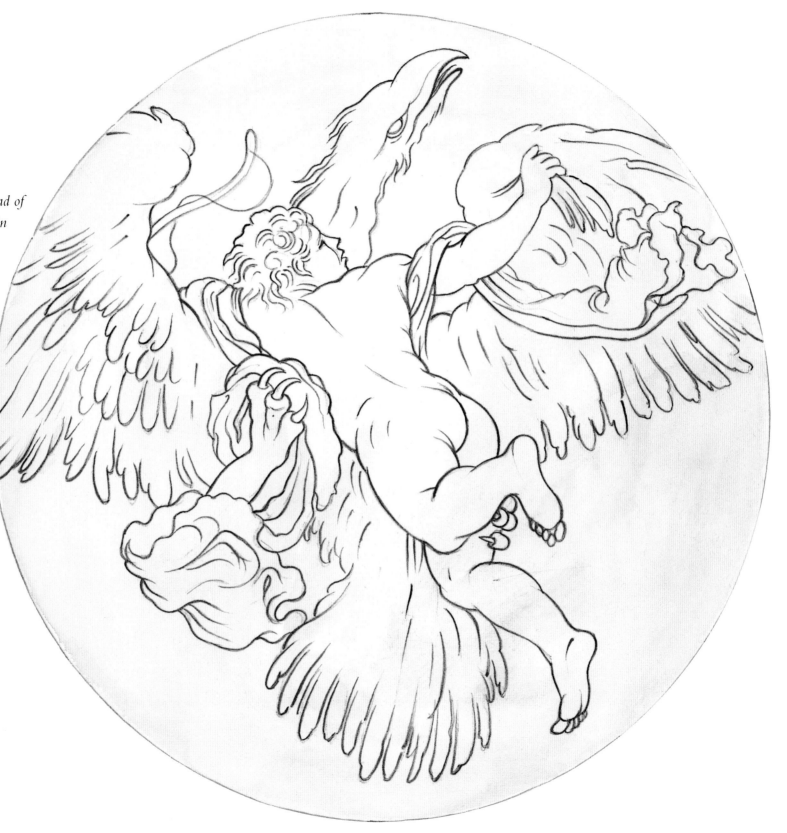

LEFT: *The view from the head of the bed. The panel was put in place under the canopy to make sure that all was well before bringing the painting to a finish. However, an added bonus in having a moveable panel is that, should the bed be dismantled, the panel could be used elsewhere. Needless to say, working on a panel on the easel certainly facilitates the work.*

RIGHT: *My line drawing of Zeus and Ganymede, after Titian. This drawing was later squared up and transferred to the panel to be painted in a monochrome of magenta.*

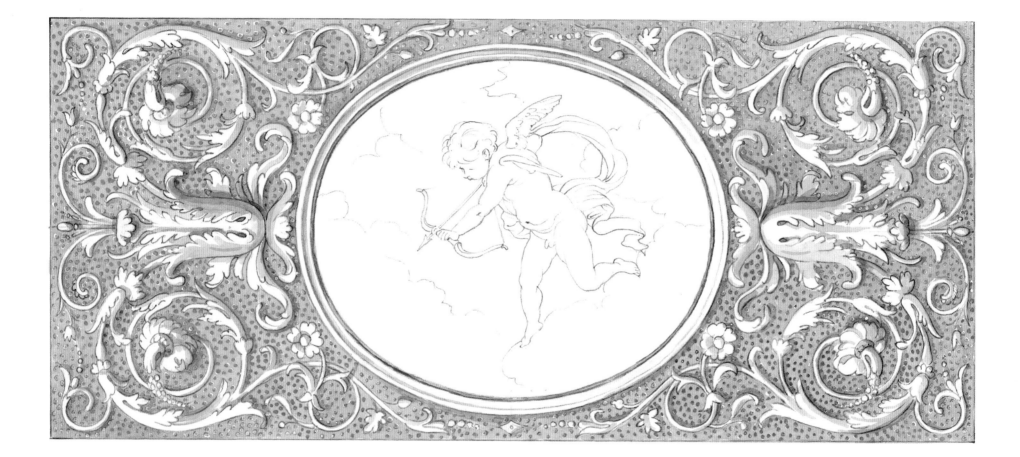

ABOVE: An alternative design for the bed canopy. A foliate decoration in umber and white surrounds a proposed polychrome painting of Cupid, as drawn in the oval.

RIGHT: This design for an entrance hall was inspired by a table inlaid in pietra dura. *I was fortunate to have a square ceiling to paint, which of course made this scheme possible. I have included a dove in the opening of the* trompe l'oeil *dome at the request of the client, although I personally prefer the clarity of a clear sky. The device of an open ceiling lends a sense of height to a modest room. This design was echoed, more simply, in marble on the entrance hall floor.*

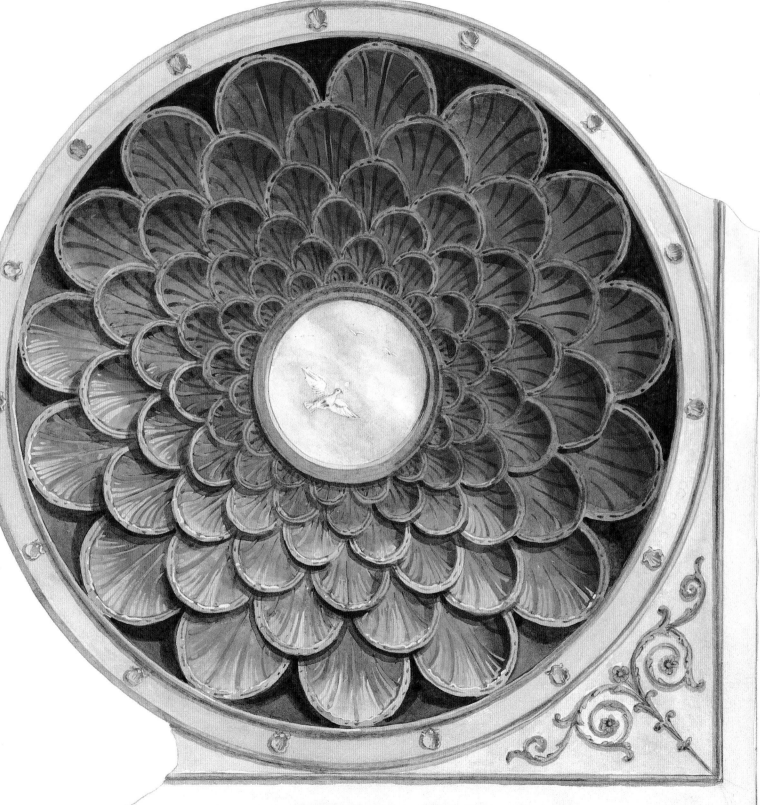

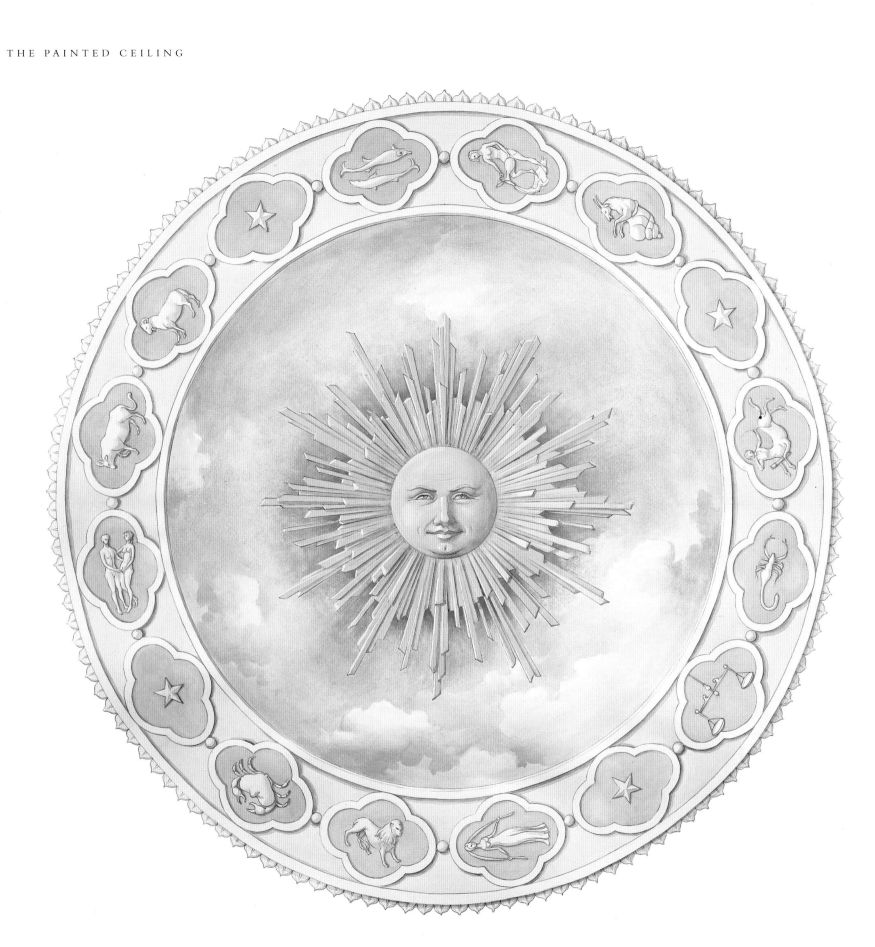

ASTROLOGICAL CLOSET

I designed two ceilings with an astrological theme for a client's Parisian apartment. The ceilings, for a pair of mirrored closets that housed, respectively, her collections of summer and winter shoes, were painted on canvas in the studio and installed *in situ* later .

LEFT: *The sun bordered by signs of the zodiac. (Right) The design for the 'summer' closet featuring the sun ceiling.*

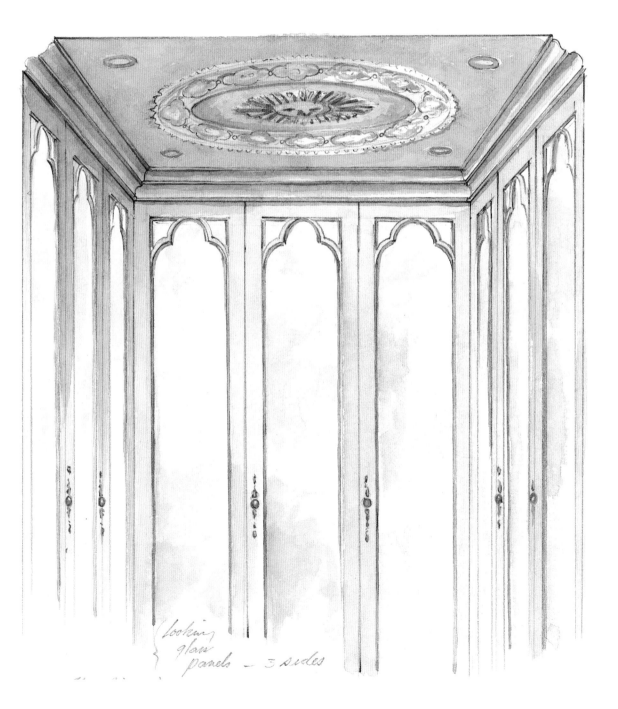

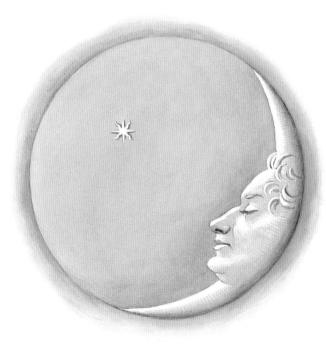

ABOVE: *The design for the moon, to be painted in the 'winter' closet, featured the profile of my client's paramour.*

EGERTON STUD

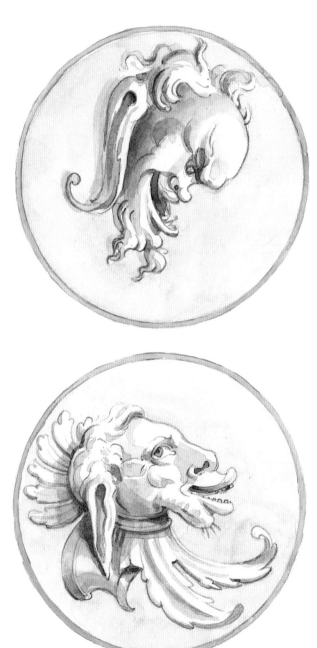

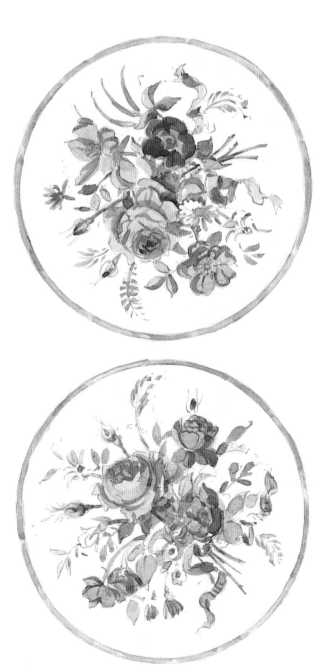

I painted the billiards room at Egerton Stud in Newmarket, with the help of David Thomas, some years ago. The stud, originally built for King Edward VII, was redecorated by the present owner, who decided to reflect the royal past in the design of this room. *Trompe l'oeil* reliefs of the monarch and his consort, Queen Alexandra, were painted as overdoors, and favourite steeplechasers, in gilded frames, painted on the walls. At one end of the room, opposite the main window, *trompe l'oeil* bookshelves housed the leather-bound stud books.

The central beam in the ceiling, which had to be incorporated into the design, determined that the ceiling would be painted to look as if it were two panelled areas, with roundels at the corners to continue the equine theme.

LEFT: *Two grotesque masks, in* grisaille, *from the fabulous collection by Gaetano Piccini.*

RIGHT: *Two compositions of flowers tied with blue ribbon. These would be particularly suitable for a morning room or bedroom ceiling.*

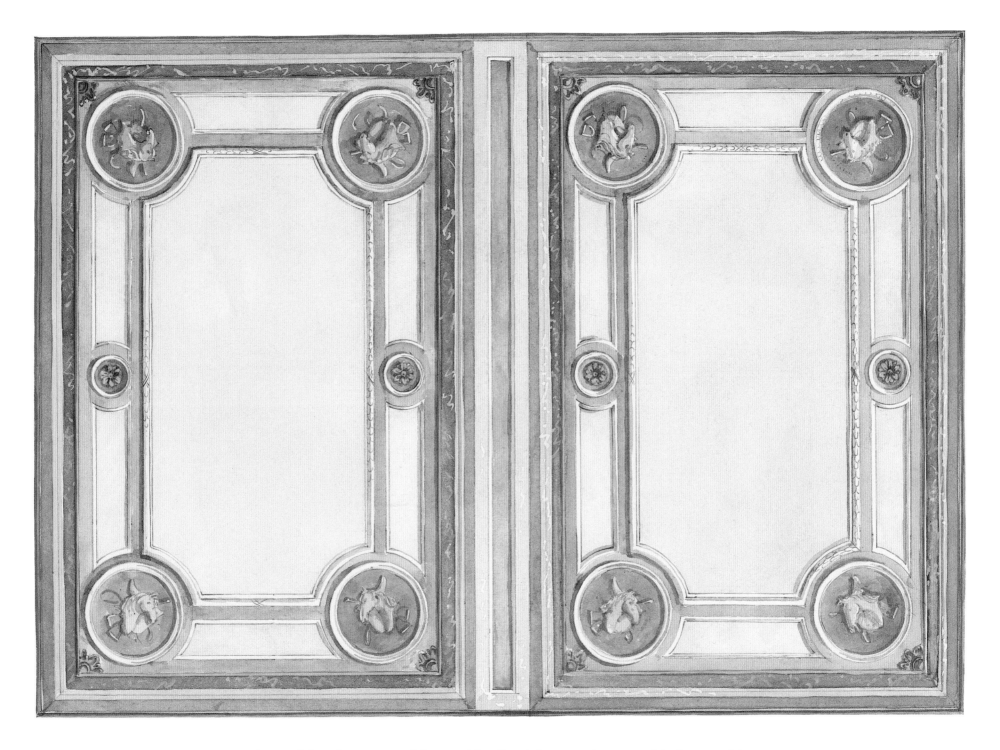

ABOVE: The subject matter of the roundels reflected the equestrian tenor of the house and its environs, however with different designs the ceiling could work happily in another setting. Opposite are examples of other themes.

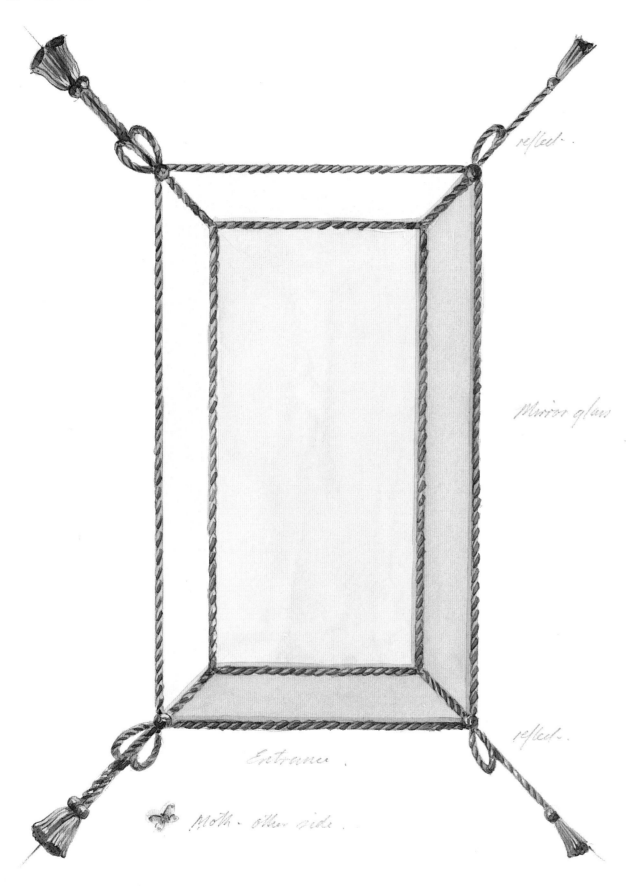

LEFT: *My design for the 'tray' ceiling at Grosvenor Square.*

GROSVENOR SQUARE

—

This ceiling, in an apartment in Grosvenor Square, London, is a good example of a simple design serving to complete the decoration of what could be a slightly baleful space. The windowless guest lavatory is quite small, as is often the case. The main decorative features are some exquisite embroidered silk, behind glass, surrounding the mirror, and two semi-precious carved stone trees in tubs. The client decided that, in this relatively tall room, the ceiling needed to be defined. The 'tray' design is tied in with the walls by the use of rope and tassels. A single loop of rope and tassel is mirrored in the glass to match the double loops and tassels in the opposite corner.

LEFT: *My design for the 'tray' ceiling at Grosvenor Square.*

RIGHT: *A photograph of the room showing the painted ceiling and tassels, with a moth on the wall.*

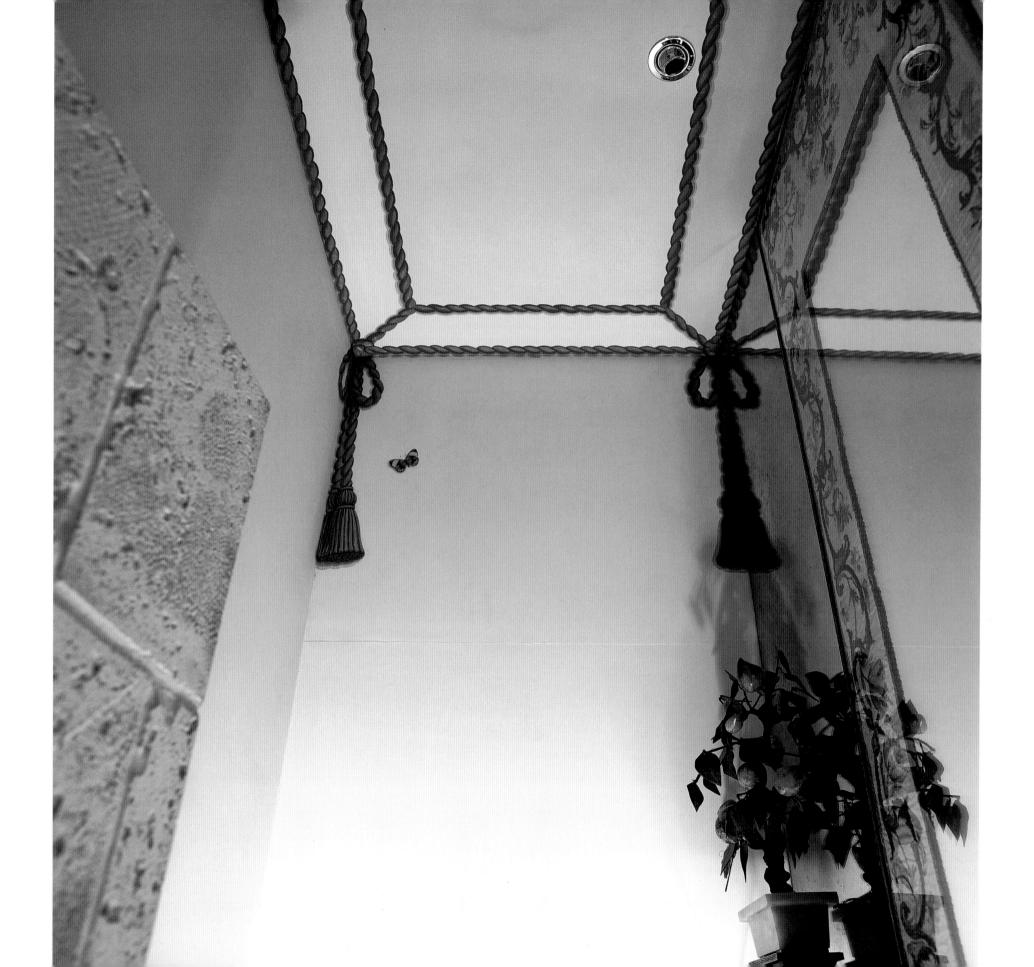

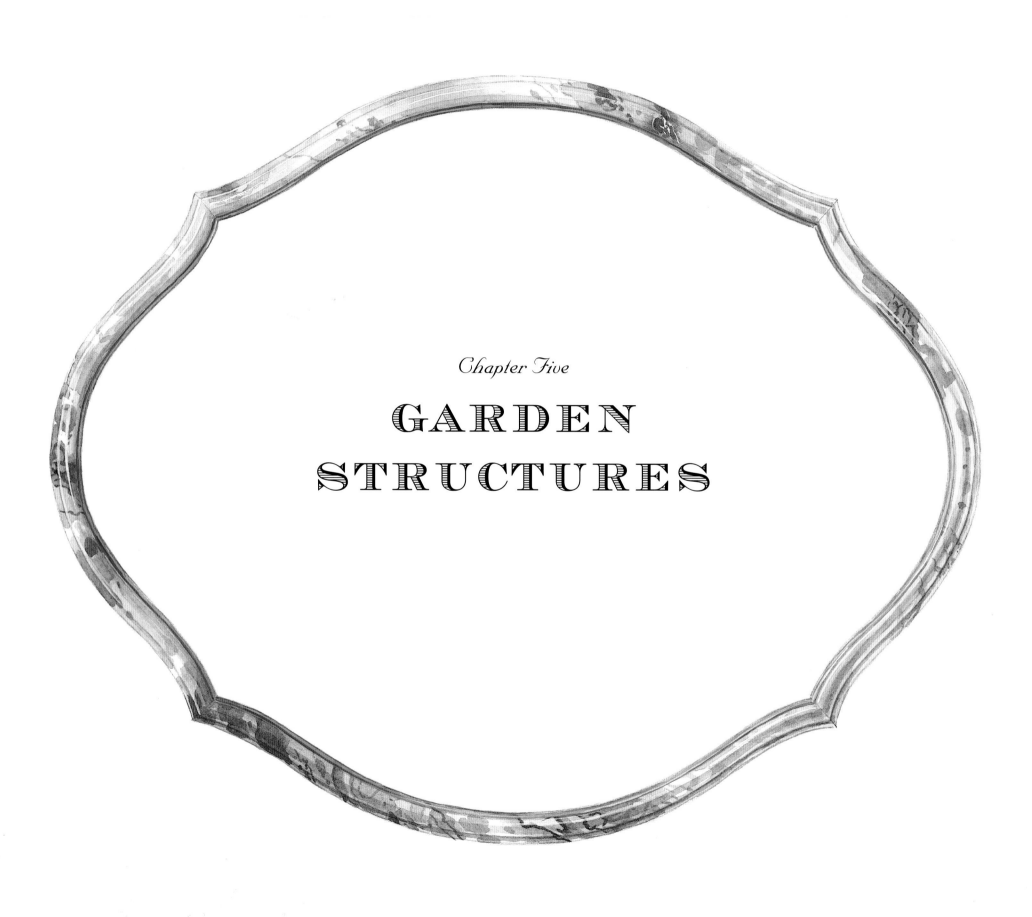

Chapter Five

GARDEN
STRUCTURES

I shall never forget the delight, having been taken to a small hunting lodge while staying at Udaipur in India, of discovering that its interior was filled with nineteenth-century Mughal paintings of flowers and animals encountered in the chase. The element of surprise was heightened by finding this treasure in a truly rustic setting.

The temple, the folly, the summer house – all are perfect places for the painter to exercise his or her imagination, whether he wishes to be restrained and discreet, or wild and exuberant. A fleeting visit or picnic in a gazebo that has a painted ceiling can only add to one's sense of magic. There is the opportunity to reflect, with the brush, the atmosphere around one, as in the case of the Indian hunting lodge.

For those of us not fortunate enough to have a summer house to decorate, there are ways to recreate the atmosphere of outdoors on interior ceilings. A ceiling can be 'opened to the elements' by effecting the ruin of the real ceiling, for

example, as in the painted interior of the monastery of Trinita dei Monti, near Rome, by Charles Louis Clerisseau. One can create the impression of a pergola or rustic support for vines or roses. A more formal architectural frame may be constructed using *treillage*.

In many instances, particularly in an urban environment, the desire to bring a little bucolic rusticity into the house is irresistible. The addition of birds, butterflies, moths and other insects can add interest here and there, even though they are not the main emphasis of the ceiling. The discovery of a butterfly on a leaf, or a bird's nest hidden in a dark corner, is bound to delight the visitor. A spider's web can intrigue, with or without the spider or her prey. However, some people do have phobias and it is worth checking before spending hours on a detail only to be told to remove it because the client 'just can't stand them'!

The tray ceiling on page 146 is painted as if fashioned from split logs, twigs and fir cones.

This type of ceiling is but one example of the ingenuity of our eighteenth- and nineteenth-century forebears' use of woodland materials to

create a variety of shapes and patterns in their gazebos, croquet huts and summer houses. These wooden patterns are similar to those created in grottoes, using shells, stone and corals, and equally satisfactory to paint in *trompe l'oeil* on walls and ceilings.

Tenting is perhaps the ideal solution if a less rustic but nevertheless *al fresco* feel is required. Tenting can vary enormously from the simulation of simple calico to rouched and pleated satins and silks, tied and be-tasselled in myriad form.

Depending on your design, and whether the walls are also part of your scheme, a pelmet can be a useful finish to a tented ceiling. It is important to take into account the differing lengths of wall before working out a module that will meet satisfactorily at the corners. These can be embellished with tassels and cords with the cast shadows helping to create the illusion of reality. There are designs on the following pages for a few of the many possibilities.

THE SUMMER HOUSE

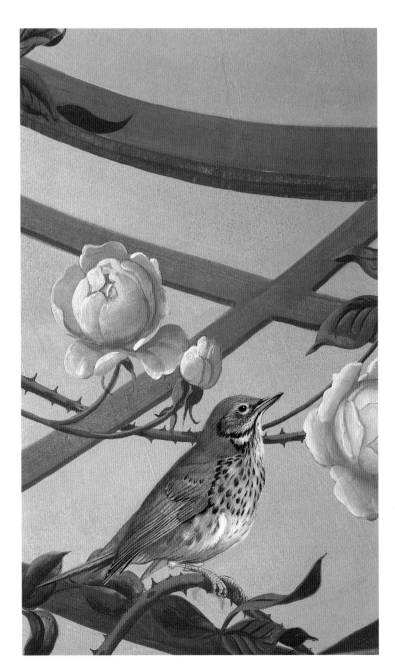

This domed summer house nestles in the grounds of a neo-classical villa in Frankfurt, set against the back drop of a woodland in a peaceful sylvan setting interrupted only by the sound of water from a nearby fountain.

The clients who commissioned this ceiling wanted the design to echo the feel of the garden. More specifically, they wanted to include some of the roses from the garden and the birds and insects that lived there. One of the hazards of working out of doors is the weather. In this case, work began in the late autumn and took just over one month to complete. Rui Paes, who worked with me painting the birds, and I stood sheltered under the dome on a light scaffold. As winter approached and the job was nearing completion, we were freezing. At other times a different menace in the form of mosquitoes can drive one mad. However, there is no substitute for working *in situ*.

LEFT: A thrush sits on the briar of a rambling rose entwined in the trellis. The sky was painted first, followed by the trellis. After this came the roses, with the final addition of the birds and insects.

RIGHT: Part of the domed ceiling of the stone summer house in Germany. The clear blue sky with a few scudding clouds is encircled by a trellis painted the colour of verdigris, which supports rambling roses, and assorted birds and insects.

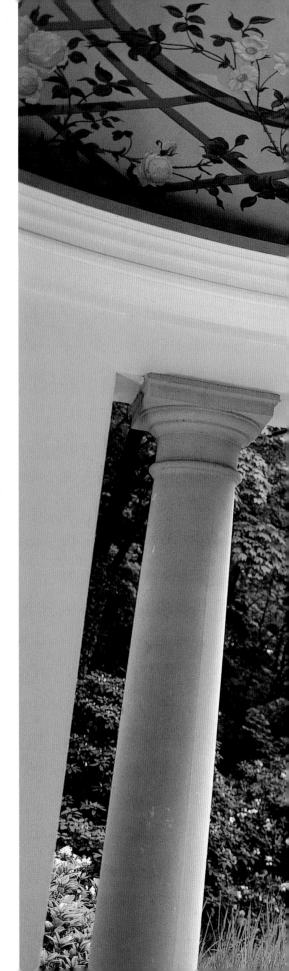

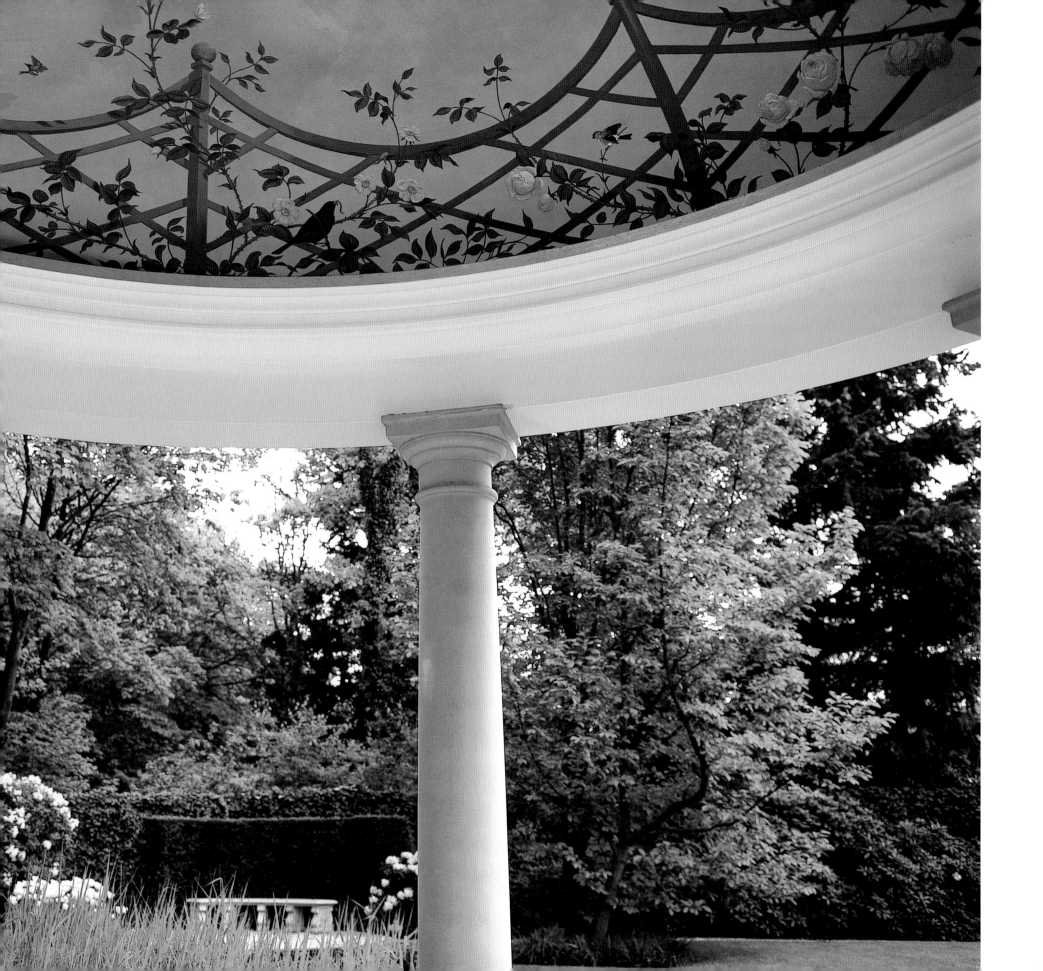

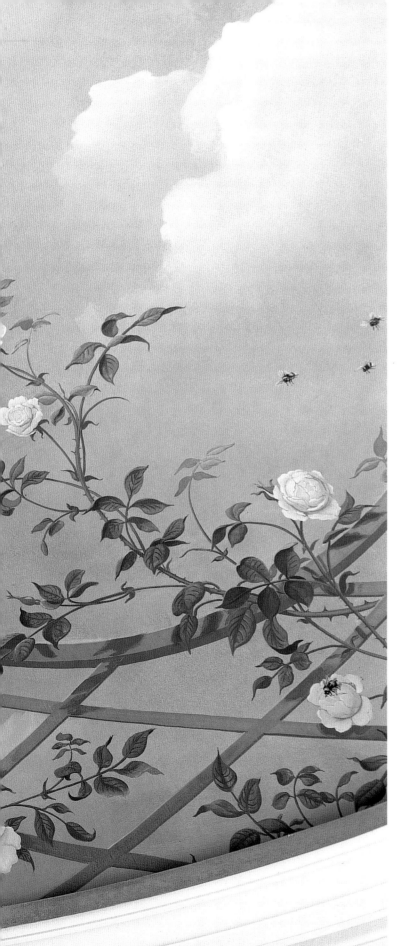

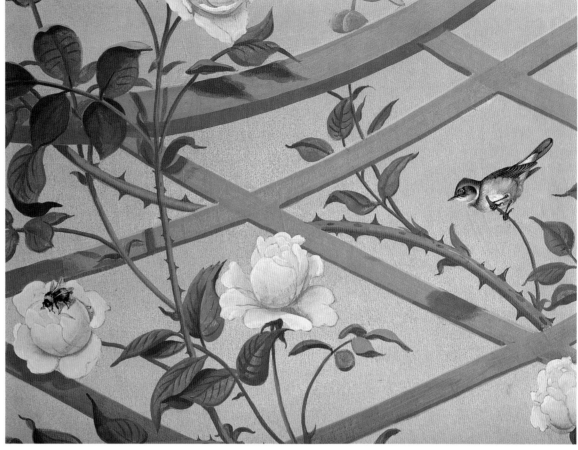

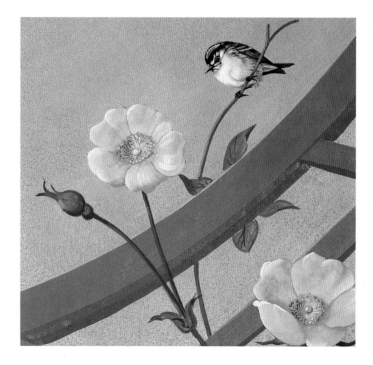

ABOVE: Roses with a bumble bee and a flycatcher. In a composition such as this, variety is essential. Try to include some birds hidden, some in flight, and some interacting, to avoid the painting becoming too static.

LEFT: 'One for sorrow, two for joy, three for a girl and four for a boy'. Settling amid the roses on the trellis, the two magpies will hopefully bring 'joy', as predicted in the traditional rhyme.

RIGHT: Single roses with a goldcrest.

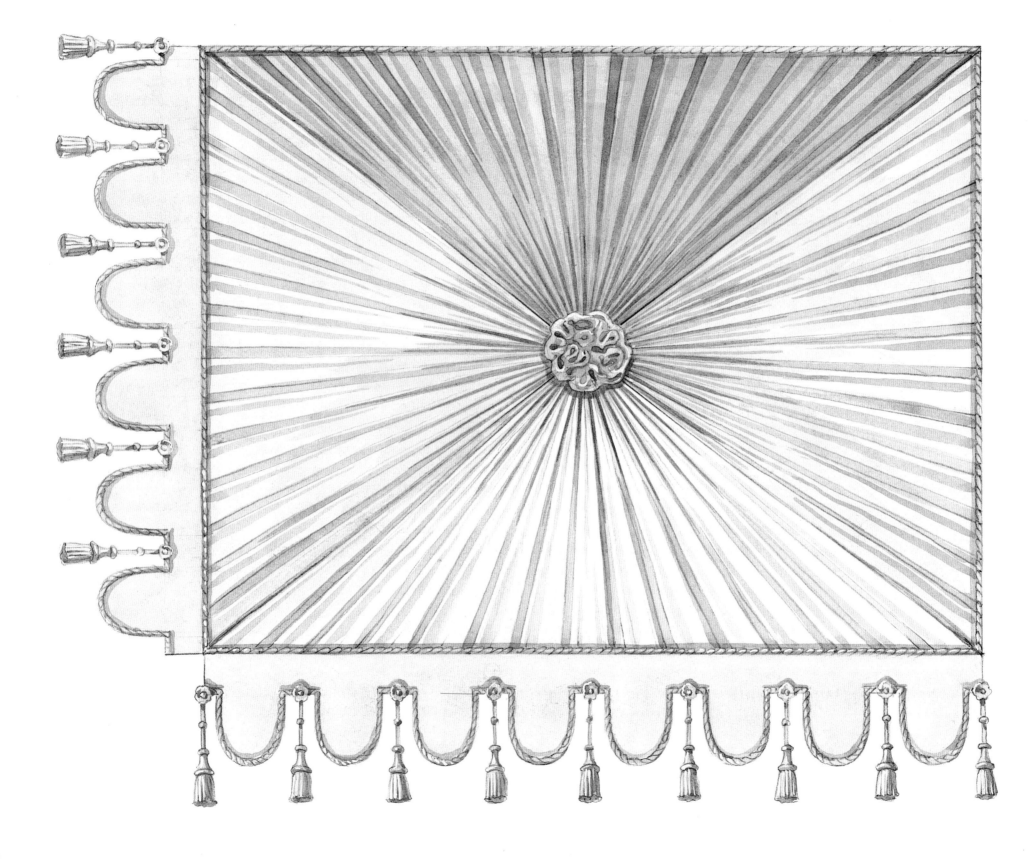

TENTED CEILING

This design for a tented ceiling was used, as was the one on the previous page, for the decoration of a ceiling in a lavatory. The bed of the ceiling was painted to appear as though of pleated, pale umber silk, held and finished at the apex with a gathered silk rose. On the walls, a pelmet edged with silk rope and tassels completes the decoration.

To help to create the illusion of a pyramid shape on a flat ceiling, the light should be such that one or two sides appear to be in shadow. If there is a window on one side of the room, it will help to clarify from which side the light source should emanate.

LEFT: The watercolour design for the ceiling, with the pelmet shown on two sides only. (Right) A section of the pelmet with tassels.

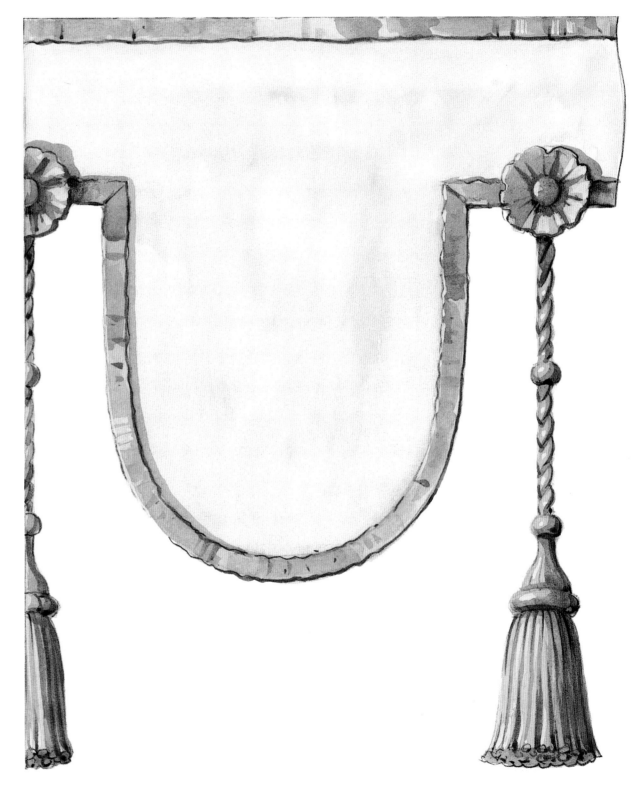

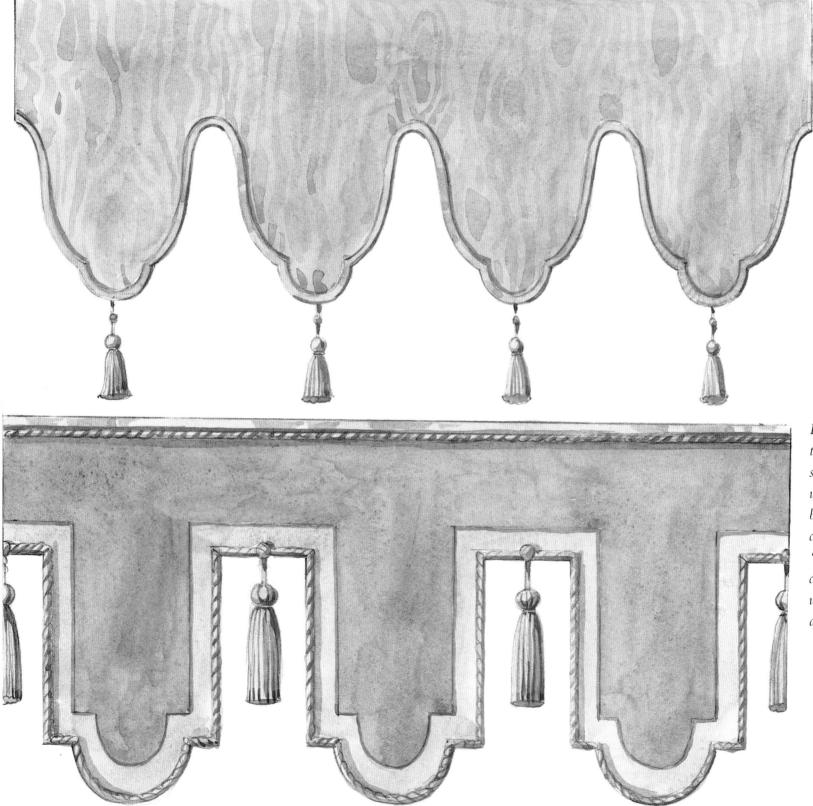

LEFT: *The soft lines of this pelmet, in watered silk, is very open, whereas the design below is more rigid and compact. A more 'masculine' feeling could be achieved by working the design in different colours.*

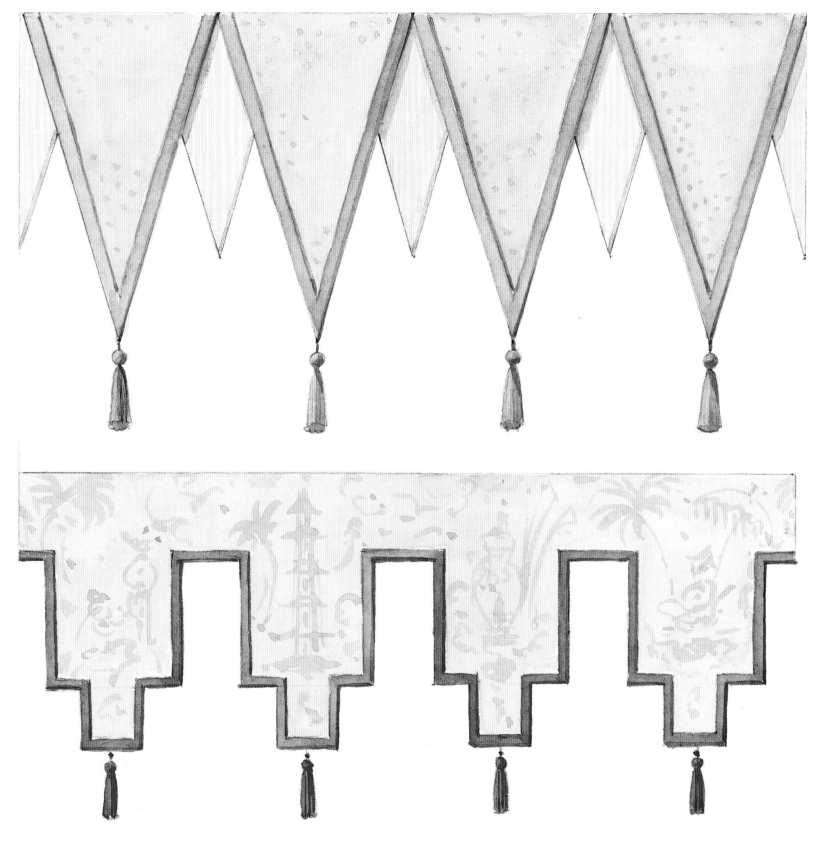

RIGHT: The sharper lines of this pelmet introduce a crisper finish and emphasise the vertical feel of the room. I used a similar design to this in a Gothick library.

Chinoiserie has always had great appeal. This example, based on a Toile de Jouy (printed cotton that is sometimes glazed) presents a more angular outline and could be painted in any colour. Many old designs are readily available today, however, eighteenth- and nineteenth-century remnants can be seen in many museums or reproduced in books.

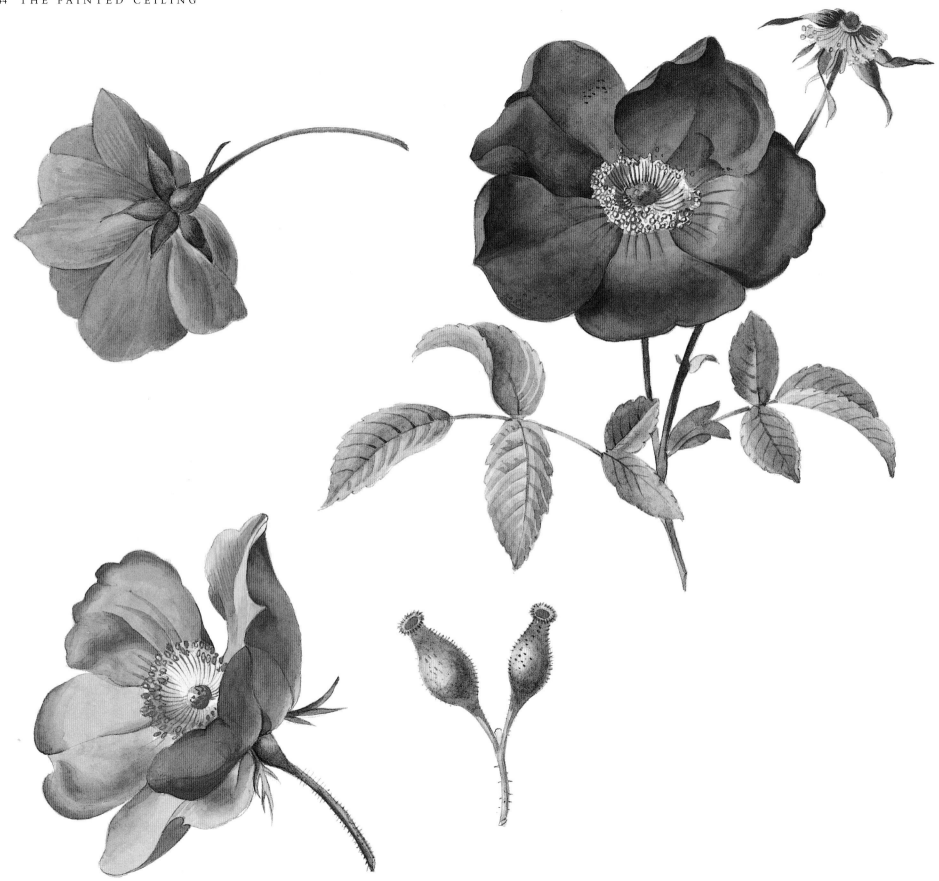

LEFT AND RIGHT: Studies of roses after Redouté. It is important to gather references for a variety of roses or other flowers. Nothing can beat making studies from life, however, it often happens that one needs a flower out of season and has to resort to using someone else's work as reference material. Photographs are little help as they do not show the structure of the plant or flower clearly.

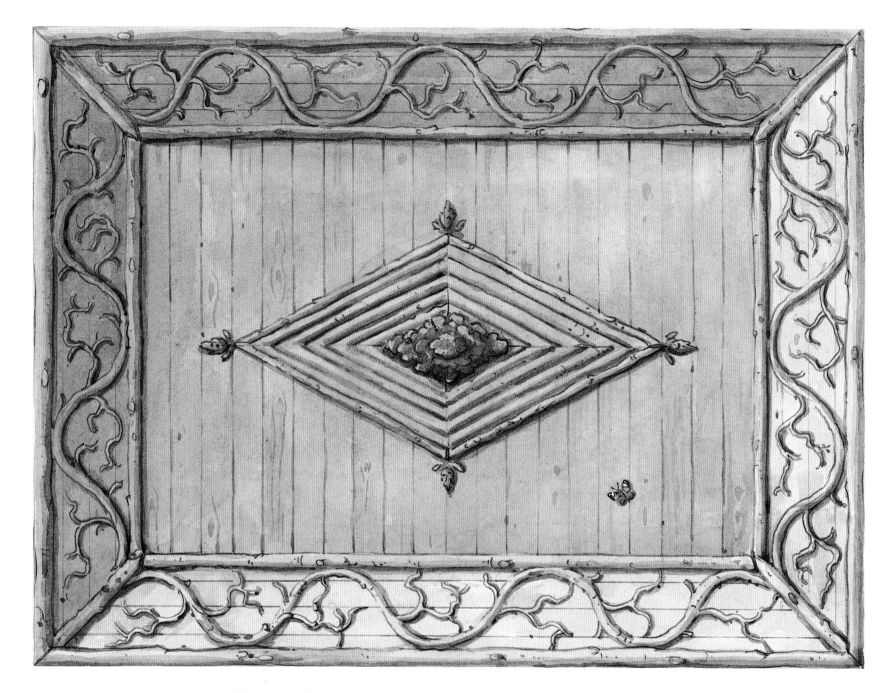

ABOVE: This design for a 'tray' ceiling for a summer house echoes the treatment of its walls: pine boards with split log and twig decoration painted in trompe l'oeil. *The butterfly adds a touch of colour to the monochromatic palette.*

RIGHT: This painted treillage *ceiling was designed for a breakfast room. On the trellis support, 'Morning glory' climbs upwards adding her heavenly blue trumpets and green leaves to the 'sky' above our heads.*

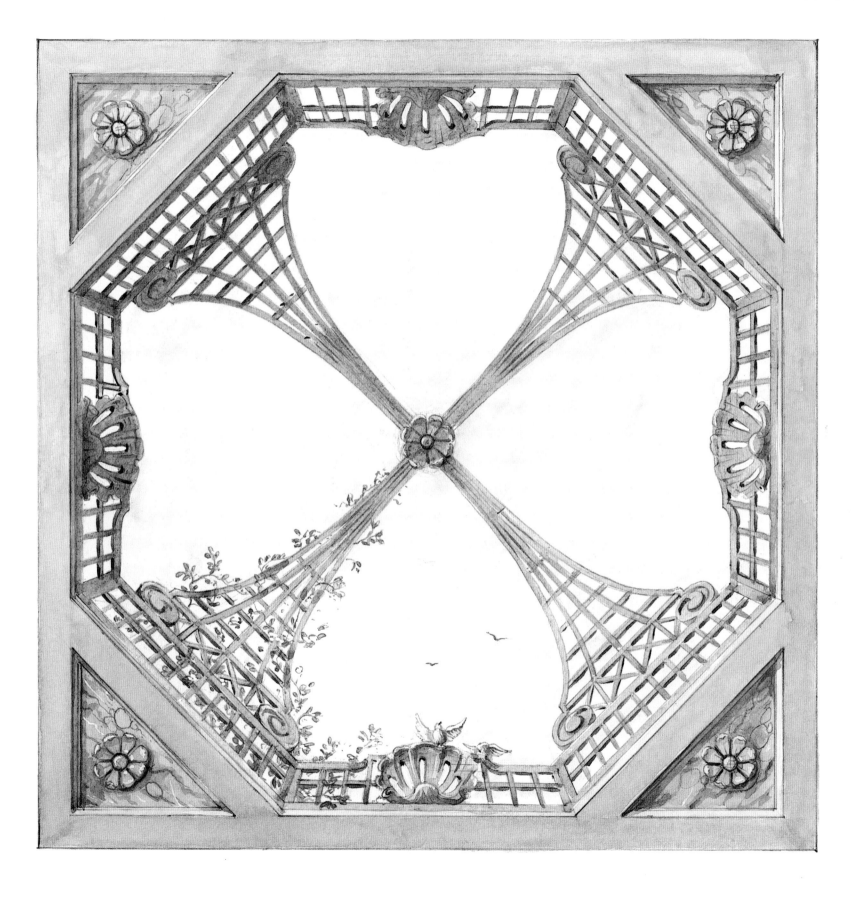

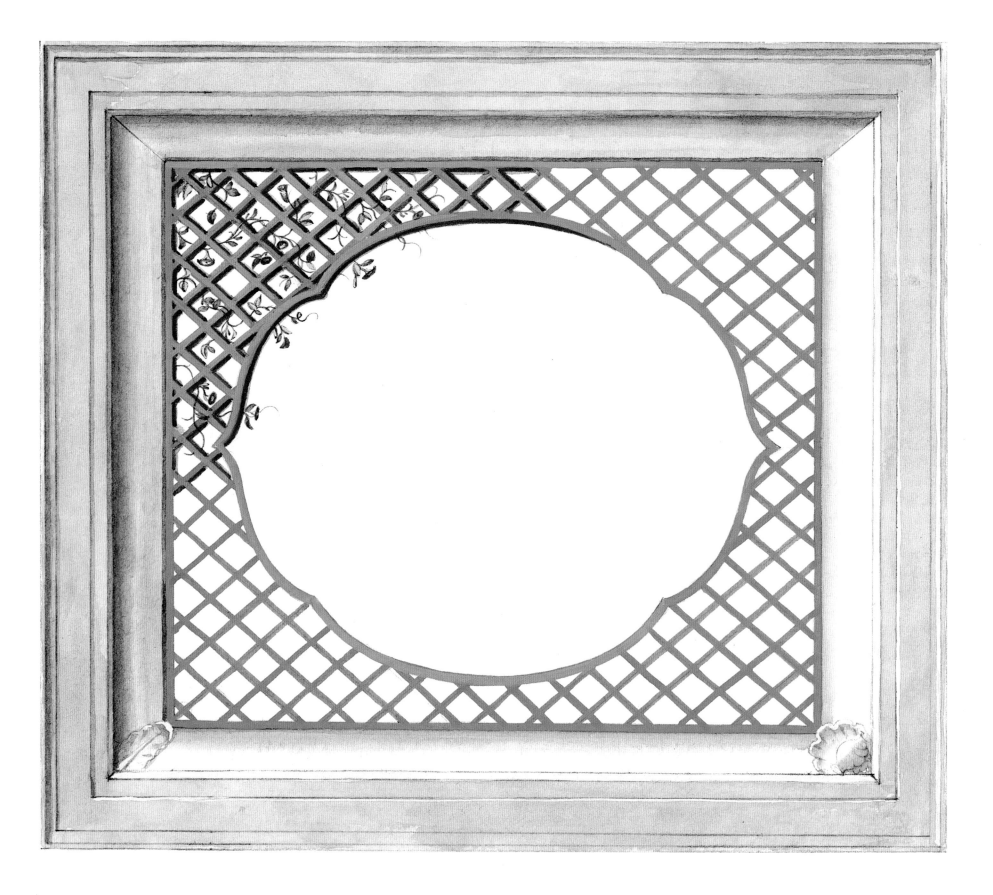

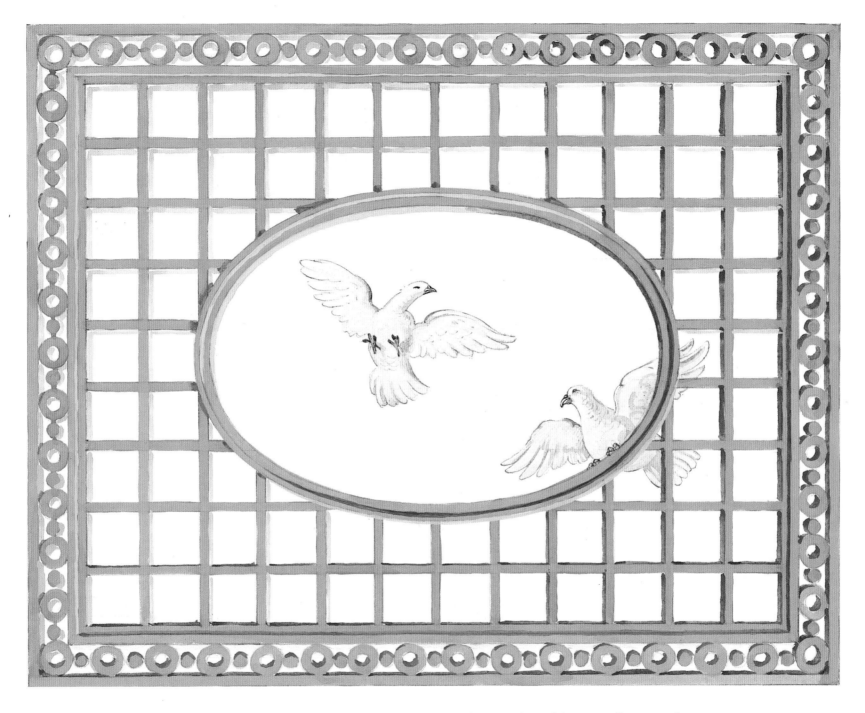

*A*BOVE: *Two doves are the focal point of this design for the ceiling of the stairwell in a small London house. The bird with its claws outstretched is far enough away from the onlooker not to appear menacing.*

*L*EFT: *A* trompe l'oeil *plaster cornice lifts the trellis up a little in this design for a low ceiling in an urban apartment.*

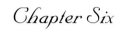

Chapter Six

PRACTICAL ASPECTS

When one is presented with a blank ceiling, there are several things to consider before letting one's imagination take flight. The first is whether painting the ceiling will enhance the room. If the conclusion is that it will, then consider the height of the ceiling from floor level, as this must, to a degree, dictate the form of decoration to take place. Many modern houses and apartments have low ceilings, and it is folly to try to paint something that needs a great distance to be viewed effectively. If the ceiling is low, an overall painted sky might be the solution, or *trompe l'oeil* plasterwork creating panels, with or without further decorative elements. A ceiling design does not have to be complicated to be effective.

If the existing decoration of the room cannot be altered, then it is best to work with it. Clients are unlikely to be satisfied if you force an unsympathetic design on them, and your work will not show to advantage.

You may have been asked to paint a ceiling with the express purpose of changing the feel of a room. The reason may be to lighten, open up or alter the character of the room, to aggrandise or impress the onlooker. In each case, thought should be given to the best way to achieve the desired result.

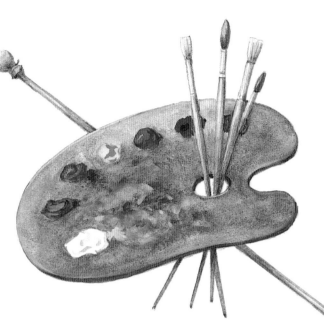

It is always helpful to produce a design to scale, bearing in mind that what is drawn on paper will be 'upside down' once transferred to the ceiling. Depending upon the extent of the area to be decorated, you will have to decide whether to divide up the ceiling into sections or opt for an 'all over' painting. It is far simpler to execute the former, as once the design is drawn out you can complete specific areas, one at a time.

In the latter, more all-embracing design on a large scale, you must be certain that you can cope with large undefined areas of painting. Covering many square feet of graduated colour, light and shade, all above your head, is not easy, even with your design to refer to. If you are uncertain of your ability to carry out a design, it is better to opt for a simple solution.

Try a clear blue sky with a few wisps of cloud and perhaps a bird or two. Once again, even with the simplest design it is imperative to produce a scaled watercolour first from which to work.

One of the practical problems to be dealt with is that of not being able to see, when at arm's length, what you are working on as a whole. This entails endless climbing up and down your scaffold to have a look from a distance. In the case of the construction of a false floor, to enable you to work close to the ceiling, it may mean moving a lot of heavy, dusty planks every time, and then replacing them.

Avoid overloading the brush as dribbling paint can be irritating, as can spilling or splashing paint on the walls. Use protective sheeting to cover the walls and floor and organise the pots of paint so that they are secure: an exploding bomb of vermilion, twenty feet below, is not always appreciated!

One last warning: it can get very hot up there, close to the ceiling. If you feel tired or faint, take a break, and always remember to do neck exercises.

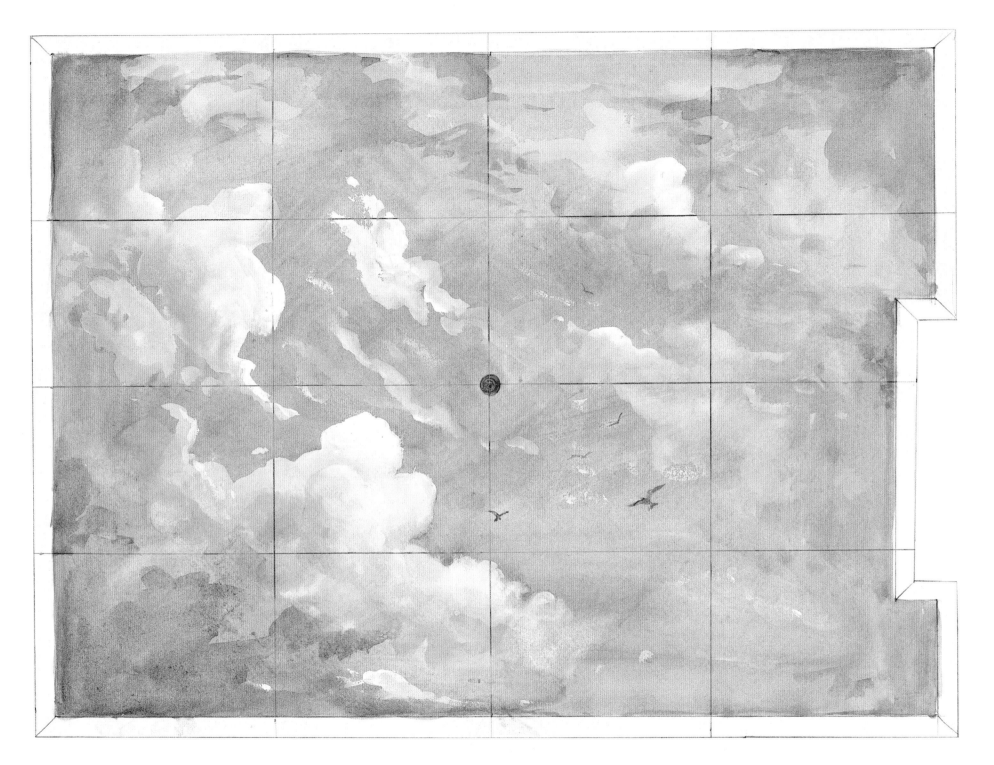

ABOVE: My design for the sky ceiling of the hall at Newfield, Yorkshire, which was painted to complete the mural decoration of the walls. Here the sketch has been squared up for transfer to the ceiling. If necessary, the grid could be further divided in the more 'busy' areas.

TECHNIQUE AND PRACTICE

Wherever I work, be it in England or overseas, I always ask the client to have the walls or ceiling prepared for me, in a white emulsion finish, by their own builders. The reasons for this are twofold. Firstly, preparing a surface can take time, and that may well be pertinent if working far afield. One does not want to fly half way across the world to be told that the preparation will take another ten days to finish: do you fly back or do you wait? Secondly, and of vital importance, you cannot be responsible for what has happened in the past. Damp, cracking or a sandwich of the wrong paints on the surface to be painted can cause havoc. I shall never forget, in my middle twenties, when working in Virginia, the horror when confronted with a blistering, peeling wall of paint on my return from a three months break in England. I was lucky that my clients were understanding and sympathetic to my plight, but it taught me how crucial it is to check that a surface has been properly prepared.

Water is always a potential hazard when painting ceilings. Overflowing baths, leaking washing machines and the inevitable burst pipe can all conspire to ruin one's work. However, as I said earlier, it is certainly easier to repair a crack or blister than to deal with unwieldy lengths of sagging paper. I would therefore suggest, where possible, that you work directly onto primed plaster.

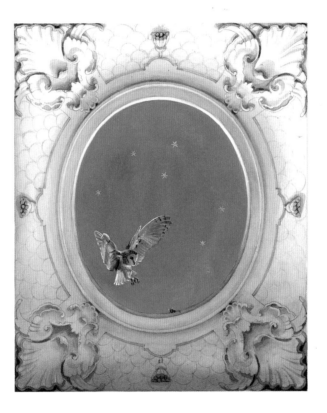

ABOVE: The finished design for the ceiling of the ante-room at Somerton.

I start work with charcoal on a white emulsion surface which is squared up in line with the squared-up design. The charcoal is then dusted off, leaving lighter, but visible lines, after which I start the process of drawing the design in charcoal onto the ceiling. When this is completed, I lightly dust off the charcoal and draw over the line in red

ochre paint, correcting and adjusting the drawing where necessary.

Making sure the paint is dry, I wash off the remaining charcoal. This can sometimes be a rather laborious job but well worth the trouble as it can take many coats of paint to eliminate a rogue charcoal line. This done, I then block in the main areas of colour and gradually work them up to a finish – a short sentence for a lot of work!

The paints I use are indelible gouache, which one can wipe with a damp cloth when dry. I never use a sealer or varnish, as it is much easier to touch up or restore the painting when one doesn't have to remove that barrier first.

The illustrations on the following pages demonstrate the order in which a design is transferred to a ceiling. The design in this case is for the ante-room in my home at Somerton. This room is really a continuation of the passage decorated with gilded clouds on a blue ground featured on pages 22 to 25. The ante-room ceiling is separated from the main passage by a depressed arch only, so I wanted it to be sympathetic in feeling. I decided that as the sky of the passage was a deep blue, I should continue the same colour as background but move on from a stylised sky to a 'real' one, thus ensuring a certain continuity. As in the passageway, I decided to continue the gilding of the cornice with two lines of gold to 'hold' the design.

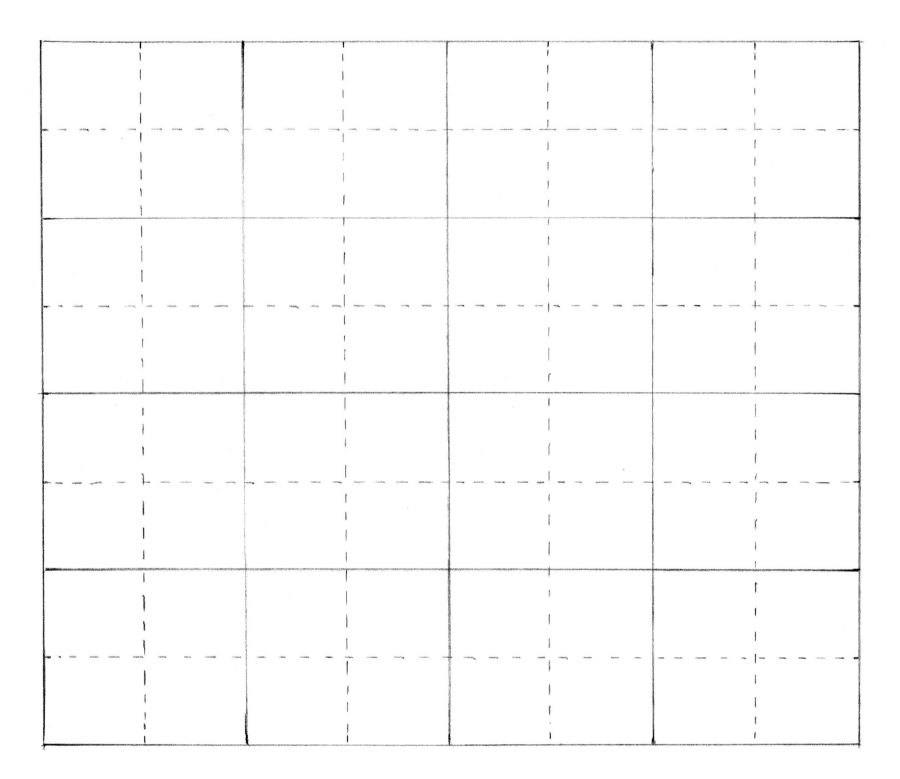

ABOVE: The ceiling area is first 'squared up' in charcoal. It is divided, whatever the proportion, in half and then in half again, and so on, rather than in squares.

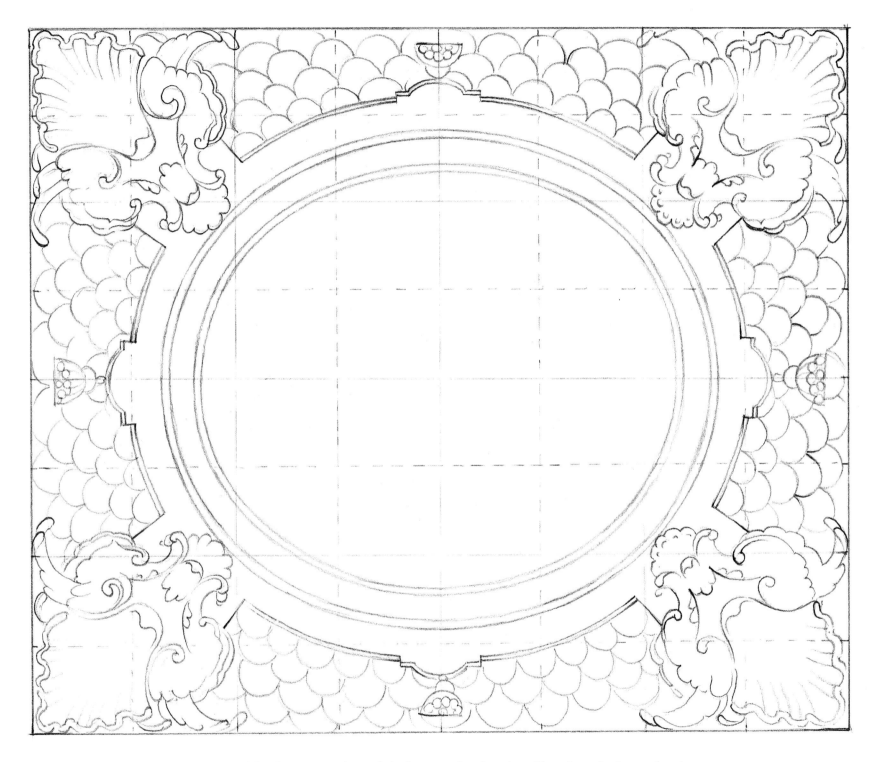

*ABOVE: The drawing, in charcoal, is then transferred to the ceiling, from the 'squared-up'
watercolour design.*

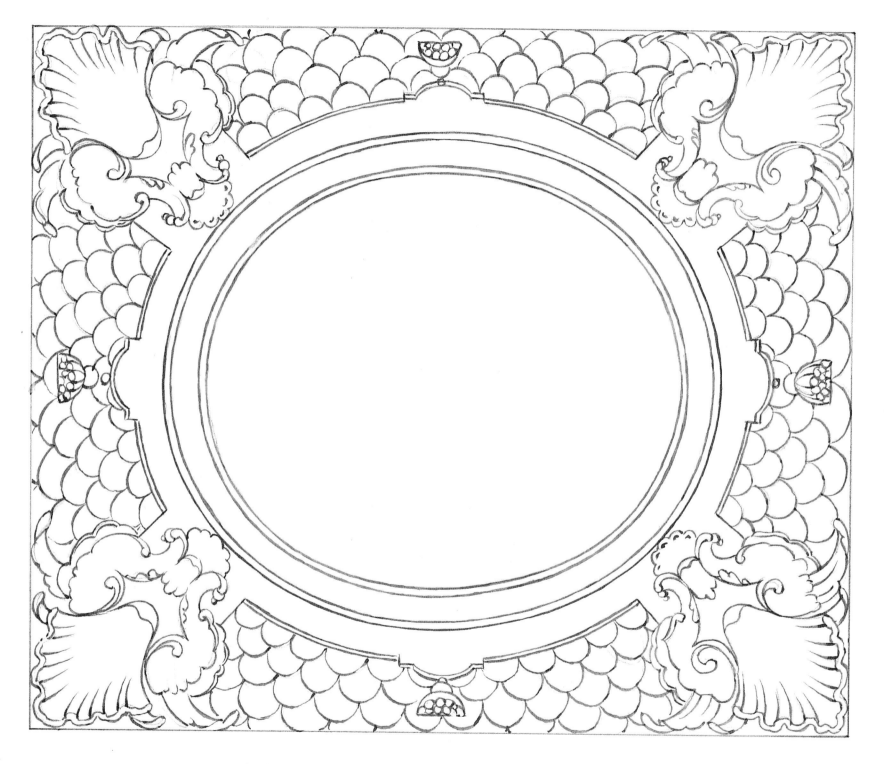

ABOVE: The drawing is painted in red ochre and the charcoal lines are washed off, to leave the line as clean as possible.

ABOVE: The central ceiling panel, is painted in and cleaned up around the edges. The ground colour was a flat cobalt blue with a little manganese and umber added to the white. Three washes of ultramarine and one of raw umber were than applied on top, to give it depth.

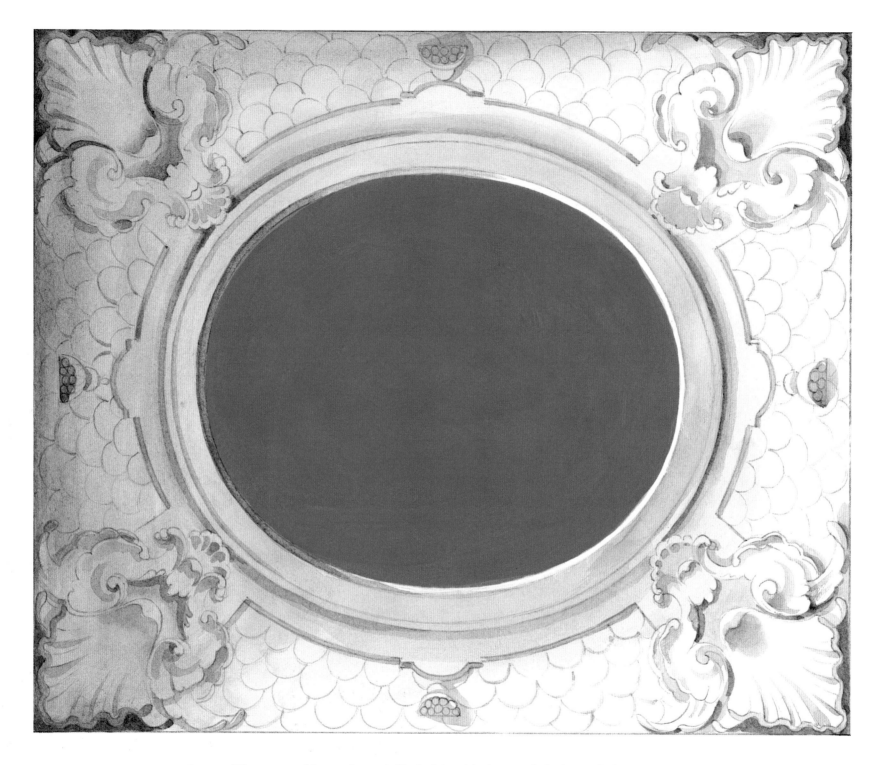

ABOVE: The outer architectural area is blocked in with the initial shading, which is in white and raw umber with the addition of a little viridian and ultramarine. This will then be worked up to the finish.

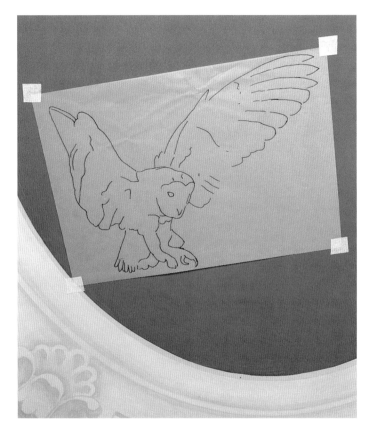

ABOVE: A paper tracing of the barn owl is placed in position ready to be transferred in charcoal and then to be drawn in paint.

RIGHT: When the owl is finished, the stars are added. On the edge of the oval, the prey, a mouse, completes the picture.

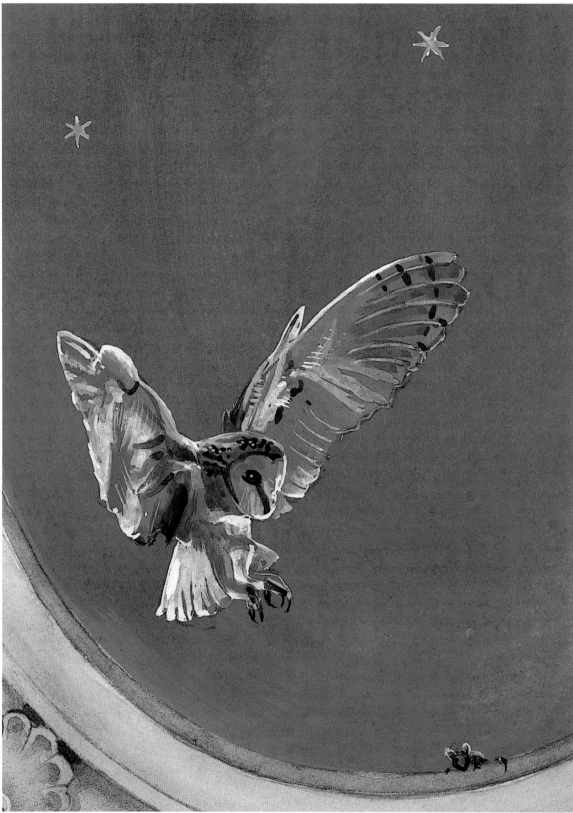

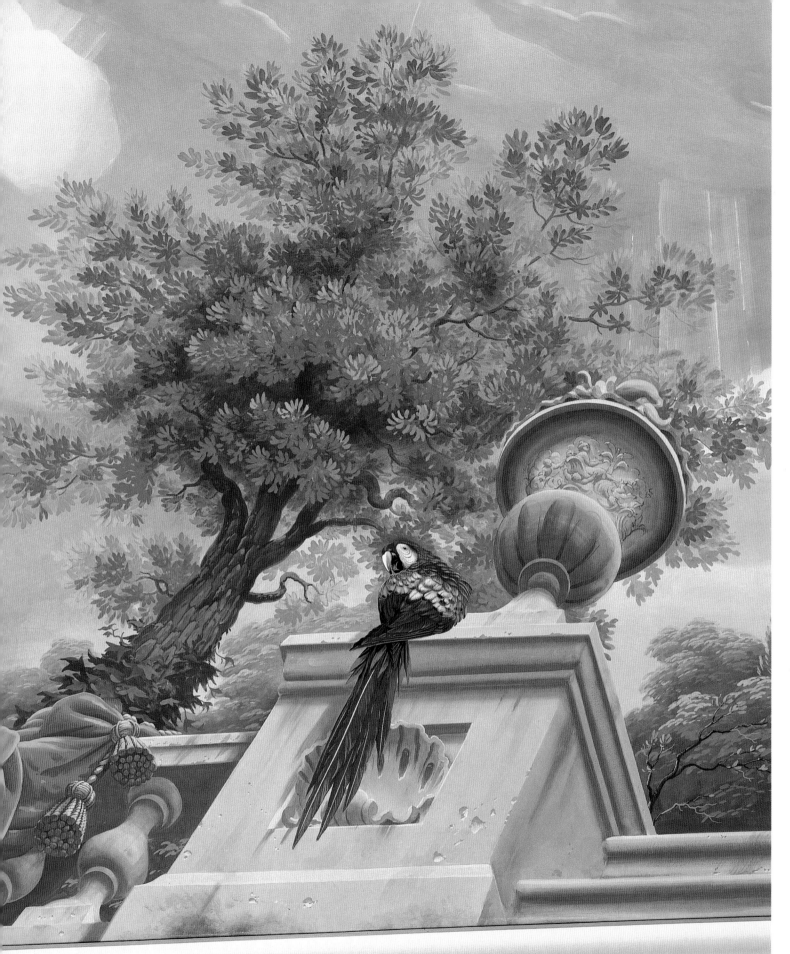

LEFT: *An urn at the end of the balustrade with a macaw from the Frankfurt ceiling. (See pages 88 to 99.) If you have difficulty capturing the perspective of an object such as this, try placing a pot on a high shelf or table at approximately the correct angle. Move around, studying it from below, before making a drawing.*

RIGHT: *On the left-hand side of the page is my rough sketch of an urn, in perspective from below, as painted by Carlo Baratta to the design of Tomasso Aldovrandini. To the right is an example of how it might look with further foreshortening.*

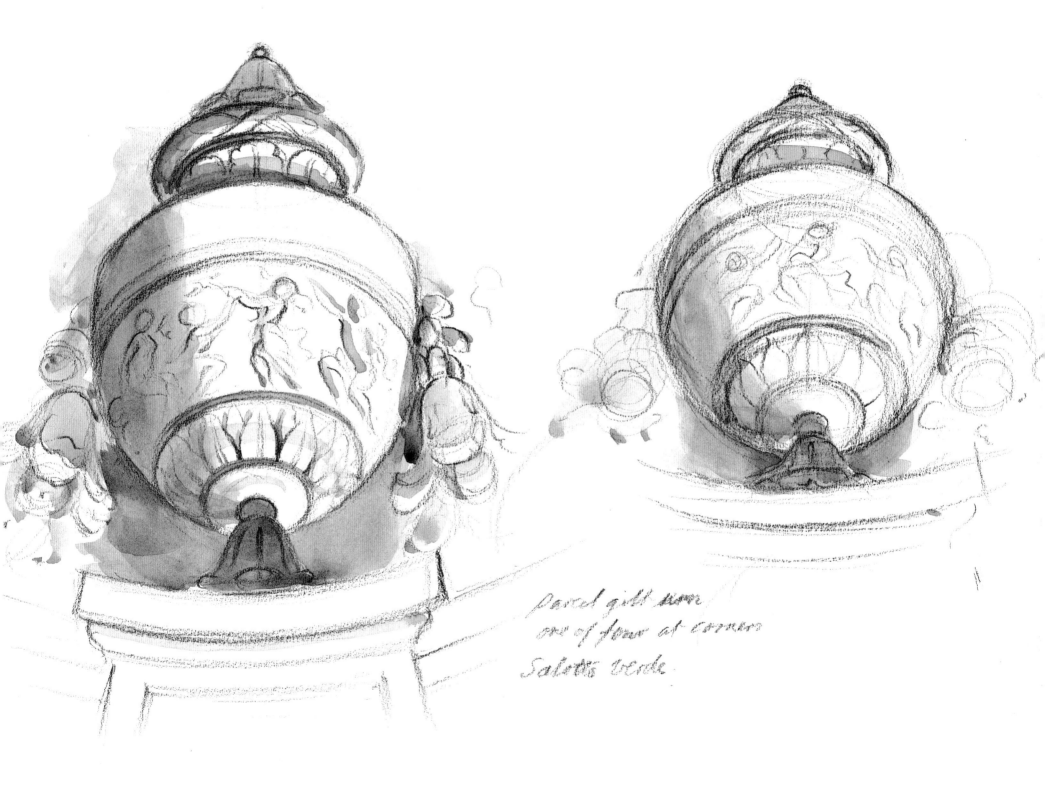

parcel gilt urn
one of four at corners
Salotto Verde

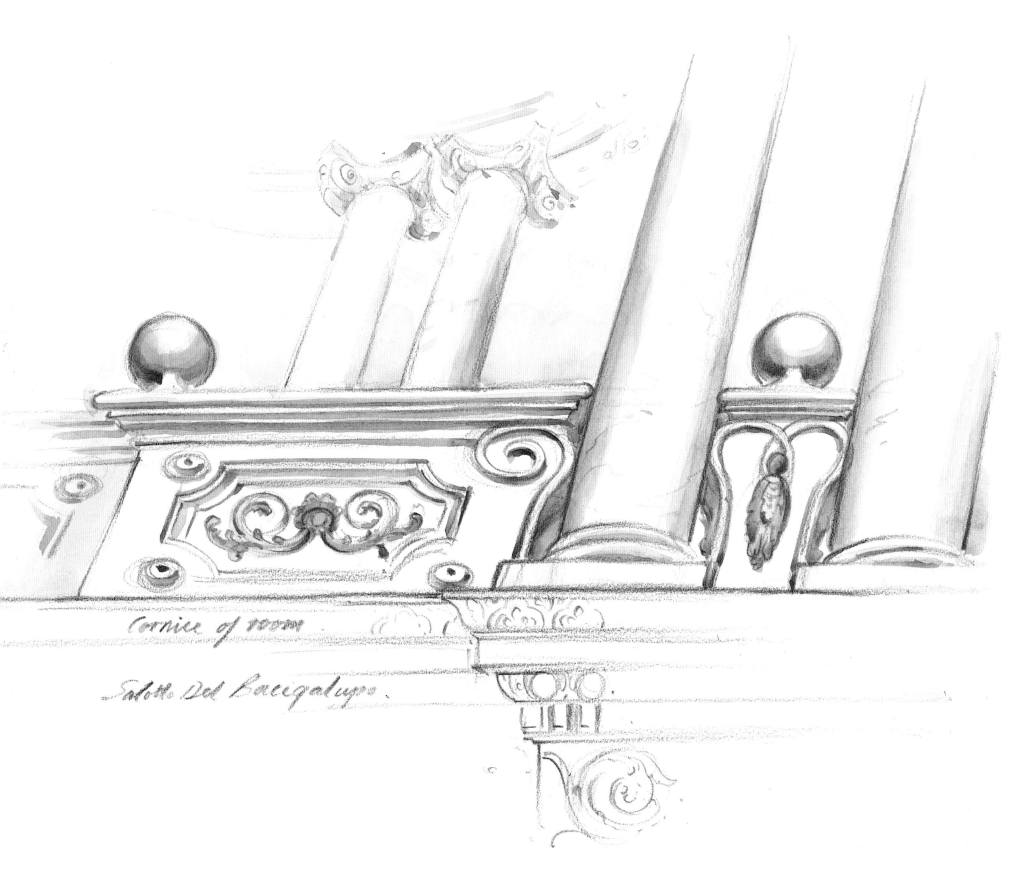

Cornice of room

Salotto Del Bacigalupo.

ABOVE: Studies of drapery, such as this, can be useful as well as decorative. Sometimes drapery can be used to help to disguise a difficult area of perspective. For instance, the join of a balustrade in the corner of a ceiling may be helped by painting drapery strategically over the difficult areas, thus making it visually more acceptable.

LEFT: An example of a solution to the problem of a balustrade meeting a column from a ceiling painting in the Salotto del Bacigalupo in Palazzo Durazzo Pallavicini. My sketch here shows how Tomasso Aldovrandini dealt with the difficult space between the two columns in the foreground.

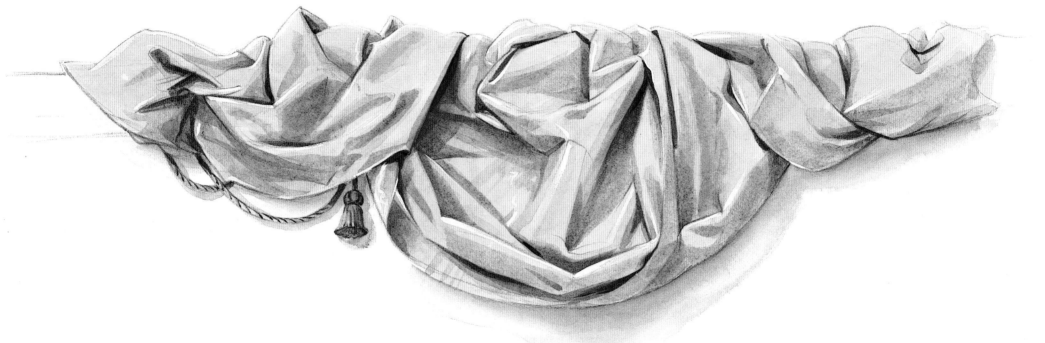

*Above: A study of drapery to hang over a balcony or balustrade. This was done in my studio by
draping the material over the gallery and drawing it from below.*

*Right: Another study of drapery to use in a different position. It is well worth taking time to
make a drawing from life, as invented drapes rarely look good, or convincing.*

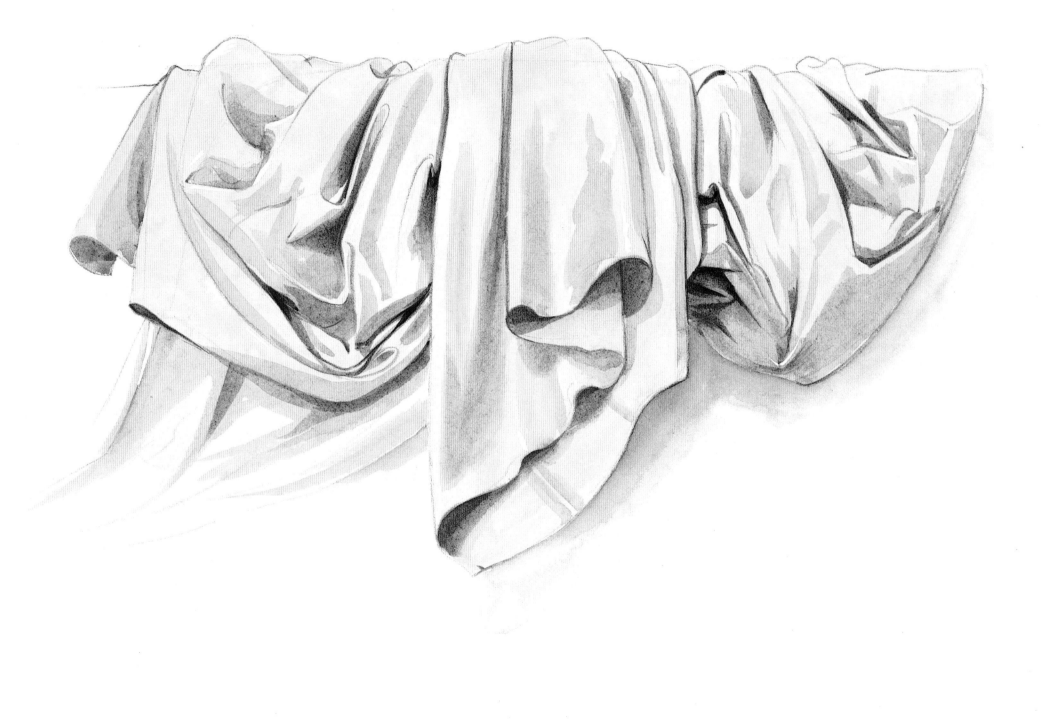

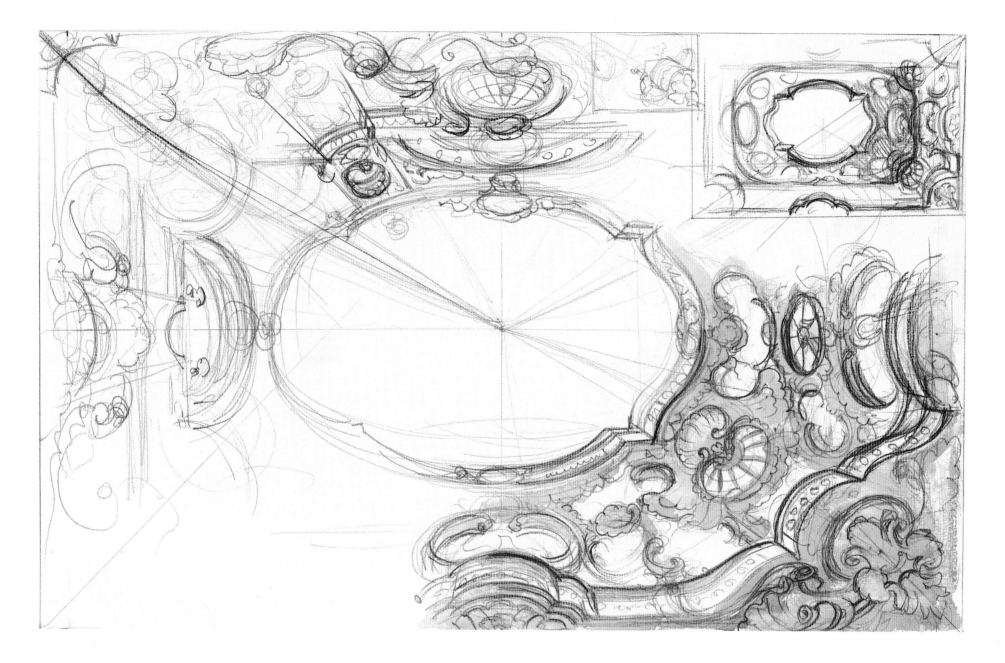

ABOVE: The sketch above is reproduced here just to show the way I work. There may be many sheets of quick doodles, such as this, before I hit upon a workable way forward. In this case, I was trying to work out the architectural disposition in space for the ceiling of my drawing room at home. The ceiling is vaulted rather than flat and where the levels change from a forty-five degree angle to the horizontal this will have to be taken into account.

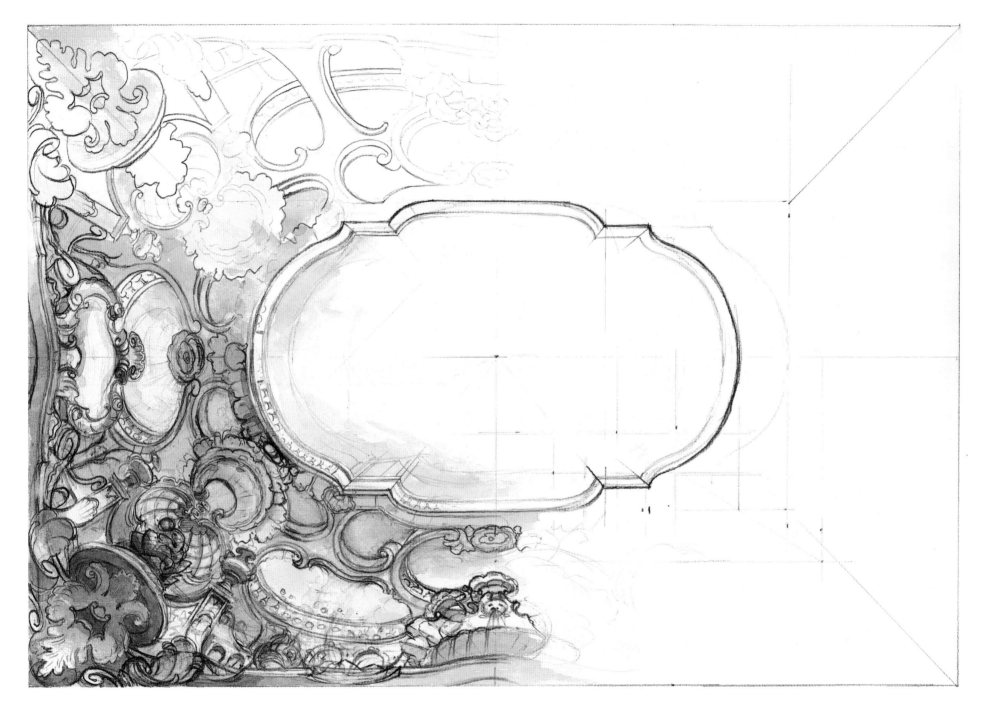

ABOVE: A further design for my drawing room ceiling, and it may well change again before a final solution is found. It is always ten times more difficult to design for oneself than for other people. Here, having drawn out a quarter of the design, it can easily be repeated as the perspective is central. The next stage, having determined the design of the architectural structure of the painting, is to compose the many figures and animals that I intend to include within this framework. I fear it may take many years.

ACKNOWLEDGEMENTS

I should like to take the opportunity to thank all the owners of my works for their generosity in allowing them to be photographed and published here.

A special thank you is long overdue to Mrs Charles Brocklebank for having the bravery to commission my very first ceiling painting, thirty-five years ago. Executed in the dining room of her apartment in Grosvenor Square the painted corners were inspired by the chinoiserie designs of J. Pillement and chosen to complement the eighteenth-century Chinese wallpaper.

Without the help of my editor, Janet Ravenscroft, and the excellent photographs taken by Shona Wood, this project would never have come to fruition. Nigel Partridge has, once again, with great skill, made sense of the many drawings and paintings to produce such a pleasing design for these pages.

Finally my thanks are due to Rui d'Andrade Paes M.A., (R.C.A.), for his paintings of birds and animals in these ceiling paintings and for his help and contribution of ideas for this book.

All paintings and designs in the book are in private collections, or in the collection of the author, unless otherwise stated.

Page 40 Coll. The Countess of Dartmouth; 50 Coll. Mr & Mrs Rupert Galliers-Pratt; 52 Coll. The Hon. Sir Richard & Lady Storey; 60, 64 Coll. Madame Yehya Ghandour; 6, 82–3, 86 (top) Coll. The Marquess & Marchioness of Hertford. All photographs by Shona Wood and © Breslich & Foss apart from: Pages 78, 79 Louise Hertford; 61, 62–3, 65, 66, 67 Jean Louis Mainguy. Author photograph: Carolyn Seymour.

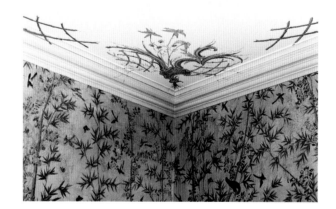

ABOVE: My first ceiling painting.